THE PICKERING MASTERS

THE COLLECTED LETTERS OF ELLEN TERRY

THE COLLECTED LETTERS OF ELLEN TERRY

EDITOR
Katharine Cockin

Volume 1
1865–1888

LONDON
PICKERING & CHATTO
2010

Published by Pickering & Chatto (Publishers) Limited
21 Bloomsbury Way, London WC1A 2TH

2252 Ridge Road, Brookfield, Vermont 05036-9704, USA

www.pickeringchatto.com

BRITISH LIBRARY CATALOGUING IN PUBLICATION DATA

Terry, Ellen, Dame, 1847–1928.
The collected letters of Ellen Terry.
Volume 1. – (The Pickering masters)
1. Terry, Ellen, Dame, 1847–1928 – Correspondence. 2. Actresses – Great Britain – Correspondence.
I. Title II. Series III. Cockin, Ka
792'.028'092-dc22

ISBN-13: 9781851961450

This publication is printed on a
National Standard for the Permanence of Paper for Printed Library Materials.

Typeset by Pickering & Chatto (Publishers) Limited
Printed in Great Britain by the MPG Books Group, Bodmin and King's Lynn.

CONTENTS

ACKNOWLEDGEMENTS

I am grateful to the National Trust, copyright holders for the unpublished works of Ellen Terry, for giving me permission to reproduce the letters; and to Mr Julian Smith, copyright holder, for allowing me to reproduce the annotations written by Stephen Coleridge on the collection of Ellen Terry's letters held at the Garrick Club and for supplying a copy of the transcripts of these letters.

A considerable amount of work and time is required to complete a project of this kind and I am therefore indebted to the British Academy, which funded this project in 2005 and 2008; and to the University of Hull, which gave me study leave to work on the project in 2008. In 2006–8 the AHRC funded the Ellen Terry and Edith Craig Database with a grant of nearly £86,000, which enabled me to complete the online catalogue of the National Trust's Ellen Terry and Edith Craig archive (see http://ellenterryarchive.hull.ac.uk). This resource, designed by Julian Halliwell of SimplicityWeb.co.uk, has made accessible descriptions of over 20,000 documents, of which the summaries of the letters (more than 700) written by Ellen Terry are most useful for this publication. However, it also provides a means of searching for related information in the National Trust's Ellen Terry and Edith Craig archive, providing a rich context for understanding the lives and work of Ellen Terry and her circle.

Staff at many institutions provided copies of letters in various forms and assisted in my enquiries. I am particularly grateful to National Trust Staff at Smallhythe Place, Tenterden, Kent. Over the years, various custodians and volunteers have contributed to the card index describing the letters of Ellen Terry at Smallhythe Place. I am especially grateful to Mr John Boyes Watson for the research he carried out on Elizabeth Rumball and her family and on Albert Fleming which informs the notes lodged with those collections.

I am grateful to repositories which have provided copies of the letters transcribed in this series: Bodleian Library, University of Oxford; British Library, London; Brotherton Collection, Leeds University Library; Honnold Mudd Library, Claremont College; Fales and Berol Collection, New York University; Folger Shakespeare Library, Washington, DC; Garrick Club, London; Harvard Theatre Collection, Houghton Library, Harvard University; Modern Books and Manuscripts Department, Houghton Library, Harvard University; Harry Ransom Center, University of Texas at Austin; Huntington Library; Pierpoint Morgan Library, New York; New York Players' Club, New York; New York Public Library; Smallhythe Place (National Trust), Tenterden, Kent; Shakespeare Centre, Stratford upon Avon; University of California, Los Angeles; University of Pennsylvania; Ben Graf Henneke Archives of Performing Arts, University of Tulsa; Victoria and Albert Museum, London.

For various advice, support and encouragement during my twenty years of work on the lives and letters of Edith Craig and her mother Ellen Terry, I am very grateful to many academics, librarians and archivists and lack of space prevents me from naming everyone. I would especially like to thank my PhD supervisor and expert on theatre history Professor Richard Foulkes, University of Leicester, and external examiner Professor Susan Bassnett, University of Warwick, for their support; Professor Nina Auerbach, University of Pennsylvania, and Sir Michael Holroyd CBE, the keynote speakers at the Ellen Terry and Edith Craig conference at the University of Hull in June 2009, along with the delegates who included relatives of Ellen Terry, Ellen Terry Craig and Marie Taylor, for sharing their enthusiasm and interest in Ellen Terry. For helpful directions on my pursuit of elusive Ellen Terry letters, I would like to thank my colleague Dr Catherine Wynne, University of Hull, for her information on letters at the Brotherton Collection. I am very grateful also to Colin Harris at the Bodleian Library, Catherine Haill and her colleagues at the Victoria and Albert Museum, Jamie Andrews and his colleagues in the Manuscripts Department of the British Library and Marcus Risdell, librarian at the Garrick Club, who facilitated my visits to their collections before Volume 1 went to press.

For assistance in typing the transcripts of over 2,500 letters, I am grateful to Pat Broughton, Fiona Childs, Dr Julie Ellam, Sophie Ottoway, Ann Riley and Mark Willcocks. I am grateful to Sue Fox, freelance researcher, who kindly photographed the Ellen Terry letters to Joe Evans held at the New York Players' Club. Dr Julie Ellam assisted in the final stages of Volume 1, helping to trace footnote information and to check the manuscript. I have benefited greatly from her exceptionally high standards of work and her good humour throughout.

Envisaged as a much smaller collection of Ellen Terry's letters confined to those from her own archive at Smallhythe Place, this project developed into a comprehensive collection of letters from at least nineteen different institutions. I am grateful to the anonymous reader of the proposal for Pickering & Chatto whose recommendation led to this change in direction. It is a much more ambitious aim than I had at the outset or would ever have formulated myself. Readers will benefit from the greater volume and range of correspondence which has resulted from this advice.

ABBREVIATIONS

General

b.	born
c.	*circa*
d.	died
ET	Ellen Terry
illeg.	illegible
Memoirs	*Ellen Terry's Memoirs*, ed. E. Craig and C. St John (London: Hutchinson, 1932)
n.d.	no date
ODNB	*Oxford Dictionary of National Biography*, ed. H. C. G. Matthew and B. Harrison, 60 vols (Oxford: Oxford University Press, 2004)
OED	*Oxford English Dictionary*
THET	*The Heart of Ellen Terry*, ed. S. Coleridge (London: Mills & Boon, 1928)

Archives

BL	British Library, London
BOD	Bodleian Library, University of Oxford
BRO	Brotherton Collection, University of Leeds
CLAREMONT	Claremont College
FALES	Fales and Berol Collection, New York University
FOLGER	Folger Shakespeare Library, Washington, DC
GARRICK	Garrick Club, London
HARV	Houghton Library, Harvard University, Massachusetts
HRC	Harry Ransom Center, University of Austin at Texas
HUNT	Huntington Library, California
NYPClub	New York Players' Club, New York
NYPL	New York Public Library
PML	Pierpoint Morgan Library, New York
SHAK	Shakespeare Centre, Stratford upon Avon

SMA	Smallhythe Place (National Trust), Tenterden, Kent
UCLA	University of California, Los Angeles
UPENN	University of Pennsylvania
V&A	British Theatre Museum collection, Victoria & Albert Museum, London
V&A Enthoven	Enthoven collection, Victoria & Albert Museum, London

ILLUSTRATIONS

Portrait of Ellen Terry. Reproduced by permission of the National Trust.

Ellen Terry in costume as Lady Macbeth (1888). Reproduced by permission of the National Trust.

GENERAL INTRODUCTION

Ellen Terry (1847–1928; hereafter ET) was always on the move. She was born into a theatrical family, to Ben and Sarah (née Ballard), while they were on tour in Coventry, England.[1] They were performers and most of their children were to follow the same line of work.[2] ET's stage debut was in the role of Mamillius in *The Winter's Tale* in 1856 in the company of Charles Kean. She had numerous roles, also appearing in London in a play by Tom Taylor. In 1862 she joined the company of J. L. Chute in Bristol. Her older sister, Kate Terry, had a successful career on the stage, retiring on marriage. Similarly, ET withdrew from the stage in 1864 when she married the artist G. F. Watts (1817–1904).[3] This was not to be the end of her career, although it was interrupted by events in her private life. After the failure of her marriage and the end of her subsequent six-year relationship with the architect and designer Edward Godwin (1833–86),[4] during which they had two children, ET was driven by expediency back to the stage. The theatre underwrote her new role off-stage as a single parent, responsible as she then was for raising her two remarkable children, Edith Craig (1869–1947) and Edward Gordon Craig (1872–1966).

ET was a survivor, adaptable to changes in her fortune and capable of learning from experience to a greater extent than most. She benefited from the advice of various mentors, such as the prolific novelist Charles Reade and the author Tom Taylor, as well as from the friendship of artists, writers, politicians, aristocrats and influential people whom she met through her marriage to Watts and her appreciative theatre audiences. She collected many admiring fans, some of whom became friends and even advisers. They provided the kind of support and fidelity which she was not to find from the men with whom she was most intimate (with perhaps the exception of Henry Irving, with whom she had a long and successful partnership).[5] Some of them happened to be extremely useful: the leading lawyers of their day provided vital legal advice; the wealthy and well-connected elite helped to increase her reputation and audiences; and artists, authors and dramatists provided her with a place in the cultural networks of the period which influenced her understanding of her stage roles. They too were influenced by her performances, which sometimes caught the spirit of the age. ET's vitality and charm characterized her acting and informed the delivery of her lines as much as the physical embodiment of the role; in the resting of a hand intimately on a male shoulder, the swaying of an auburn plait; in a glance or a glittering robe.

ET was one of the first modern stars of the British stage. A contemporary of Eleanora Duse and Sara Bernhardt, she acted opposite Henry Irving at the Lyceum Theatre from 1878 to 1902. She had an international reputation, touring the United States, Canada and Australia. ET was adored by the public and she was honoured by royalty, government and academia. She was recipient of the award of an honorary doctor of letters at the University of Aberdeen in 1922 and Dame of the British Empire in 1925. She has become an icon of Victorian womanhood. She held a secure place in the landscape of the Pre-Raphaelites and Impressionists: G. F. Watts, John Singer Sargent, J. F. Pryde and W. G. Robertson. From 1868 to 1875 she set up home with one of the leading architects of the arts and crafts movement, Edward Godwin. In 1871 Godwin designed and built a house for their family at Fallows Green, Harpenden, Hertfordshire.

As Lady Macbeth ET's portrait is on display in the Tate Gallery in London, caught by John Singer Sargent in a moment of self-coronation. A gesture not seen in the play, it dominates the composition, indicating the challenge Lady Macbeth posed to Victorian femininity and ET's power in the realization of the role when it was first performed at the Lyceum Theatre on 29 December 1888. G. F. Watts probably idealized her in life as in his portrait of her selecting a bloom (*Choosing*, now in the National Portrait Gallery in London). In an apparently melancholy mood, she is arrested by the camera of Julia Margaret Cameron. Before the advent of reliable photographic or film recording of performance, the actor's work was inevitably ephemeral. As Virginia Woolf put it in one of the last things she wrote, her biographical portrait of ET: 'What remains is at best only a wavering, insubstantial phantom – a verbal life on the lips of the living'.[6] Hence, critics had considerable power and responsibility in recording and publicizing their experiences, bearing witness to the magical transformation of person into persona. ET, like many of her contemporaries, published an autobiography, but it is in her letters that she reveals her natural facility with the written word, liberated from any directorial control.

ET's reputation as a witty and charming correspondent was a treasured secret of her friends and acquaintances. It became widely established after her death by the posthumous publication of selections from her correspondence with George Bernard Shaw.[7] According to Virginia Woolf these were 'some of the best letters in the language'.[8] The controversies of ET's private life were numerous – elopement, cohabitation, single-motherhood, two marriages with significant age differences – yet she maintained, simultaneously and without duplicity, the public- and self-image of a thoroughly feminine woman. ET's life story exemplifies the transition between the Victorian and modern worlds. In the preface to their correspondence, Shaw said, 'we presently became occupied with one another in a paper courtship, which is perhaps the pleasantest, as it is the most enduring, of all courtships'.[9] Although ET seemed to prefer her lovers in more substantial form (her third and final husband, James Carew (1876–1938), was 29 years her junior), her paper portfolio was not restricted to Shaw. The lengthy and intimate correspondence with Stephen Coleridge is worthy of comparison and is presented here in full in print for the first time.[10] Letters to her friends of either sex were also exuberant. As Shaw summarized:

> One may say that her marriages were adventures and her friendships enduring. And all these friendships had the character of innocent love affairs: her friends were her lovers in every sense except the technical one; and she was incapable of returning their regard coolly: she felt either warmly or not at all.[11]

The Collected Letters of Ellen Terry therefore provides an opportunity to appreciate the extent of Terry's playful exchanges with other correspondents.

ET's correspondence provides an insight into the dynamics of the theatre as a field of employment, the mechanisms of patronage and affiliation and the impact on the health of the performer of a rigorous schedule. As Henry Irving's leading female performer at the Lyceum Theatre, ET toured many times with the company to the United States and Canada and independently toured Australia during the First World War. There are many famous addressees in this correspondence (distinguished theatrical figures such as A. W. Pinero, Bram Stoker and Charles Reade, for example) but the most intriguing letters are often those to the least auspicious of addressees. Nina Auerbach has analysed in detail the correspondence between ET and Audrey Campbell which ran from 1897 to 1912.[12] In many letters ET conveys fleeting but incisive comments on her illustrious contemporaries and these revealing gems sit alongside fascinating accounts of daily news. ET's correspondence with her close female friends, such as Pauline Chase (the actress noted for her performance as Peter Pan) and Bertha Bramley, are of particular interest for their revelations of ET's intimate feelings about work and family, providing evidence of her delightful sense of humour as well as her maternal devotion.

ET's name and her image were fixed in the public consciousness in the inter-war years. After her death in 1928, her daughter, Edith Craig,[13] transformed her mother's Kent house into the Ellen Terry Memorial Museum. Given to the National Trust in 1939, it is now known as Smallhythe Place. The annual memorial performance at the Barn Theatre in the grounds of the house drew distinguished actors and audiences and it was a focus of much cultural and social activity. Edith Craig and her partners, (Clare) Tony Atwood and Christopher St John (Christabel Marshall) socialized with many fascinating and controversial local figures, such as Vita Sackville West, Virginia Woolf, Radclyffe Hall and

Una Troubridge. There is a context for reading ET's correspondence, therefore, in the broad fields of women's studies and lesbian history as well as literary modernism. Virginia Woolf was fascinated by both mother and daughter. While the main character, Miss LaTrobe, in Woolf's last novel, *Between the Acts*, may be modelled on Edith Craig,[14] one of the last things Woolf wrote in 1941 was a biographical essay on ET. In this essay Woolf recognized the value of ET's letter-writing. She seems to have agreed with Edith Craig that ET was 'one of the most fascinating letter-writers that ever lived'.[15]

The Collected Letters of Ellen Terry will provide scholars with a rich context in which to reassess ET's life writings and her lectures alongside her work as a performer. New work has developed over the last decade on the New Woman, women in theatre, gender and performance and the history of the women's suffrage movement.[16] However, ET's ambiguous position has not yet been fully appreciated. In the first issue of the radical journal the *Freewoman* in 1911, ET was the only named role model cited in the editorial. This same publication debated political issues, such as women's rights and vivisection: cultural events, including theatrical productions; as well as the ethics of free love, contraception and masturbation. However, any claim for a radical ET should be qualified by evidence of her ambivalence towards political movements and the views she expressed in private, in correspondence, which appear sometimes contradictory.[17] Consistency of position is an ideal which may not always be practicable.

ET's letters reveal the difficulties of life for both the Victorian woman in general and for this exceptional woman who maintained a public profile as a successful international performer while raising two children who, in this period, would have been designated 'illegitimate'.

After ET's death, her daughter Edith Craig advertised in the national press for her mother's letters (or 'Ellen Terry relics') to be returned so that they could be published. The vast collection of letters at Smallhythe Place has a curious history. Although the collection has been subjected to censorship in later years by means of selective destruction, over seven hundred letters have, nevertheless, survived. While the letters from Smallhythe Place are unusual from an archival point of view, the other letters from ET follow the expected life of such documents, being located in the archives of their addressees. This edition draws on the holdings in at least nineteen different institutions. Significant collections include letters to Stephen Coleridge held at the Garrick Club, London, and letters to ET's son, Edward Gordon Craig, held at the Harry Ransom Center, University of Austin at Texas. Many of these are presented in Volume 1. Other correspondence includes that to Joe Evans, Mary-Anne Hall, Mrs Nettleship, Sir Albert Seymour, Audrey Campbell, Bertha Bramley and Mrs Elizabeth Rumball (Boo).

Letters have been selected on the principle of including as many as may be of interest to readers. Careful consideration has been given to those very few which have been omitted. Since many of ET's letters, especially those to significant male intimates and to others in certain periods of her life, appear to have been destroyed there are gaps in her life story. Those letters which may at first appear to be relatively trivial have been included if they provide clues about her whereabouts or contribute to the wider narrative of her life. Letters which have been omitted are those which offer no clues whatsoever and whose content is indisputably uninformative (e.g. those which are both undated and have no address and with minimal content). The other omissions relate to the collection of letters to Anna Methven, the smaller collection to Edward Ladd, and to May Ward for which it has not yet been possible to obtain permission from the owners. The attempt to produce 'The Complete Letters of Ellen Terry' would be a thwarted undertaking. ET seems to have written letters in every spare moment in her long life. It is known that some of her correspondence is held privately and anonymously and it is therefore impossible to include these letters. Pickering & Chatto's decision to publish these volumes annually makes it possible to include in the last volumes some latecomers. Anyone in possession of letters written by ET is therefore invited to contact the editor with a view to having them included in the series.

The Collected Letters of Ellen Terry therefore brings together for the first time letters which reveal the fascinating spirit of this exceptional woman of the theatre, loved by her audiences and sustained by her many friends through gruelling schedules and the difficulties of failed marriages, ill health and bereavements.

Readers may have encountered some of ET's correspondence which appeared in two published editions: *The Heart of Ellen Terry*, ed. Stephen Coleridge (1928); and *Ellen Terry and Bernard Shaw – A Correspondence*, ed. Christopher St John (1931). After her death, Stephen Coleridge published a selection of ET's side of the correspondence: twenty-six letters she sent to him covering the period 1878 to 1917. Coleridge provided explanatory notes. He lightly edited the letters, standardizing the paragraphing and rendered some of the vocabulary slightly less colloquial. In one or two instances he excised significant material. In 1931, George Bernard Shaw provided Christopher St John, Edith Craig's partner, with selected letters from both sides of his correspondence with ET, which began in 1892, several years before they met. This publication was regarded by ET's son, Edward Gordon Craig, as an act of indecent exposure, misrepresentation and betrayal. In *Ellen Terry and Her Secret Self* (1932), Edward Gordon Craig claims for himself the authorized portrait of his mother, privileged access to her 'secret self' not available to his sister. George Bernard Shaw defended the publication of the correspondence on the grounds that ET occupied an alternative moral universe. Evidence of the extent of her awareness of this is revealed in her letters and presented here for the first time.

In the new light of *The Collected Letters of Ellen Terry*, Shaw's forceful summary of ETs philosophy and *modus vivendi*, formulated as it is in characteristically provocative and extreme expression, appears now to have miscast her to some extent:

> All this has to be grasped before the lay reader can understand how Ellen Terry could be a woman of very exceptional virtue without having the smallest respect for the law. She did not care enough about it to have even a prejudice against it. If the man of her choice was free, she married him. If the marriage was not a success, she left him. She had many enduring friendships, some transient fancies, and five domestic partnerships of which two were not legalized, though they would have been if the English marriage law had been decently reasonable.[18]

This summary, rather than the publication of the letters themselves, seems worthy of Gordon Craig's censure.

If ET was an outlaw, it was on a part-time basis only. She had, in her circle of friends, various aristocrats and lawyers; she had private correspondence with royalty; and a very long-standing and intimate correspondence with the son of the Lord Chief Justice of the day. She made use of the law, to protect herself in her separation from her second husband, to prevent him from squandering her money and, according to Stephen Coleridge, from molesting her.[19] George Bernard Shaw is quite definitely wrong that she 'did not care enough' about the law or social conventions. She most certainly did. But she lived within the constraints imposed upon her, which had limited her opportunities and affected the choices she made. ET's life began with the difficulties, as well as the rich experiences, derived from her place within a large theatrical family, being a child-worker, presented before the paying public from the age of nine years. She was largely self-educated. In 1875 she applied for a reader's ticket for the British Museum. Her letters demonstrate her wide reading and lively interest in contemporary art and culture. She was a patron of the New Gallery, founded by Joe Comyns Carr. Her letters are characterized by a creative and imaginative impulse, written by someone who loves language and delights in communication with others. Her occasional uncertainty is revealed at moments of epistolary tension, when blots appear and apostrophes stray. She was a student of the plays in which she appeared and it is to the good fortune of her appreciative audiences that these included the works of Shakespeare.

ET married young to a much older man who failed to appreciate her. His rejection and their separation brought her humiliation and censure at a very young age. The fact that G. F. Watts was highly educated and one of England's most distinguished artists may have accentuated the gulf which opened between them, making their separation more visible and harder for ET to negotiate. The repercussions were to last a lifetime. Nearly twenty years later she faced ostracism in some quarters when she returned to the United States for the second Lyceum Tour in 1884. Stephen Coleridge felt compelled to defend her and his stern words appear to have settled the matter to her benefit. ET was loved passionately by many and adored at a greater distance by many others. Her family members were devoted to her and, as often occurs, took her for granted. But she also acquired an increasingly large circle of dependants, obliging her to continue to tour the world into the years which should have been set aside for rest and retirement. Her attitude to her work was consistently serious and conscientious, even puritanical. She regularly found her health compromised by rigorous schedules but she was committed to the realization of the performance and respected the responsibility which she had in her relationship with the paying audience. Although in some of her letters she expressed worries about different aspects of her work, these do not seem to have been founded upon serious doubts about her abilities as a woman in the field of work.

ET's attitude to letters seems to have changed over time. She indicated that she would destroy some of her correspondence, such as that to Elizabeth Rumball, her long-term housekeeper and companion. She asked Clement Scott to destroy the letter she sent him. But she carefully preserved others, annotating them for posterity with her own comments and dates. As an avid collector of autographs and letters, she owned a letter written by General Gordon as he entered Khartoum which was kept in her handbag, 'Quex'. She treasured her correspondence and she clearly had a sense of its long-term historical value. Letters seem to have been part of the fabric of her life, a private script for the performance of the stories of her life.

Notes:

1. ET's life story was published as *The Story of My Life* (London: Hutchinson, 1908), and revised after her death as *Ellen Terry's Memoirs* (London: Hutchinson, 1932), co-edited by her daughter, Edith Craig, and Christopher St John. The principal biographies of ET include: E. G. Craig, *Ellen Terry and Her Secret Self* (London: Sampson Low, Marston, 1931); M. Steen, *A Pride of Terrys* (London: Longman, 1962); T. Prideaux, *Ellen Terry: Love or Nothing* (1976; New York: Limelight Editions, 1987); R. Manvell, *Ellen Terry* (London: Heinemann, 1968); N. Auerbach, *Ellen Terry: Player in Her Time* (London: Phoenix House, 1987); J. Melville, *Ellen and Edy* (London: Pandora, 1987); J. Melville, *Ellen Terry* (London: Haus, 2006); M. Holroyd, *A Strange Eventful History: The Dramatic Lives of Ellen Terry, Henry Irving and their Remarkable Families* (London: Chatto & Windus, 2008).
2. M. Webster, *The Same Only Different: Five Generations of a Great Theatre Family* (London: Gollancz, 1969), provides a detailed history of the lives of this theatrical dynasty. See M. S. Barranger, *Margaret Webster: A Life in the Theater* (Ann Arbor, MI: University of Michigan Press, 2004).
3. V. F. Gould, *G. F. Watts: The Last Great Victorian* (New Haven, CT: Yale University Press, 2004).
4. See S. W. Soros (ed.), *E. W. Godwin: Aesthetic Movement and Architect and Designer* (New Haven, CT: Yale University Press, 1999).

5. The principal biographies of Henry Irving include: A. Brereton, *The Life of Henry Irving* (London: Longmans Green & Co., 1908); L. Irving, *Henry Irving: The Actor and His World* (London: Faber & Faber, 1951); M. Bingham, *Henry Irving and the Victorian Theatre* (London: George Allen & Unwin, 1978); and J. Richards, *Sir Henry Irving: A Victorian Actor and His World* (London: Hambledon, 2005). See also the collection of essays from the international conference on Henry Irving held at Leicester University in 2005: R. Foulkes (ed.), *Henry Irving: A Re-Evaluation of the Pre-Eminent Victorian Actor-Manager* (London: Ashgate, 2008).
6. V. Woolf, 'Ellen Terry', *The Collected Letters of Ellen Terry Volume IV* (London: Hogarth Press, 1967), pp. 67–72, on p. 67. See P. Farfan, 'Freshwater Revisited: Virginia Woolf on Ellen Terry and the Art of Acting', *Woolf Studies Annual*, 4 (1998), pp. 3–17; and P. Farfan, *Women, Modernism and Performance* (Cambridge: Cambridge University Press, 2004).
7. See M. Holroyd, *George Bernard Shaw*, 3 vols (London: Chatto & Windus, 1988–90); G. G. Longstreth, 'Epistolary Follies: Identity, Conversation, and Performance in the Correspondence of Ellen Terry and Bernard Shaw', *Shaw: The Annual of Bernard Shaw Studies*, 21 (2001), pp. 27–40.
8. Woolf, 'Ellen Terry', p. 70.
9. G. B. Shaw, 'Preface', in *Ellen Terry and Bernard Shaw: A Correspondence*, ed. C. St John (London: Constable & Co., 1931), pp. vii–xlv, on p. xliii. See S. Peters, 'A Paper Courtship: Bernard Shaw and Ellen Terry', *Annals of Scholarship*, 9:3 (1992), pp. 327–40.
10. See F. Hughes, 'The End of a Quest: Letters of Stephen Coleridge and E.T.', *First Knight: The Journal of the Irving Society*, 9:1 (June 2005), pp. 13–26; and J. H. B. Irving, 'Quest for Missing Ellen Terry Letters', *First Knight: The Journal of the Irving Society*, 5:2 (December 2001), pp. 44–51. The Stephen Coleridge collection is now held at the Garrick Club, London.
11. Shaw, 'Preface', p. xvii.
12. Auerbach, *Ellen Terry*, pp. 408–13.
13. See the biography of Edith Craig: K. Cockin, *Edith Craig (1869–1947): Dramatic Lives* (London: Cassell, 1998). An early *festschrift* was published, E. Adlard (ed.), *Edy: Recollections of Edith Craig* (London: Frederick Muller, 1949). For a study of Edith Craig's theatre work, see R. Gandolfi, *La Prima Regista: Edith Craig, fra rivoluzione della scena e cultura delle donne* (Rome: Bulzoni, 2003). For Edith Craig's work with the Pioneer Players, see the chapters in J. Holledge, *Innocent Flowers: Actresses on the Edwardian Stage* (London: Virago, 1981); the essay by C. Dymkowski, 'Entertaining Ideas: Edy Craig and the Pioneer Players', in V. Gardner and S. Rutherford (eds), *The New Woman and Her Sisters* (Hemel Hempstead: Harvester Wheatsheaf, 1992), pp. 221–33; and the book by K. Cockin, *Women and Theatre in the Age of Suffrage: The Pioneer Players* (London: Palgrave, 2001).
14. See J. Marcus, 'Some Sources for Between the Acts', *A Virginia Woolf Miscellany*, 6 (1977), pp. 1–3, on p. 2; and Holledge, *Innocent Flowers*, p. 161, both discussed in Cockin, *Edith Craig*, p. 9.
15. *Memoirs*, p. v.
16. See J. Stokes, M. Booth and S. Bassnett, *Bernhardt, Terry, Duse: The Actress in Her Time* (Cambridge: Cambridge University Press, 1988); T. Davis, *Actresses as Working Women: Their Social Identity in Victorian Culture* (London: Routledge, 1991); S. T. Barstow, 'Ellen Terry and the Revolt of the Daughters', *Nineteenth-Century Theatre*, 25:1 (1997), pp. 5–32; Gardner and Rutherford (eds), *The New Woman and Her Sisters*.

17. K. Cockin, 'Ellen Terry and Women's Suffrage Agitation', in C. Bland and M. Cross (eds), *Gender and Politics in the Age of Letter-Writing 1750–2000* (London: Ashgate, 2004), pp. 201–12.
18. Shaw, 'Preface', p. xvii.
19. See the Garrick Club correspondence.

EDITORIAL PRINCIPLES

ET's idiosyncratic handwriting displays such features as multiple underlining and dashes. Her single or double underlining has been exactly reproduced. Further multiple underlinings are indicated by asterisks enclosing the relevant text. Other annotations and the insertion of text by ET are described in the notes.

ET uses unconventional notations. There are dashes of different lengths and a variety of signs for 'and'. These have been reproduced as faithfully as possible. She frequently uses superscript for abbreviations such as Mr, cd and shd. For ease of reading, these have been rendered in normal font. Her spelling is sometimes uncertain and apostrophes sometimes go adrift. No silent corrections have been made and where an unusual feature occurs, the academic convention of [*sic*] is employed. The layout on the page has been reproduced as closely as possible and an indication of each new page of text is provided. Crossed out text has been reproduced as such, and inserted text has been indicated by placing the words inside angled brackets < >.

Since her letters record the fatigue and physical pain she endured from neuralgia, rheumatism and poor eyesight, it is not surprising that some letters are characterized by occasional illegibility. Where the text can be deduced but there is a degree of uncertainty, the relevant material is enclosed in square brackets. Where the text is indeed illegible, this is recorded by the abbreviation [illeg.].

ET was usually scrupulous with regard to dating her letters and indeed implores her relatives to date theirs. However, it is natural that in the course of a busy day she has failed to follow her own advice and in many letters dates have therefore been omitted. The dating of letters with confidence is based on the date given on the letter itself. The treatment of undated letters has proceeded with caution. Where the accompanying envelope is the only clue, the postmark date may be used and this will be made explicit in a note. Some postmarks may be indistinct and the abbreviations for the month on the postmark stamp may have caused some confusion. Where there is internal evidence to ascertain the date, for instance where a specific production of a play or an event is mentioned, the letter will be included in the relevant volume and the estimated date given in square brackets. However, where there is no or insufficient evidence to date a letter precisely, these will be located in the final volume of the series.

A subject's change of permanent address acquires the greatest importance in the dating of letters. However, in the case of ET, a performer regularly on tour and often staying with friends, a woman wealthy enough for many years to own or rent more than one property, the address from which she writes changes unusually frequently. For many years she lived in the Earls Court area of London. After her separation from Edward Godwin, ET lived at 211 Camden Road and 44 Finborough Road. On her marriage certificate to Charles Wardell in 1877, Terry's address is given as 44 Finborough Road while Wardell's is 33 Longridge Road. The date of ET's move from 33 Longridge Road to 22 Barkston Gardens has caused some confusion. ET refers to her move to Barkston Gardens in a letter in August 1888 but the actual move seems to have been somewhat delayed, at least until after October and probably later in the year. The purchase of property has also been used to locate ET geographically and therefore date some letters. In 1899 she bought The Farm at Smallhythe in Kent and in 1902 she bought 215 King's Road, Chelsea.

WORKS CITED

Adlard, E. (ed.), *Edy: Recollections of Edith Craig* (London: Frederick Muller, 1949).

AHRC Ellen Terry and Edith Craig archive, at http://www.ellenterryarchive.hull.ac.uk.

American National Biography, gen. ed. J. A. Garraty and M. C. Carnes, 24 vols (New York: Oxford University Press, 1999).

Auerbach, N., *Ellen Terry: Player in Her Time* (London: Phoenix House, 1987).

Barranger, M. S., *Margaret Webster: A Life in the Theater* (Ann Arbor, MI: University of Michigan Press, 2004).

Barstow, S. T., 'Ellen Terry and the Revolt of the Daughters', *Nineteenth-Century Theatre*, 25:1 (1997), pp. 5–32.

Bingham, M., *Henry Irving and the Victorian Theatre* (London: George Allen & Unwin, 1978).

Brereton, A., *The Life of Henry Irving* (London: Longmans Green & Co., 1908).

Cockin, K., *Edith Craig (1869–1947): Dramatic Lives* (London: Cassell, 1998).

—, *Women and Theatre in the Age of Suffrage: The Pioneer Players* (London: Palgrave, 2001).

—, 'Ellen Terry, the Ghost Writer and the Laughing Statue: The Victorian Actress, Letters and Life-Writing', *Journal of European Studies*, 32 (2003), pp. 151–63.

—, 'Ellen Terry and Women's Suffrage Agitation', in C. Bland and M. Cross (eds), *Gender and Politics in The Age of Letter-Writing 1750–2000* (London: Ashgate, 2004), pp. 201–12.

—, 'Ellen Terry and Henry Irving: A Working Relationship', in R. Foulkes (ed.), *Henry Irving: A Re-Evaluation of the Pre-Eminent Victorian Actor-Manager* (London: Ashgate, 2008), pp. 37–48.

Coleridge, S., *Memories with Portraits* (London: John Lane, 1913).

—, *Famous Victorians I Have Known* (London: Simpkin, Marshall Ltd, and Cardiff Western Mail Ltd, 1928).

Craig, E., *Gordon Craig: The Story of His Life* (London: Victor Gollancz, 1968).

Craig, E. G., *Ellen Terry and Her Secret Self* (London: Sampson Low, Marston, 1931).

Davis, T., *Actresses as Working Women: Their Social Identity in Victorian Culture* (London: Routledge, 1991).

Dymkowski, C., 'Entertaining Ideas: Edy Craig and the Pioneer Players', in Gardner and Rutherford (eds), *The New Woman and Her Sisters*, pp. 221–33.

Farfan, P., 'Freshwater Revisited: Virginia Woolf on Ellen Terry and the Art of Acting', *Woolf Studies Annual*, 4 (1998), pp. 3–17.

—, *Women, Modernism and Performance* (Cambridge: Cambridge University Press, 2004).

Foulkes, R., *Lewis Carroll and the Victorian Stage* (London: Ashgate, 2005).

— (ed.), *Henry Irving: A Re-Evaluation of the Pre-Eminent Victorian Actor-Manager* (London: Ashgate, 2008).

Gandolfi, R., *La Prima Regista: Edith Craig, fra rivoluzione della scena e cultura delle donne* (Rome: Bulzoni, 2003).

Gardner, V., and S. Rutherford (eds), *The New Woman and Her Sisters* (Hemel Hempstead: Harvester Wheatsheaf, 1992).

Gielgud, K. T., *Kate Terry Gielgud: An Autobiography* (London: Max Reinhardt, 1953).

Gould, V. F., *G. F. Watts: The Last Great Victorian* (New Haven, CT: Yale University Press, 2004).

Hart, J. D. (ed.), *The Oxford Companion to American Literature*, 5th edn (New York: Oxford University Press, 1983).

Hartnoll, P. M. (ed.), *The Concise Oxford Companion to the Theatre* (Oxford: Oxford University Press, 1972).

Hatton, J., *Henry Irving's Impressions of America Narrated in a Series of Sketches Chronicles and Conversations*, 2 vols (London: Sampson Low, Marston, Searle & Rivington, 1884).

Holledge, J., *Innocent Flowers: Actresses on the Edwardian Stage* (London: Virago, 1981).

Holroyd, M., *George Bernard Shaw*, 3 vols (London: Chatto & Windus, 1988–90).

—, *A Strange Eventful History: The Dramatic Lives of Ellen Terry, Henry Irving and their Remarkable Families* (London: Chatto & Windus, 2008).

Hughes, F., 'The End of a Quest: Letters of Stephen Coleridge and E.T.', *First Knight: The Journal of the Irving Society*, 9:1 (June 2005), pp. 13–26.

Irving, H., *English Actors: Their Characteristics and Their Methods: A Discourse by Henry Irving Delivered in the University Schools at Oxford on Saturday June 26, 1886* (Oxford: Clarendon Press, 1886).

Irving, J. H. B., 'Quest for Missing Ellen Terry Letters', *First Knight: The Journal of the Irving Society*, 5:2 (December 2001), pp. 44–51.

Irving, L., *Henry Irving: The Actor and His World* (London: Faber & Faber, 1951).

Longstreth, G. G., 'Epistolary Follies: Identity, Conversation, and Performance in the Correspondence of Ellen Terry and Bernard Shaw', *Shaw: The Annual of Bernard Shaw Studies*, 21 (2001), pp. 27–40.

Mackenzie, J. H., *Orientalism: History, Theory and the Arts* (Manchester: Manchester University Press, 1995).

Manvell, R., *Ellen Terry* (London: Heinemann, 1968).

Marcus, J., 'Some Sources for Between the Acts', *A Virginia Woolf Miscellany*, 6 (1977), pp. 1–3.

Melville, J., *Ellen and Edy* (London: Pandora, 1987).

—, *Ellen Terry* (London: Haus, 2006).

Noszlopy, G. T., *Public Sculpture of Warwickshire, Coventry and Solihull* (Liverpool: Liverpool University Press, 2003).

Oxford Dictionary of National Biography, ed. H. C. G. Matthew and B. Harrison, 60 vols (Oxford: Oxford University Press, 2004).

Partridge, E., *A Dictionary of Slang and Unusual English*, 5th edn (London: Routledge & Kegan Paul, 1961).

Peters, S., 'A Paper Courtship: Bernard Shaw and Ellen Terry', *Annals of Scholarship*, 9:3 (1992), pp. 327–40.

Prescott, A., 'Brother Irving: Sir Henry Irving and Freemasonry', *First Knight: Journal of the Irving Society*, 7:2 (December 2003), pp. 13–22.

Prideaux, T., *Ellen Terry: Love or Nothing* (1976; New York: Limelight Editions, 1987).

Richards, J., *Sir Henry Irving: A Victorian Actor and His World* (London: Hambden, 2005).

Skolout, P. F., 'Queen Palmer', *Cheyenne Edition*, 9 June 1995, pp. 17–18.

Soros, S. W. (ed.), *E. W. Godwin: Aesthetic Movement and Architect and Designer* (New Haven, CT: Yale University Press, 1999).

Steen, M., *A Pride of Terrys* (London: Longman, 1962).

Stokes, J., M. Booth and S. Bassnett, *Bernhardt, Terry, Duse: The Actress in Her Time* (Cambridge: Cambridge University Press, 1988).

Terry, E., *The Story of My Life* (London: Hutchinson, 1908).

—, *The Heart of Ellen Terry*, ed. S. Coleridge (London: Mills & Boon, 1928).

—, *Ellen Terry's Memoirs*, ed. E. Craig and C. St John (London: Hutchinson, 1932).

Terry, E., and B. Shaw, *Ellen Terry and Bernard Shaw: A Correspondence*, ed. C. St John (London: Constable & Co., 1931).

Webster, M., *The Same Only Different: Five Generations of a Great Theatre Family* (London: Gollancz, 1969).

Winter, W., *Henry Irving* (New York: George J. Coombes, 1885).

Woolf, V., 'Ellen Terry', *The Collected Letters of Ellen Terry Volume IV* (London: Hogarth Press, 1967), pp. 67–72.

INTRODUCTION: VOLUME 1

This volume begins with letters written in 1865, when ET was eighteen years old, already a well-known performer and in the uncertain position of having separated from her husband. The first letters presented here are to a female artist friend, Mary-Anne Hall, to whom ET writes in great confidence. There are letters to Mrs Wigan, to whom ET is grateful for her professional advice, acknowledging Mrs Wigan's influence on the development of her acting technique. During the Wigans' management of the Queen's Theatre, Long Acre, London, ET had performed with Henry Irving for the first time, in David Garrick's adaptation of *The Taming of the Shrew*. ET could have been a footnote in regional theatre history. However, her determination was always to learn, to develop and to *work* at her roles. She was committed to making the most of every opportunity and it yielded great results, giving her a significant place in nineteenth-century culture as well as theatre history. For many readers of this volume, it will be her involvement in the performances of Shakespeare's plays with Henry Irving and his Lyceum Theatre Company that provides the greatest interest. The volume spans twenty-three years, ending in December 1888 in the period when ET faced one of the greatest challenges of her career: the performance of Lady Macbeth.

The collection of ET's letters represents certain periods in great detail, with letters sometimes written to several people on the same day, while other periods are completely silent. There are, therefore, presumed gaps in the correspondence relating both to specific periods of her life and to specific addressees. It is frustrating that so few letters have emerged from the early years: during her marriage to G. F. Watts, her 'six year vacation', as she describes it in her autobiography;[1] when she lived with Edward Godwin, the father of her two children; and during her marriage to Charles Wardell (who acted in the theatre under the name Kelly). Godwin and Wardell were men whom her daughter was to describe as polar opposites:

> All through her life the man of brains competed for her affections with the man of brawn. But this man of brawn, although a good fellow in some ways – he had a genuine affection for his wife's children, who for a time bore his name – had a violent and jealous temper which Ellen Terry eventually found intolerable.[2]

The nature of ET's relationships and the general tendency of relatives to take a protective stance when dealing with the effects of the deceased make it likely that some of her letters have been destroyed. There is evidence still visible in her archive of paperwork having been burnt. Furthermore, ET appears to have had a consistent approach to her letter-writing, expressing concern when she is unable to write or obliged to dictate a letter to be sent on her behalf, so any lack of coverage in a particular period of time invites some scrutiny and cautious interpretation.

Some individuals feature in this volume as regular recipients of ET's letters. In the early letters, written when ET was a young woman, Mary-Anne Hall is treated to an intimate revelation of ET's feelings about her husband, G. F. Watts, from who she was separated. Roger Manvell quoted from these letters in detail in his biography of ET.[3] The energetic tone of Terry's correspondence with her close female friends is also apparent in her letters to her mentor, the novelist Charles Reade. The annotations which he, apparently, made on these letters convey his determination to write back, to record for posterity his reaction to her forceful and manipulative demands. Some indication is provided here of the personality of the lively young woman who had provoked such a strong reaction in G. F. Watts.

ET's friends were drawn from a very wide social group. Perhaps her closest and most long-standing friend was Elizabeth Rumball (1823–1913), née Bocking, wife of James Quilter Rumball, surgeon of Harpenden. She was the stalwart companion and housekeeper to ET, known in the family as 'Boo'. She was nearby and had assisted when Edith Craig was born. Boo's family members also became part of ET's circle, notably Catherine Elizabeth Powell (1849–1936), also known as Bo or Kitty, Boo's niece, and her husband Joe (Joseph) Powell (1850–1927), who was a blacksmith at Brancaster, Norfolk. Their children were Kittie (Pussie), Ellen E. (Nellie), Edie (married Gascoigne; d. *c.* 1951) and Joe (J. E. C.) Powell (d. 1957). Boo was given the responsibility of taking care of ET's children and was entrusted with ET's confidences. Of relevance to a later volume in this series is ET's purchase of land in Brancaster, Norfolk, presumably as a form of pension for Boo. ET attempted to mask the identities of donor and recipient by purchasing the land for Boo's niece Catherine Powell. This was the site of The Limes, which was to become a refuge for one of the younger generation of the Terry family.

Two close female friends of ET, Bertha Bramley and Elsie 'Queen' Palmer, feature in the correspondence but not in ET's published autobiography. Queen Palmer was a wealthy American friend who had been a singer before her marriage to a military man with whom she settled on a vast plot of land in the United States which was to become Colorado Springs. In poor health, Queen Palmer relocated to Britain. ET's tours of the United States with the Lyceum Theatre Company had given her the opportunity to develop a circle of friends across the

Atlantic. Other American female friends included Mrs Gillespie, Mrs Fields and Mrs Beecher, wife of the famous preacher Rev. Henry Beecher.

ET also enjoyed the company and friendship of men. She enjoyed a long correspondence with Albert Fleming, of Elterwater in the Lake District, which appears to have begun in 1885. Fleming taught Edith Craig and ET to spin, providing an authentic dimension to ET's scenes as Margaret in *Faust*. Fleming had been influenced by John Ruskin in his interest in spinning and weaving and he occasionally supplied ET with linen,[4] as well as the Lake District daffodils from which he acquired his nickname from her, Daffy.

Where there was the frisson of potential or realized intimacy with men, the epistolary exchange is perhaps more vital and dramatic. Joe Evans had been part of an admiring audience group at the Star Theatre, New York, and became a close friend, corresponding with both mother and daughter, teaching Edith Craig to paint and visiting them in England. ET's correspondence with Evans reproduced here has been subject to censorship, the circumstances of which are not known, but some parts of the letters have been excised. ET's friendship with Stephen Coleridge also began in the theatre. In their long-standing and very regular correspondence, which has only recently been located and made available to researchers, ET provided her intimate thoughts. She expressed concern for him on his travels abroad. On his marriage to Geraldine, ET recalibrated her discourse, embracing 'Gill' as well as Stephen and expressing her devotion to the entire Coleridge family in a sincere desire to maintain contact. She relied on Coleridge's sound advice and guidance, especially during the upbringing of her son, Edward Gordon Craig, the vicissitudes of his education and her separation from her second husband, Charles Wardell (Kelly). The letters to Coleridge in this volume give an insight into the extremely distracting and distressing events occurring backstage in ETs personal life. This provides the context for the period when she was complying with a rigorous schedule of rehearsals and achieving great things in performance.

ET's relationship with her children, Edith Craig and Edward Gordon Craig, was often maintained by letter while she was away on tour. This long-distance parenting created its own pressures and anxieties which are most apparent in letters to her son. Extremely detailed instructions and demands, circumscribing minute details of behaviour, appear now to be extraordinarily oppressive. Yet these letters were a substitute for the conversations which she was unable to have with him. She enlisted the help of trusted teachers to take on the education of her children. Letters included here give an insight into the education received by Edith Craig from Elizabeth Malleson at her home in Gloucestershire. Edith Craig was then sent to Germany, accompanied by Mrs Malleson's daughter Mabel, and was taught music by Alexis Hollaender. ET was dismayed to find that her son's progress at school in Heidelberg was not promising and was devastated by his expulsion. Her attempts to find out exactly what had happened and to take control of the situation involved her in close consultation with Stephen Coleridge. Her strategy was to deprive her son of contact with her for some time, until arrangements had been made for his continued education elsewhere. All of this turmoil was taking place when she could least afford the time and emotional energy. This was the period leading up to her performance as Lady Macbeth at the Lyceum Theatre in December 1888.

ET developed epistolary relationships with the leading drama critics of the day on both sides of the Atlantic, responding to their reviews of her performance. In this volume examples are included from letters to William Winter and Clement Scott, with whom ET endeavoured to maintain contact. She was aware of the dependence of the business of theatre on both the critics and the paying audience and she achieved a rapport with her critics. The equivalent of networking was an essential part of the life of the theatre and the rising status of the acting profession brought ET and her colleagues into the social circles of the aristocracy. Henry Irving was a member of several London clubs, including the Savage Club and the Garrick Club. He became a freemason but refrained from joining the Drury Lane Lodge associated with Drury Lane Theatre.[5] Meanwhile ET benefited from her association with various well-connected individuals such as Sir George Lewis, the leading lawyer associated with cases of great controversy, and aristocrats such as Lady Gordon, Lady Jeune and Lady Lewis.

Chapter 1 of the present volume covers the period 1865–77, during which ET returned to the stage following her separation from G. F. Watts, and began her relationship with Edward Godwin, which ended in the year of her second marriage, to the actor Charles Wardell (Kelly). What is immediately striking is the absence of letters in the years 1869–73, the period when her children were born. Most of the early letters are to her close friend Mary-Anne Hall, including one which should be treated with some caution, as an unsigned copy, the original of which has not been seen. Others include letters to Charles Reade, John Hare and the American author Shutz Wilson.

Chapter 2 begins with the year 1878: a turning point for ET in several different ways. This was the year when Henry Irving invited her to join him at the Lyceum Theatre, bringing her a regular and substantial income. Her success in the role of Olivia in the dramatization of Oliver Goldsmith's *The Vicar of Wakefield* provided her with one of several identities she adopted in her epistolary life, signing herself in the name of the stage role. For the public too, she became Olivia, achieving great popularity and acclaim. Another change of identity and name occurred at this time, in her decision to marry again, to actor Charles Wardell (Kelly). It also affected her family. Mother and children took the new name Wardell, trying it on for size. For the children, this involved putting aside the names which had been conjured from the Scottish island of Ailsa Craig.

Armed with such rugged personae, they had protected themselves against the opprobrium of illegitimacy. This is also the year when the extant correspondence begins between ET and Stephen Coleridge, her admirer, intimate friend, mentor and legal adviser. Coleridge was to be a stalwart assistant in her extrication from the Wardell marriage, which had become untenable and even dangerous. The chapter begins with ET's witty but acerbic acknowledgement of her husband's controlling behaviour.

In 1881, ET enlisted the help of Stephen Coleridge to arrange her separation from Wardell and letters relating to this distressing period punctuate Chapter 3. Meanwhile her successes on the stage continued and she refers to performances in Tennyson's *The Cup*, *The Merchant of Venice* and *Romeo and Juliet*. She used her position to help her colleagues on many occasions, evidenced here by her letter to Janet Achurch, which demonstrates ET's support of a performer at the start of her career.

Chapter 4 features letters from the period of the first two Lyceum Theatre Company tours. These momentous transatlantic tours to the United States and Canada began in 1883. They were of great importance for Anglo-American relations and for their impact on the history of nineteenth-century theatre. The departures and arrivals of the company were major public events, attracting dignitaries and the press. ET, as the leading female performer in the company, attracted great attention and had no means of concealing her trepidation and home-sickness on arrival in New York. The press shamefully recorded her tearful response to questions about those she had left behind. ET's separation from her children must have taken its toll. This is recorded by the journalist Joseph Hatton, who provided the detailed and lively account of Henry Irving's travels to the United States, giving a sense of the excitement and publicity which had been built up for the first tour.[6] In autumn 1883 Henry Irving, ET and their colleagues had a most extraordinary adventure. Irving and Terry were invited to meet Rev. Henry Beecher and his wife. They learnt about the politics of the American civil war and the abolition of slavery. They were delighted by the illumination of Brooklyn Bridge by night but the train journey to Baltimore in snow and ice was fraught and, in Hatton's terms, 'wild'.[7] In Canada in February 1884 the snow brought novelty and exhilaration when ET took to the ice at the Toronto Toboggan Club. She had some difficulties to face in this period, too. Some emotional turmoil and financial difficulties were created by her estranged husband, Charles Wardell, who persisted in a theatrical tour which was to be financial disastrous, incurring further debts for her. Communication from G. F. Watts had resumed in Easter 1882 and in the summer of 1883 a brief but poignant letter reproduced here indicates the depth of feeling she still held for him.

The second Lyceum Tour in the winter of 1884–5 took Henry Irving, ET and their colleagues away from home at Christmas but the rigorous schedule and difficulties of travelling were offset by their critical acclaim. The impact of these first two tours is measured by the efforts of William Winter, the leading drama critic in the United States. In 1885, Winter's book appeared, dedicated to the Garrick Club, London. It detailed Henry Irving's productions in New York and endorsed his reputation with a study of his acting.[8] Not only a major cultural event, Irving's tours also prompted a reflection on theatre and performance and the state of the art in the United States at that time. ET's place in the rise of Irving's status was assured but assumed to be a supporting, if indispensable role.

ET could not always be relied upon to behave with composure on formal occasions. Mirth might take over at any moment. For that reason she absented herself from Irving's part in the ceremony to unveil the fountain at Stratford upon Avon although she would have liked to have attended his lecture at Oxford University in 1886.[9] She would have been captivated as he explored the methods of the most distinguished actors in Britain and their relationship to the eternal tension between nature and artifice. She would have endorsed Irving's public declaration as an autodidact: 'The only Alma Mater I ever knew was the hard stage of a country theatre'.[10]

The years 1885–6, represented in Chapter 5, brought thoughts of mortality very much to the fore. ET was devastated by the unexpected death in October 1886 of Edward Godwin, the father of her children and unique in her affections. She gained comfort especially from her daughter. Before ET left for the United States on the third Lyceum tour in October 1887, Edith Craig had accompanied her mother to Godwin's grave. During ET's tours abroad her letter-writing became a source of sustenance, in maintaining contact with friends and family. In 1887, the subject of Chapter 6, ET was very much concerned with her children's education, both of whom were educated in Germany with different degrees of success. Not surprisingly the year 1888 is very well represented with letters and Chapter 7 is devoted to it. The year began with reports of activities in wintry Chicago. It ended with ET's concerns about Edward Gordon Craig's expulsion from school in Heidelberg and her need to concentrate on the demanding and nerve-wracking performance of Lady Macbeth. The letters available for this year provide a sense of ET's breadth of interest, the variety of correspondents with whom she was maintaining contact and the unfolding of developments in various supportive relationships, such as with Joe Evans and Stephen Coleridge. The letters of maternal surveillance to her son are well represented too. Family relationships were changing as the children were finding their ways in the world and coming to terms with their identity as individuals. In 1887 they were christened in Exeter Cathedral by the bishop. They had adjusted to the official status accorded by the patronymic from Wardell in spite of the difficulties the marriage brought to their mother. Having gained one father, they lost two: Wardell through separation and Godwin through unexpected death.

Other male figures had a significant presence in their lives – Henry Irving, Bram Stoker and Stephen Coleridge – but it was their mother who was to dominate. She was growing in status, establishing a role for herself in society as well as on the stage with considerable charm and influence. She had indeed become, in Oscar Wilde's terms, 'Our lady of the Lyceum'.[11]

Notes:

1. E. Terry, *The Story of My Life* (London: Hutchinson, 1908), ch. 4.
2. Ibid., pp. 116–17.
3. R. Manvell, *Ellen Terry* (London: Heinemann, 1968).
4. *Memoirs*, p. 186.
5. A. Prescott, 'Brother Irving: Sir Henry Irving and Freemasonry', *First Knight: Journal of the Irving Society*, 7:2 (December 2003), pp. 13–22.
6. J. Hatton, *Henry Irving's Impressions of America Narrated in a Series of Sketches Chronicles and Conversations*, 2 vols (London: Sampson Low, Marston, Searle & Rivington, 1884).
7. Ibid., vol. 2, p. 15.
8. W. Winter, *Henry Irving* (New York: George J. Coombes, 1885).
9. H. Irving, *English Actors: Their Characteristics and Their Methods: A Discourse by Henry Irving delivered in the University Schools at Oxford on Saturday June 26, 1886* (Oxford: Clarendon Press, 1886).
10. Ibid., p. 2.
11. Quoted in M. Holroyd, *A Strange Eventful History: The Dramatic Lives of Ellen Terry, Henry Irving and their Remarkable Families* (London: Chatto & Windus, 2008), p. 214.

CHRONOLOGY (1865–88)

Year	Date/Month	Event
1847	27 February	Birth of ET at 44 Smithford St, Coventry (see *ODNB*)
1848	27 February	Presumed birth date of ET during her lifetime
1856	28 April	ET's stage debut in London
1857	summer	Terry family stay in Ryde, Isle of Wight
1861		ET's sister Kate performs opposite Charles Fechter in *Hamlet*
1862		ET joins J. L. Chute's company in Bristol
		G. F. Watts meets Kate and Ellen Terry; portrait *The Sisters*
1864	20 February	ET marries G. F. Watts in St Barnabas Church, Kensington, London; portrait *Choosing*
		Portrait of ET by Julia Margaret Cameron
	21 December	ET meets Lewis Carroll
1865	26 January	ET separates from G. F. Watts
	7 April	Lewis Carroll visits the Terry family
1866	spring	ET travels to Paris, for the first time, with Mrs Marie Casella
		ET lives at 24 Caversham Road, Kentish Town Road, London
1867		Kate Terry marries Arthur Lewis
	26 December	ET acts with Henry Irving for the first time
1868	10 October	ET leaves the stage; elopes with Edward Godwin
1869	15 July	Henry Irving marries Florence O'Callaghan
	9 December	Birth of Edith Craig
1870	15 July	Birth of H. B. Irving
1871		E. W. Godwin designs house for ET, Fallows Green, Harpenden, Hertfordshire
	25 November	Henry Irving separates from his wife Florence
	December	Birth of Laurence Irving
1871–8		Henry Irving performs in Lyceum Company, managed by the Batemans
1872		Henry Irving moves to 15a Grafton Street
	16 January	Birth of Edward Gordon Craig
		Birth of Elsie Palmer, first child of Mary (Queen) Palmer
1873		Godwin takes ET and Edith Craig to France
1874		Charles Reade persuades ET to return to theatre
		ET lives with Godwin at 20 Taviton Street, Gordon Square, London
	April	ET meets Charles Wardell (Kelly)
1875		ET separates from Godwin
1876		Birth of James Carew, ET's third husband
	4 January	Godwin marries Beatrice Philip
	18 February	Death of Charlotte Cushman
1876–*c.* 1880		ET's residence at Rose Cottage, Hampton Court Road, London

Year	Date/Month	Event
1877	13 March	G. F. Watts divorces ET
	6 November	ET's decree absolute
		ET lives at 44 Finborough Road before her marriage to Wardell
	21 November	ET marries Charles Wardell; lives at 33 Longridge Road, London
1878		ET's role in *Olivia*, under the management of John Hare, relaunches her career
	July	Henry Irving visits ET at Longridge Road
	August	ET on tour with Wardell; stays in County Durham at her father-in-law's house
	30 December	ET begins working with Henry Irving at the Lyceum
1878–1917		Correspondence with Stephen Coleridge
1879		Death of Laura Seymour, Charles Reade's companion
		George Terry, ET's brother is her manager during her tour
1880		Henry Irving buys The Grange, Brooke Green
		Death of Tom Taylor
		William Terriss joins the Lyceum Company
1881	October	ET is advised by Stephen Coleridge on her separation from Charles Wardell
1882	Easter	ET's correspondence with G. F. Watts resumes
		Florence Terry marries William Morris
c. 1882		Queen Palmer moves to England.
1883		Edith Craig boards at Mrs Cole's school, Foxton Road, Earls Court
		Louise Jopling's portrait, *Ellen Terry as Portia*, exhibited at Grosvenor Gallery
	January	Edward Gordon Craig boards at Southfields Park, Rev. Wilkinson's school
	29 May	First Actors' Benevolent Fund Matinee, Drury Lane Theatre
	summer	ET writes to G. F. Watts
	29 October	First Lyceum company tour of USA and Canada opens in New York; ET and Henry Irving meet Rev. Henry Beecher
1884	February	ET at the Toronto Toboggan Club, Canada
	April	ET and Lyceum company return to England
		Publication of Joseph Hatton's book on Irving's tour of USA
		Death of Charles Reade
	30 September	Second Lyceum company tour, opens at the Academy of Music, Quebec, Canada
1885	14 January	Edward Gordon Craig's first speaking role, in *Eugene Aram* in Chicago, USA
	17 April	Death of Charles Wardell
		Publication of William Winter's book on Henry Irving
		ET's correspondence with Joe Evans
1886	June	Henry Irving's lecture at Oxford University
	August	ET and Henry Irving on holiday
	6 October	Death of Edward William Godwin
1886–7		Edward Gordon Craig educated at Bradfield College

Year	**Date/Month**	**Event**
1887		Death of Mrs Sara Prinsep
	11 January	Edith Craig and Edward Gordon Craig christened at Exeter Cathedral by the bishop
	8 March	Death of Rev. Henry Beecher
	August	Death of Palgrave Simpson
	autumn	ET and Edith Craig visit Godwin's grave
	7 November	Third Lyceum company tour of USA (New York, Philadelphia, Chicago and Boston), opening at the Star Theatre, New York; Edith Craig accompanies ET
1887–1912		ET's correspondence with Audrey Campbell
1888	26 June	Edith Craig performs for Mummers Society, St George's Hall (ET is president of the society)
	July	ET in Germany and Venice; on holiday with Edith Craig and Henry Irving in Lucerne, Basle, Cologne and Berlin in August
	October	Edward Gordon Craig expelled from Heidelberg College
	November	Edward Gordon Craig is educated by Mr Wilkinson
	autumn	Edith Craig is taught music by Alexis Hollaender in Berlin, where she sings in a concert in November
c. autumn 1888–1902		ET's main residence at 22 Barkston Gardens, London

MAJOR ROLES PLAYED BY ELLEN TERRY (1865–88)

The first performance in a significant role is given. Repeat performances are given for the tours in United States and Canada only when these signify the move from one city to another during the tour. Where a play programme is held in the National Trust's Ellen Terry and Edith Craig archive, the reference number is given in the final column.

Year	Date/Month	Play	Role	Venue (in London unless specified)	Archive Reference
1856	20 April	*The Winter's Tale*	Mamillius	Princess's (produced by Charles Kean)	
	October	*A Midsummer Night's Dream*	Puck	Princess's	[ET-Pm]
1857		*The White Cat*	Goldenstar / Dragonetta	Princess's	
1858		*King John*	Prince Arthur	Princess's	
1859–60	on tour (managed by Ben Terry in Illustrative and Musical Drawing Room Entertainment)				
1860	29 June		prologue	Campden House	[ET-D2074]
	1 August		prologue	Kingston	
	29 August	*Home for the Holidays*		Literary Institution, Ventnor	[ET-D1]
1861	November	Eugene Sue, *Atar Gull*	Clementine	Royalty Theatre	
1862	15 September	*Endymion*	Cupid	Theatre Royal, Bristol (managed by J. H. Chute)	
1863	4 March	*A Midsummer Night's Dream*	Titania / Spirit of Future	Theatre Royal, Bath	

Year	Date/Month	Play	Role	Venue (in London unless specified)	Archive Reference
1863	19 March	*The Little Treasure* (adapt. from *La Joie de la Maison*)		Haymarket	
	(other roles at the Haymarket: Hero in *Much Ado About Nothing*; Lady Frances Touchwood in *The Belle's Stratagem*; Julia in *The Rivals*; Mary Meredith in *Our American Cousin*)				
1866	20 June	Sheridan Knowles, *The Hunchback* (Kate Terry's benefit)	Helen		[ET-D6]
1867	11 May	Tom Taylor, *A Sheep in Wolf's Clothing*			
	8 June	*The Antipodes or The Ups and Downs of Life*		Theatre Royal Holborn	
	24 October	Charles Reade, *Double Marriage*		New Queen's (managed by the Wigans)	
	14 November	*Still Waters Run Deep*	Mrs Mildmay	New Queen's	
	26 December	David Garrick, *Katherine and Petruchio* (ET acts for first time with Henry Irving)	Katherine	New Queen's	[ET-D7]
1868	February	*The Household Fairy*		New Queen's	
1874	28 February	Charles Reade, *The Wandering Heir* (ET's return to the stage)		New Queen's	
	30 April	Charles Reade, *It's Never Too Late To Mend*	Susan Merton	Theatre Royal, Westminster Bridge Rd	[ET-D10]
1875	17 April	*The Merchant of Venice*	Portia	Prince of Wales (managed by the Bancrofts; designed by E. W. Godwin)	[ET-D12]
	29 May	*Money*	Clara Douglas	Prince of Wales	[ET-D13]
	19 June	*A Happy Pair*	Mrs Honeyton	Prince of Wales	
	7 August	*The Lady of Lyons*	Pauline	Princess's	[ET-D14]
	6 November	Tom Taylor and Charles Reade, *Masks and Faces*	Mabel Vane	Prince of Wales	[ET-D15]

Year	Date/Month	Play	Role	Venue (in London unless specified)	Archive Reference
1876	6 May	*Ours*	Blanche Haye	Tottenham Court Rd	
	4 November	Charles F. Coghlan, *Brothers*	Kate Hungerford	Court (managed by John Hare)	[ET-D16]
	2 December	Tom Taylor and A. W. Dubourg, *New Men and Old Acres*	Lilian Vavasour	Court	[ET-D17]
1877	1 March	*Money* (Henry Compton benefit; ET's first appearance at Drury Lane)	Georgina Vesey	Drury Lane	[ET-D18]
	6 October	Lord Lytton, *The House of Darnley*	Court	[ET-D19]	
1878	26 January	Tom Taylor, *Victims*	Mrs Merryweather	Court	[ET-D20]
	30 March	W. G. Wills, *Olivia* (ET performs opposite William Terriss)	Olivia	Court	[ET-D21]
	summer	ET toured the provinces in *Olivia*; *The Cynic's Defeat or All is Vanity*; Charles Reade's *Dora*, adapted from Tennyson's poem			
	23 August	Charles Reade, *Dora*		Prince of Wales, Liverpool	
	30 December	*Hamlet*	Ophelia	Lyceum (ET's first appearance at the Lyceum, managed by Henry Irving)	[ET-D23]
1879	17 April	Edward Bulwer Lytton, *Lady of Lyons*	Pauline	Lyceum	
	6 June	W. G. Wills, *The Fate of Eugene Aram*	Ruth Meadows	Lyceum	[ET-D24]
	27 June	W. G. Wills, *Charles I*	Queen Henrietta Maria	Lyceum	[ET-D22]
	4 July	Charles Reade, *The Lyons Mail*	Jeanette	Lyceum	
	25 July	*Richard III* (Act I)	Lady Anne	Lyceum	
	25 July	Kenney, *Raising the Wind*	Peggy	Lyceum	
	summer	ET toured the provinces in *New Men and Old Acres*; *The Merchant of Venice*; Lady Teazle in *The School for Scandal*			

Year	Date/Month	Play	Role	Venue (in London unless specified)	Archive Reference
1879	12 September	Alice Comyns-Carr, *Butterfly* (adapt. from *Frou-Frou*)	Butterfly	Glasgow	
	1 November	*The Merchant of Venice*	Portia	Lyceum	
1880	20 May	*The Merchant of Venice*	Portia	Lyceum	[ET-D28]
		and W. G. Wills, *Iolanthe* (second benefit for ET)	Iolanthe		
	23 July	*The Hunchback* (one scene)	Helen	Lyceum	[ET-D29]
	3 September	*Much Ado About Nothing*	Beatrice (ET's debut in the role)	Grand Theatre, Leeds	
	autumn	ET toured the provinces in *Much Ado About Nothing*			
1881	3 January	Alfred, Lord Tennyson, *The Cup*	Camma	Lyceum	
	16 April	Hannah Cowley, *The Belle's Strategem*	Letitia Hardy	Lyceum	
	2 May	*Othello*	Desdemona	Lyceum	[ET-D31]
	23 July	Sheridan Knowles, *The Hunchback* (scene)	Helen	Lyceum	[ET-D937]
1882	8 March	*Romeo and Juliet*	Juliet	Lyceum	[ET-D39]
	24 June	*Romeo and Juliet* (benefit for ET and the 100th performance of play)	Juliet	Lyceum	[ET-D42]
	11 October	*Much Ado About Nothing*	Beatrice	Lyceum	[ET-D44]
1883	2 June	Charles Reade, *The Lyons Mail*	Jeanette	Lyceum	[ET-D54]
	14 June	Charles Selby, *Robert Macaire* (in aid of the Royal College of Music)	Clementine	Lyceum	[ET-D551a]

Year	Date/Month	Play	Role	Venue (in London unless specified)	Archive Reference
1883	30 October	W. G. Wills, *Charles I*	Queen	Star Theatre, New York, USA	[ET-D590]
	(several other productions of *The Merchant of Venice* were given in New York, ending on 24 November 1883)				
	26 November	*The Merchant of Venice*	Portia	Chestnut St Opera House, Philadelphia, USA	[ET-D595]
	10 December	*The Merchant of Venice*	Portia	Boston Theatre, USA	[ET-D598]
	29 December	*The Merchant of Venice*	Portia	Academy of Music, Baltimore, USA	[ET-D601]
	31 December	*The Merchant of Venice*	Portia	Haverly's Theatre, Brooklyn, USA	[ET-D602]
1884	2 January	*The Merchant of Venice*	Portia	Star Theatre, Broadway and 13th Street, New York, USA	[ET-D2002]
	21 January	Hannah Cowley, *The Belle's Stratagem*	Letitia Hardy	Olympic Theatre, St Louis, USA	[ET-D607]
	28 January	Casimir Delavigne, *Louis XI*		Grand Opera House, Cincinnati, USA	[ET-D610]
	6 February	Hannah Cowley, *The Belle's Stratagem*	Letitia Hardy	English's Opera House, Indianapolis, USA	[ET-D611]
	13 February	*Hamlet*	Ophelia	Haverly's Theatre, Brooklyn, New York, USA	[ET-D614]
	18 February	Hannah Cowley, *The Belle's Stratagem*	Letitia Hardy	Whitney's Grand Opera House, Detroit, USA	[ET-D616]
	23 February	W. G. Wills, *Charles I*	Queen	Grand Opera House, Toronto, Canada	[ET-D617]
	26 February	W. G. Wills, *Charles I*	Queen	Boston Theatre, USA	[ET-D618]
	3 March	Casimir Delavigne, *Louis XI*		National Theatre, Washington, DC, USA	[ET-D509]
	22 March	*Much Ado About Nothing*	Beatrice	Chestnut Street Opera House, Philadelphia, USA	[ET-D625]

Year	Date/Month	Play	Role	Venue (in London unless specified)	Archive Reference
1884	31 March	*Much Ado About Nothing*	Beatrice	Star Theatre Broadway, New York, USA	[ET-D626]
	8 July	*Twelfth Night*	Viola	Lyceum	[ET-D63]
	8 October	*The Merchant of Venice*	Portia	Grand Opera House, Toronto, Canada	[ET-D631]
	14 October	*Much Ado About Nothing*	Beatrice	Academy of Music, Buffalo, New York, USA	[ET-D632]
	24 October	*The Merchant of Venice*	Portia	Globe Theatre, Boston, USA	[ET-D634]
	13 November	*Much Ado About Nothing*	Beatrice	Star Theatre, Broadway, New York, USA	[ET-D636]
	8 December	*Twelfth Night*	Viola	Chestnut Street Opera House, Philadelphia, USA	[ET-D640]
1885	16 January	*Twelfth Night*	Viola	Haverly's Theatre, Brooklyn, New York, USA	[ET-D643]
	3 February	*The Merchant of Venice*	Portia	Albaugh's Grand Opera House, Washington DC, USA	[ET-D649]
	16 February	W. G. Wills, *The Fate of Eugene Aram*	Ruth Meadows	Globe Theatre, Boston, USA	[ET-D650]
	25 February	*Much Ado About Nothing*	Beatrice	Chestnut Street Opera House, Philadelphia, USA	[ET-D655]
	7 March	*Much Ado About Nothing*	Beatrice	Brooklyn Theatre, New York, USA	[ET-D656]
	10 March	W. G. Wills, *The Fate of Eugene Aram*	Ruth Meadows	Star Theatre, Broadway, New York, USA	[ET-D657]
	2 May	*Hamlet*	Ophelia	Lyceum	[ET-D66]
	27 May	W. G. Wills, *Olivia*	Olivia	Lyceum	[ET-D70]
	19 December	W. G. Wills, *Faust*	Margaret	Lyceum	[ET-D75]

Year	Date/Month	Play	Role	Venue (in London unless specified)	Archive Reference
1887	1 June	Byron, *Werner* (benefit for Dr Westland Marston)	Josephine	Lyceum	[ET-D87]
	7 June	Alfred C. Calmour, *The Amber Heart*	Ellaline	Lyceum	[ET-D89]
	7 November	W. G. Wills, *Faust*	Margaret	Star Theatre, New York, USA	[ET-D662]
	12 December	W. G. Wills, *Faust*	Margaret	Chestnut Opera House, Philadelphia, USA	[ET-D665]
1888	23 January	W. G. Wills, *Faust*	Margaret	Boston Theater, Boston, USA	[ET-D666]
	28 February	*Olivia*	Olivia	Star Theater, Broadway, New York, USA	[ET-D667]
	21 March	*The Merchant of Venice*	Portia	Star Theater, Broadway, New York, USA	[ET-D668]
	7 July	*The Amber Heart* (ET's benefit performance)		Lyceum Theatre	[ET-D98]
	29 December	*Macbeth*	Lady Macbeth	Lyceum	[ET-D99]

1 RETURN TO THE STAGE (1865–77)

1. To Mary-Anne Hall, 3 February [1865]

Friday morning =
February = 3rd

Dearest Marion[1] =

I went to the Olympia Theatre last night (to meet Mrs Simon, and Boo)[2] and I made my bad cough very very bad in doing so I suppose for I hardly slept at all, all night – my chest was so very sore, & bad this morning, that Mama[3] advised me not to go out – in fact she said she wd not let me go out being "quite sure that Miss Hall wd be sorry if you" (I) "were ill": and Oh! Marion

[p. 2]

dear it is so foggy!!!

Dear Mrs Simon was so kind to me Marion – didn't scold me a bit for not having written to her – and asked Katie,[4] & me to come to her at Blackheath on Sunday next, sleep there (3 in a bed. Oh! how nice) Sunday night and come away the next day =

Little Boo was charming – as usual – I enclose you a Photo= of myself

[p. 3]

If you will please to have it =

It is the only "Private" one that I have ~~of~~ in the house =

Good bye dear little Marion my clever little (I hate the word Artist)[5] Painter = Believe me always

Your very loving friend
Ellen Alice Watts[6]

N.B. Better known as "Poor Nell" =
No news dear =
"Ah me I am a weary, & I wish that I were dead= No dear Marion I have much

[p. 4]

To live for even now =

"Nil desperandum"[7] is my motto =
I have youth (I'm not very old rather) and I have great great hope – oh! So much and I can't believe that all is lost yet = I have faith too dear = for I cannot but think that help will, must come to me someday = Hope – Faith – Two great things – but Charity! Ah! Ellen, Ellen, I'm afraid you have not one particle of that, the most beautiful of all, all feelings or you wd not feel as you do

[p. 5]

Towards a person of flesh & blood & that person a Woman. God forgive her[8] for I can not do so =

I suppose Im [*sic*] very, very, wicked to feel so but indeed Marion I think , & think what have I done that she sd[9] use me so = God knows I'd forgive anyone that even killed me if I loved them = But "Hope on, hope ever"
& don't be selfish Nell =
You are talking to your self!

[p. 6]

Pray forgive me, for this is selfishness =

I believe the great business of life is to be merry & wise = and the best way to "keep up one's self" is to go out, to leave the sorrow & troubles of others which must make one forget one's own = & still be merry & wise, to relax the ugliness of those furrows, & wrinkles, which sorrow ploughed in the fair forehead of Gods creation =

Oh! What an "idiot" I am!
God bless you dear –
Nelly Watts =

V&A

The last two pages are marked 1) and 2) and have probably been presumed hitherto to have constituted a separate letter.

1. Mary-Anne Hall was an artist and a close friend of ET at this time. See T. Prideaux, *Love or Nothing: The Life and Times of Ellen Terry* (1976; New York: Limelight Editions, 1987), p. 58.
2. Mrs Elizabeth Rumball (1823–1913), née Bocking, ET's long-standing companion, nurse and friend, was the wife of James Quilter Rumball, surgeon of Harpenden. ET's son, Edward Gordon Craig (1872–1966), apparently named her 'Boo', the name by which she was known by ET and her family and derivatives of which were used to name her niece Catherine Elizabeth Powell (1849–1936), known as Bo or Kitty.
3. Sarah Terry (1817–92), née Ballard, actor who married Ben Terry (1818–96), also an actor. Of their eleven children, five worked in the theatre, notably ET, her sisters Kate, Marion and Florence and their brother Fred. The family toured the provinces

and worked with Charles Kean, whose company was at the Princess's Theatre. See *ODNB*.

4. ET's older sister, Kate Terry Lewis (1844–1924), appeared on stage at age eight as Prince Arthur in *King John* with Charles Kean. She left Kean in 1859 to join the Bristol stock company. Her notable performances in a highly respected career on the stage were as Ophelia opposite Charles Fechter in 1861 and in various plays by Tom Taylor. Retiring in 1867 on her marriage to Arthur Lewis, she briefly returned to the stage in 1898 in *The Master* by G. Stuart Ogilvie. Her daughter Kate was the mother of John Gielgud.
5. ET's first husband, G. F. Watts (1817–1904) was one of the most distinguished artists of his generation. He married ET on 20 February 1864 at St Barnabas, Kensington. The marriage failed within the year. The divorce proceedings went to court on 13 March 1877; decree absolute was issued on 6 November 1877; see J. Melville, *Ellen Terry* (London: Haus, 2006), p. 40. Her personal experience of artists may inform the distinction ET makes here between artists and painters.
6. ET is continuing to use her married name at this time.
7. 'Do not despair' (Latin).
8. Mrs Sara Prinsep (1816–87), née Monckton, daughter of James Pattle, sister of Julia Margaret Cameron and Virginia, Countess of Somers, married Henry Thoby Prinsep on 14 May 1835. G. F. Watts, ET's first husband, lived with the Prinseps at Little Holland House, Kensington, for twenty-one years and this is where ET lived as his wife (*ODNB*). Mrs Prinsep appears to have interfered in Watts's relationship with ET to ET's disadvantage.
9. Should.

2. To [Mary-Anne Hall], 14 February [1865]

"Good morrow! 'tis St Valentines day" = (ahem! Shakespere=) and "the doctor" (Mr Simon) wont let me go out! Oh! Marion dear what a "bother"= is'nt it? No! positively! I'm not to go to town with dear Mrs Simon!
Oh! Bye, the by, Marion I've just been in her bed-room to give the pleasant (?) tidings, & I saw

[p. 2]

her (Mrs Simon) with her hair down!!! She looked charming! I wish she cd always wear it so! Oh! It was so fine too & soft – not that I felt it, but I saw that it was so =

[p. 3]

Now I call Mr S – very hard-hearted = don't you? (????) Writing makes me cough = (or something else does) so "fare thee well! My Dove" = my little painter[1] =

Always with much love
Our affectionate
Nelly Watts[2] =

Oh! I cough'd so much last night – a good thing that you were not there – I'm afraid I kept Mrs Simon awake with the nasty noise I made =

[p. 4]

Oh – o-o-o-o-o---
It s-o-o-o-o-o
c-c-c-c-c-c-c-cold =

———

Eleanor Alicia Watson =
my new name[3] =

———

V&A

1. ET alludes to the reference made in her previous letter to the distinction she made between artists and painters.
2. ET refers to herself frequently as Nelly.
3. Her letters are often signed in different names which she invents for herself, usually playing with her first name 'Ellen'. See K. Cockin, 'Ellen Terry, the Ghost Writer and the Laughing Statue: The Victorian Actress, Letters and Life-Writing', *Journal of European Studies*, 32 (2003), pp. 151–63. Here ET also draws attention to her married name, 'Watts', by changing it and may have derived some comfort and sense of empowerment by this creative self-reinvention in her correspondence.

3. To Mary-Anne Hall, [1865?]

Do not mention what I've written to you to any one else – please!

at/
W. Carr Esq.
Stackhouse
Settle.

My dearest friend

I have been away from home (my yorkshire home) and did not receive your letter until Friday night, when I returned. Darling Mary Anne it is so good of you to write to me such nice long letters: Oh dear I'm so sorry we shall have no more happy talks in the little Studio in Belgrave St. Well dear and how have you been? The last time I saw you it was at the top of Eaton Square since that time you have been at one end of the world, and I, at another! and here we are again writing to each other! How has the world treated you my dearest chick? I've been treated very well indeed – have found more (new) friends, who seem as anxious to love me and to be of use to me as I know my old and tried friends to be – I've seen more beautiful scenery than I ever imagined existed, and I am trying

(I feel I shall succeed) to quite forget the one dark cloud which a little while ago hung over my whole life, and all I did and felt, and hoped, and thought! I have never been so truly contented as now, and so I feel sometimes that it has been all for my ultimate good that this ill has happened to me for at least it has taught me patience – I bear no malice – but I feel no love toward Mr Watts[1] – He is to me now, as if he did not exist!! I daresay you will wonder what has changed my feelings so completely[;] I'll tell you – reports meet me on every side down here in this quiet place – in Manchester – and all about, of what Mr Watts has said of me – all most cowardly – and most untrue!! There is no shadow of doubt (for it has been proved to me) that he and not Mrs Princep[2] [*sic*] only has said these things! (I cd have forgiven the spite, and vexation of an angry, and not good woman) but not the untruths of one whose constant care was to make every one think me untruthful and one to whom I was devoted heart and soul – and for one I tried to make fond of me by every power I cd think of, and whom I wd not have left, (if all the world had wished it) had he not desired it also – although I thought at the time it would be my death. But enough of this wild way of talking [–] suffice it that Mr Watts has now become to me a mere ordinary person who has been, once upon a time[,] a source of the only unhappiness I ever felt – who has taught me a lesson (and I pray to God most earnestly I may take the lesson (a severe one) to heart, and profit by it –) But I forgive him most entirely!! For he had bad advisers: The reports concern my physical state, Darling don't laugh at me, I don't know how to put it in words in a letter – I cd tell you in a very plain words and quite make you understand me if I were with you! Talking! But *try* to understand me when I tell you that he (Mr W.) has not said I was not everything that was good to him, in fact he has not brought brought [*sic*] any charge against me at all that says I was not true to him in every way, and that I did'nt [*sic*] do my best to please him, but he simply says he cd not live with me! There dearie, I can't say more in a letter than I have done= I can but say this[:] he has said things which make me positively blush when I think, sometimes and things which might stand in my way for the future, and also in the way of all my sisters = Sweet-heart forgive me for talking all about myself in this way – still – still more of myself. I am very well in health upon the whole. Some very bad weak, and nervous days I have, but that falls to the lot of most people. My cough has quite left me, and the one unhappiness I had (my love for him – which was quite thrown away) has left me also = Now! having given you a satisfactory account of my health will you tell me how you are? Don't write if you are not quite well for it will make you worse and make me unhappy – "Where ignorance is bliss"[3] etc, etc =! But if you are well, and ever feel inclined and it does not weary you to

talk to me a bit, know that poor Nell will always be so very much pleased to hear from her dear young friend Mary Anne Hall
With very much affection

Your loving
Nell W.[4]

Please excuse this dreadful writing and the blot.

SMA, ET-Z2,201
Typed unsigned copy of letter. Annotated '1865' and 'From Nell Watts (Ellen Terry) to Mary Ann Hall'.

1. G. F. Watts; see n. 5 to letter 1, above.
2. See n. 8 to letter 1, above.
3. Last lines of Thomas Gray, 'Ode on a Distant Prospect of Eton College' (1747), ll. 99–100: 'where ignorance is bliss, / 'Tis folly to be wise'.
4. ET varied her signature in her correspondence depending on her relationship with the addressee. Here her signature incorporates the familiar 'Nell' and the initial of her married name, 'Watts'. She made reference to ink blots in her letters, obviously self-conscious about the impression made on the addressee and sometimes dealing with them in an imaginative way; see K. Cockin 'Ellen Terry and Women's Suffrage Agitation', in C. Bland and M. Cross (eds), *Gender and Politics in The Age of Letter-Writing 1750–2000* (London: Ashgate, 2004), pp. 201–12.

4. To Mary-Anne Hall, 27 April 1866

24 Caversham Rd
Friday 27. 4. 66

Nelly

Dearest Mary Anne –

After a long & unsuccessful search for Janie Faulkners [*sic*] letters I write to tell you that I truly cannot remember whether she has written to me, since the first of February, or not = I know she has not done so since the 19 of that month, for I've not heard

[p. 2]

from her since I started for Bradford =
Her letters have never contained one atom of harm in them further than the wish to conceal the fact of having written them – from her Auntie = why – I cannot imagine – for they were most simple – childlike, & loving = & altogether were what a child of her age with a good heart – loving

[p. 3]

Disposition, & not which knowledge wd be expected to write "out of her own head" – I have these letters put away some where, on a screw to keep, but where I can have put them, I can't imagine – But I'm determined to find them & (when I do, I'll be sure to send them to you, ear to read, just to see how foolish it is to wish to keep such letters as they are a secret from her Auntie.

[p. 4]

another little girl I know has written me within 3 weeks no less than 11 letters which remain unanswered by me, simply because tho' there is no real harm in any one of them, I do not like to answer to her cousins house, instead of to her Fathers =

I hope poor Boo is well not having heard from her, for so long, I don't know =

I wrote to dear Mrs Simon the other day trying to thank her for her kindness

[p. 5]

in sending me to Dr Quain & of course dear, I might at the same time to have said how deeply I grieved for – & sympathized with her – for the loss of her dear mother as I do, most sincerely & truly = (Do you know dear, I never wrote to her about it at all but she sent me cards, & I felt as if it were a reproach to me, for never have written –) Well as I was saying,

[p. 6]

I would'nt, even when I did write, mention the subject for I never can write all I feel, & I thought it wd only pain the poor dear Mrs Simon – No dear – I did'nt like even to write the word "mother" & I said – what was very stupid "somebody else, instead of Kate, took me to Dr Swain," when I should have said, Mama took me to Dr Quain =

Tell me please dear, do

[p. 7]

you think I might, even now to write – or do you think she wd not think it unkind of me not to do so? I ask your advice my dear Mary, for you, know her so well & you always do give me advice & good advice – I enclose a letter I wrote some days ago – which was never posted – Do let me hear about yr picture =

[p. 8]

With very much love,
Hoping you are well, & that I shall see you soon,
Believe me dearest Mary

Yours faithfully
(I like the term)
Ellen W=

I write this in a great hurry = please excuse bad writing, & all sorts of mistakes =

V&A

5. To Mary-Anne Hall, 6 [June] 1866

Dearest Mary-Anne –

How long it is since I've seen you! I write now to tell you that after the 20 of this same month I shall be able to sit to you for "the" Portrait – If you can spare time to paint then =

On the 20th of this month

[p. 2]

I play for my sister's benefit[1] =

S. Knowls 's is the author of the evening – "The Hunchback" – the piece selected = Kate plays "Julia" I in "Helen" !!! An address by Tom Taylor, & a farce, will conclude the evening's entertainments.

There dear – having told you all that is to be – I hope – now to what has not passed.

I have been staying with

[p. 3]

dear, kind, Mrs Simon = not a very long visit but enough to prove more than ever, what a dear good lady she is = Miss O'Meara was most kind to me also = I had a very sweet little letter from Boo Daisy when I was there =

I was glad to hear from her =

Dearest old thing how are you?

[p. 4]

Well? Likely? Perhaps? [?] Eh? All this I expect to find "Little Mary" when I see her!

Shall I? In the mean-time her very affectionate (this in strict confidence=)

Nelly Watts,

Would be glad to hear from her =

V&A

Headed notepaper with 'EAW' (Ellen Alice Watts) monogram.

1. See n. 4 to letter 1, above.

6. To Mary-Anne Hall, 22 June 1866

Friday-22-6-66
24 Caversham Rd

Dearest Mary-Anne

I hear from Mr Taylor[1] you were "in front" on Wednesday.[2] I looked for you when my sister was speaking the address but could'nt see you – before that time, I looked for no body. I was so very very nervous, & oh so really unwell – on the stage I laughed as you know, but when I reached

[p. 2]

My dressing-room I positively cried, with pain in my side – I am however very much better now –

I think people were most kind to me that evening (in your part of the building I mean –) Of course it was only what my sister Kate had a right to expect, being an acknowledged favourite with the Public but I was quite an amateur =

Dear dear chick –

[p. 3]

When shall I come (to sit for the portrait) to your studio? I am most anxious for you to do it – a truthful, un-varnished portrait – if you will do it please let me know when I shall come – I wish you did'nt [*sic*] live so far away.

With very best love dear

Believe me always affectionately

Yours/ Nelly Watts =

Did you see Mrs Dalrymple[3] in a Private Box?

V&A

1. Tom Taylor (1817–80), educated at Trinity College, Cambridge University, and trained as a barrister, was a prolific dramatist and editor of *Punch* magazine. He was committed to popular theatre and adapted many plays, including dramatizations from the works of Charles Dickens. Several of his plays were produced at the Lyceum Theatre.
2. ET refers to her sister, Kate Terry's benefit performance in which ET participated and reports on her disappointing performance.
3. Mrs Dalrymple (Lady Sophia) (1829–1911), née Pattle, was one of the seven daughters of James Pattle of the East India Company. Three of her other sisters, Mrs Prinsep, Lady Somers and Mrs Julia Margaret Cameron, photographer, were known as 'Beauty, Dash and Talent'.

7. To Mr Bean, 15 October 1866

Dear Mr Bean

Will you send me two Cartes de visites of myself (done by your Photographer) the best you have of me – & send them to "Mrs G. F. Watts – (at W. Carr Esqre –) Stackhouse – Settle" – & if you wd let me know at the same time what I am indebted to you for them

[p. 2]

you wd oblige me – & I wd send stamps to the amount.

I saw you in the Stalls of the Olympic Theatre on the night of my sisters [*sic*] (Miss Terry's) benifit[1] [*sic*] – & I hope you were pleased – you looked so –

Hoping you will forgive me for troubling you about the Photo's [*sic*] (I did not know how to get them without writing to you)

Believe me
Faithfully yours
Ellen Watts – (Terry)

Yorkshire – October 15th/66 –

UPENN, MsColl. 585 F.145

Handwritten and signed (henceforth, all letters are handwritten and signed, unless indicated otherwise). Decorative notepaper with engraving by W. Banks, Edinburgh, depicting Windermere from Lowood Hotel.

1. See n. 2 to letter 6, above.

8. To Mary-Anne Hall, [1866?]

Dearest Mary-Anne!

Thanks for yr letter. I will send you 2 stalls in a few days = but not until I have first booked them dear, as that will prevent confusion & give you a good seat!! I am so nervous about this affair, that I get quite feverish about it.

I had tickets sent me for a concert on Saturday last – instead of going however,

[p. 2]

I stayed in bed the whole day long, & food never passed my lips! I felt much better on Sunday, & went to Mrs Tom Taylor's – To day a very heavy re-hearsal did not improve me! – Oh dear, oh dear! Here I am grumbling about my own stupid self, & never so much as saying, that I hope you are well, you dear old chick! You know I hope well for you ever dear however – Now Mary, when you see me on

[p. 3]

the Stage, you must please not mix me up, in yr thoughts, with the character I am playing! For she ("Mistress Helen Heartwell") is not a very desirable person to be! I think! Although no harm in her!

With many, many, *many* kisses

Always your loving

Nell =

Please excuse this silly letter & put it in the fire.

V&A

Headed notepaper with 'EAW' (Ellen Alice Watts) monogram; annotated '?/66'.

9. To [Sir] Leslie [Ward], [1866]

My dear Leslie.

I want you to do some little sketch for my album – I have had a beautiful one given to me – if you wd send me some thing (ever so small) I sd be very much obliged.

I have been "stay

[p. 2]

-ing North" for the last two months.

My address is "– Mrs G. F. Watts – at W. Carr Esqre – Stackhouse – Settle –Yorkshire ="

I've a great deal of impudence have'nt [*sic*] I Leslie, coolly asking you for a sketch in this manner?

Nevertheless – I hope you'll forgive me –

I have been very ill the last two days & am writing this in bed – so please forgive this short selfish note – Hoping you are well & that all your family are so, also,

With best regards/Believe me sincerely yours

Nelly Watts

PML, LHMS Misc Ray 188742 MA 4500

Decorative notepaper with engraving by W. Banks, Edinburgh, depicting Upper Beach of Ullswater.

10. To unidentified man, 8 August 1867

14 Caversham Rd

N.W

Dear Sir – I beg your pardon for my rudeness in not answering your letter before – I with pleasure comply with your request

Yours truly

Ellen A. Watts – (nee Terry)[1]

Thursday – August 8th 1867.

FOLGER, Y.c.434 (1–400)

1. ET's reference to her birth name 'Terry' may reflect the change in her marital status at this time. Although still married to Watts, by 1864 they had separated.

11. To [Mary-Anne Hall], 1 January 1868

Nellie

God bless the 1st day of the New Year – 1st January 1868

My little darling –

I too earnestly & fondly wish you a happy New Year –

I sd have written yesterday but dear Marion I have a really dreadful cough – & I am at times quite convulsed by it – yesterday I sat down after dinner with my writing desk but found it was of no use whatever – I coughed, & coughed, all the afternoon, in the

[p. 2]

theatre all the time I was acting, & all night long in bed! I feel as weak as can be this morning, but am happy to say have coughed but very little as yet, & it's now 12 o'clock – I shall sleep I hope this after noon, or my "shrewishness" will be tame to night – is'nt [*sic*] it horrid, Mary-Anne dear, having to

[p. 3]

act that thing – "Katherine" –?

Cd you contrive my Mary to come to me some day either Friday or Saturday this week or the beginning of next week to come in the morning – go down in the brougham with me in the evening – be put in a private box with, either Mama, my little sisters, or your own friends to take care of you come back with me & go away when you liked next day – cd you, & wd you

[p. 4]

do this Mary-Anne, you wd delight me very much – for now we never see one another & I'm beginning to feel we are drifting slowly away from each other – & I cn't bear that my darling – So do come, if you possibly can – make it by some means a useful visit to town, & let us shop together – Oh! Mary-Anne I wish we lived nearer, for write I cannot much, & one can't establish private telegraphs from house to house – !

I'm so sorry you were writing to me when you

[p. 5]

were tired – Don't do it again sweet – I am now going to see the kind Doctor Quain – so must not write any more.

With very kind remembrances to your family & my best wishes for their happiness in this New Year, & with a fond embrace for you, believe me ever darling, your truly affectionate

Nelly Watts.

P.S. Don't be afraid that I am ill dearie – I sd be on the contrary very well but for this terrible cough!

E.W.

V&A

Headed notepaper, marked 'Nellie'.

12. To [Mary-Anne Hall], [2 April 1868]

Thursday –

Moray Lodge,
Campden Hill
Kensington

My little dear –

Our baby told us only yesterday that "a lady" had called "one day" when we (Mama & I) were out. The servants didn't say anything at all about the matter 'till I spoke to them & then said "Oh! Yes miss – some lady did call" but they cd not remember the

[p. 2]

name – I put several names to baby & he "thinks", it was Miss Hall"! Was it dear? If so, I'm so truly sorry I was from home – I'm quite idle now – doing no work at the theatre & staying with my Kate – can't I come & see you my darling somewhere?

[p. 3]

Harley St? Wandsworth? Newman St or somewhere?

I have not seen our sweet Mrs Simon for ever so long. I'm afraid she is much grieved by Mrs Faulkner's death – Poor darling.

Kate is waiting for me I can write not more now – Ever with fond true love, Your devoted

Nelly Watts –

V&A

Headed notepaper for 'Moray Lodge, Campden Hill, Kensington'.

13. To Mary-Anne Hall, [6 May 1868]

Darling Mary – I forgot the foot-muff & the rug for your poor little knees! I am so sorry – Why I didn't come up to your "Box" last night to see you was because the Stage Manager wdn't let me pass – at which piece of overstrained duty I was much riled: & hope for Mrs Wigan's speedy return[1] = You

[p. 2]

promised you know dear Mary-Anne, you wd not be disgusted with me when you saw "Katherine the shrew" didn't you? So I hope you kept your promise! I was glad for you, to see yr brothers join you so early = Did you see Dr Quain opposite your box with his wife!? I hardly coughed at all last night I'm happy to say – & so am particularly well to day – I have so many letters to answer so

[p. 3]

forgive me this tiny letter, & with my dearest love believe me sweet plump Mary

Most affectionately yours
Nelly Watts –

V&A

1. Mrs Leonora Wigan, née Pincott, married Alfred Wigan, with whom she managed the New Queen's Theatre, Long Acre, under the direction of Mr Labouchere. ET recalls Mrs Wigan as a mentor who influenced the development of her acting style, emphasizing the significance of each glance and gesture; *Memoirs*, p. 59.

14. To [Charles Reade],[1] [1874]

20. Taviton Street. Gordon Square[2]

Thursday –

I wrote a long letter sometime ago to you telling you why I cd not come to see you – telling you no end of things, amongst others how much I did love you. Then I thought – "ah!" He – (I always think of you with a capital letter –) "HE will think I don't only care for him, but that I want an engagement – that I have some design <upon him>" (for I know you <are> a naughty suspicious sweet lovely man, & you do take for humbug sometimes, what is in truth most devoted gratitude & that the bungling expression <shd> create doubt is not to be wondered at. I think of you at times, & your kindness comes before me so palpably that I see in the glass that I'm smiling & crying

[p. 2]

& wish that for my art I cd have at command such expression of face, & then off fly the thoughts from you, & I grimace in the glass with all might but I never get the look back again.

Will you think me very stupid – so you shall. I can write a word or two to you now because I don't want an engagement – & I send you a picture – Isn't it nice? I sat for it! You may dis-believe if you will – but I did. I send that girl to you – & a big bit of my love – some to Mrs Seymour[3] – but more to you, if you & she don't mind please. Whether the love will be left, outside on the doorstep or be taken in & warmed I can't tell. I sometimes do wonder whether ~~your thoughts~~ the leavings of your thoughts ever go me-wards – in

[p. 3]

charity – spite of my seeming indifference & ingratitude – I pray God so – for I do love you & reverence you so much. I may not be able to write to you but I may be able to come some day. I shall try if you will think me "an ungrateful Toad" & send me from your door. I will send back Master Philip's clothes next week [–] I am ashamed not to have done so before. Mr G.[4] is in the Isle of Wight <&> returns on Sunday & I am up to my pate[5] in work of various kinds (the mystery will unfold itself in course of time – Ha!) Both my little ones[6] have severe colds but I am as brave – as brave as ever I was! – Kiss Mrs Seymour for me. Do – & ask her to kiss you too (& two!) for me.

Your tired & dearly loving

Philippa[7] – not Mrs Wood – the other one

SMA, ET-Z2,229b

1. Charles Reade (1814–84), author and dramatist to whom ET attributed the role of having brought her back to employment in the theatre in 1874 after her retirement

and seclusion in Hertfordshire while she was cohabiting with Edward Godwin. See *ODNB*.

2. ET and Edward Godwin (1833–86) lived together at this rented property in 1874.
3. Mrs Laura Seymour lived with Charles Reade from the 1850s until her death in 1879; see *ODNB*.
4. Edward Godwin had apparently stayed with a friend in the Isle of Wight to avoid creditors; Melville, *Ellen Terry*, p. 72.
5. Head, especially crown; origin unknown; archaic and humorous (*OED*); ET means she is overloaded.
6. In 1874 ET's children, Edith Craig and Edward Gordon Craig, were respectively five and two years old.
7. ET performed the role of Philippa Chester in Charles Reade's *The Wandering Heir* on 28 February 1874 at the New Queen's Theatre. She took over the role from Mrs John Wood, who had been successful in the provincial tour. The play was based on the Tichborne case (*Memoirs*, p. 76).

15. To unidentified men, 16 March 1874

Queens Theatre.
March 16th. 74.

Dear young gentlemen.[1]

Your expressions of welcome touched me. & I do thank you both. I've recd[2] many kind letters but none from young people – but dear me! – perhaps you are both old people by this time! if so I ask your pardon – & can only excuse my self by saying that I can not think of either of you but as big boys!

[p. 2]

Yes I do remember – the old I. of W. days[3] – I do remember the "broken head" days, & the grief of poor Palgrave Simpson[4] for "his boy".

Will you both be glad to hear for my sake that the present days (my present days) are the best of all? I think you will.
I'll tell you (both) a secret – I hate writing!

[p. 3]

So with affectionate remembrances
Believe me

Very truly yours
Ellen Terry.

NYPL

1. ET received many letters from admiring fans and took trouble to respond to many of them personally. On 28 February 1874, two weeks before the date of this letter, she had performed as Philippa Chester in *The Wandering Heir* at the New Queen's Theatre, London.
2. Received.
3. ET had stayed at Freshwater in the Isle of Wight with her new husband G. F. Watts for their honeymoon at Julia Margaret Cameron's house. Watts had painted a portrait of Virginia Pattle, sister of Sarah Prinsep, and of Julia Margaret Cameron, photographer. He had met Kate and ET in 1862, painting *The Sisters* and several others using ET as model when she sat for him at Little Holland House, London. ET first met Alfred, Lord Tennyson, at Freshwater.
4. John Palgrave Simpson (1807–87) was an author and dramatist, educated at Corpus Christ, Cambridge University. His writings were informed by his travels, including a novel about Hungary and an eyewitness account of the 1848 revolution in France. He was an amateur actor and secretary of the Dramatic Authors' Society in 1868–87. See *ODNB*. His obituary in *The New York Times*, 20 August 1887, highlighted Simpson's biography of Karl Maria von Weber (1865) and the publication of over forty plays in England and the United States, the most successful of which were *The World and the Stage*, *Second Love* and *Sybilla or Step by Step*. Simpson was a contributor to *Blackwood's Magazine*, *Fraser's Magazine* and *Bentley's Miscellany*.

16. To [Shutz] Wilson, 31 December 1875

The last day of this dear old
year = 1875 =

Our dear Mr Wilson[1]

We send you a few leaves of our hearts ease. We have so much of that same hearts ease we can spare a little & feel no loss – but rather gain = We all wish you may be very well, very happy & have all your heart's desires in the little New Year that is coming –

Believe that we are
affectionately yours
"Boo" & Ellen, Edith, & Edward Watts[2]

CLAREMONT

1. Henry Shutz Wilson was an author of several books: *Studies and Romances* (1873), *Alpine Ascent and Adventures* (1878), *Poets as Theologians* (1888) and *History and Criticism* (1896).
2. It is significant that ET is still using her married name at this point.

17. To [John] Hare, 30 March 1876

Wednesday March 30 76=

Dear Mr Hare[1]

I pray you to excuse my silence – my terms are £30 a week, and as I have lately experienced many unpleasantnesses I could not possibly have anticipated, I wd rather that my

[p. 2]

next engagement shd be for the run of a play than for a season

There is a measure of justice on both sides in such an arrangement too – is there not? –

Will you kindly let

[p. 3]

me hear from you soon?

Believe me very truly yours

Ellen Terry

V&A Enthoven

1. John Hare (1844–1921), né Fairs, was a renowned actor manager. In 1877 he cast ET as Olivia in W. G. Wills's adaptation of *The Vicar of Wakefield*, a role which relaunched her career and brought her to the attention of Henry Irving. In 1879 Hare went into partnership in theatre management with W. H. Kendal and Madge Kendal. He was knighted in 1907. See *ODNB*.

18. To unidentified, 24 [no month] 1876

221. Camden Road

Monday – 24th – 76.

Will you tell me where I can get one of those very cleverly drawn advertisements of you – Or will you give me one. It's lovely – I never but once before saw anything of the kind that was good. Poor Freddy Walker[1] did that one. Who did this I wonder –

Your brother? –

[p. 2]

Do let me know how I can get one – How is the good Papa – Give him my love & warm wishes for this cold weather –

I saw Miss Coghlan[2] on Saturday (looking even more beautiful off than on the stage) & was glad to hear from her how well "All for ~~him~~ her"![3] was doing at the St James', –

[p. 3]

If you know where Herman can be found let me know by just a line like a kind good sun-shiny fellow as you always were – Your ears ought to tingle, for Mrs Casella[4] & I are always talking about you when we meet – & that's not seldom. I dine there again next Sunday

[p. 4]

but I don't live at Weatherby Rd.
Yours verily & sincerely
Ellen Terry.

FOLGER

1. Frederick Walker (1840–75), artist and illustrator whose work was widely known through illustrations of Thackeray and Dickens in publications such as the *Cornhill Magazine*, *Good Words* and *Once a Week* and publications of Dickens's *Hard Times*. Walker had died of consumption the year before ET was writing this letter; see *ODNB*.
2. Miss Coghlan may be related to Charles Coghlan, who performed Shylock with ET as Portia in the three-week production in April 1875 of *The Merchant of Venice* at the Prince of Wales Theatre under the management of Mrs Bancroft, which revitalized ET's career. Edward Godwin designed the production.
3. *All For Her* was a dramatization of Charles Dickens's *A Tale of Two Cities*, co-authored by Herman Merivale and J. Palgrave Simpson (produced on 18 October 1875).
4. Mrs Marie Casella, ET's long-standing friend, with whom she travelled to Paris for the first time in spring 1866; see Prideaux, *Love or Nothing*, p. 64. Her daughters Ella and Nelia also became close friends of ET's.

19. To [Shutz] Wilson, 30 April 1877

Court Theatre
Monday 30 – April . 77.

My dear Mr Wilson–

I shall be out tomorrow so shd you have kindly thought of calling, this is to warn you not to come. I will write to you about Mr Wyndham – now the play's the thing[1]

In great haste hoping you are well

=Most sincerely Yrs
Ellen Terry
I'm "called" ! –

CLARAMONT

1. In 6 October 1877 ET appeared as Lady Juliet Darnley in *The House of Darnley* by Lord Lytton at the Court Theatre.

20. To Shutz Wilson, [before 1877]

221 . Camden Road. N.W.
Wednesday .

Dear Mr Shütz Wilson had I but a Secretary like Mr Schütz Wilson, I shd not be at the present moment in despair for want of words to reply to the pretty, kindly & far too flattering letters greeting me on every side –
Indeed I am surprised – for I am not at all satisfied with my own endeavours.

[p. 2]

Be kind enough to accept ~~my~~ the most gratefulest [*sic*] thanks imaginable for your too kindly letter & believe me

Sincerely yours
Ellen Terry

CLAREMONT

Undated but presumably before 1877, as ET lived at this address before she married Charles Wardell; see M. Holroyd, *A Strange Eventful History: The Dramatic Lives of Ellen Terry, Henry Irving and their Remarkable Families* (London: Chatto & Windus, 2008), p. 81.

21. To Shutz Wilson, [1877?]

Thursday = 221 – Camden Rd

Dear Mr Wilson

Such a delightful parcel of books just arrived – so very many thanks. I'll take the greatest care of them & return them un-injured when our feast is over – our – for Boo[1] & I, I see it plainly, will quarrel

[p. 2]

over them there books!

With kind love from us all Always yours sincerely
Ellen Terry .

CLARAMONT

1. Elizabeth Rumball; see n. 2 to letter 1, above.

22. To [Schutz Wilson], [1877?]

[...] my little woman to call upon you last – Monday, I think – when I looked up at your window & saw a gentleman so we passed on – Whenever we are near Rep. St Edie[1] wants me to "go & see Mr Wilson" & so do I ! – only as we are

[p. 2]

often in Rep. St it wd hardly do ! –

Thank you very much for what you said in yr last letter about having spoken to your housekeeper telling her to make me "comfy" sd[2] I arrive a weary traveller – So just like you ! & arranged so just like you –

[p. 3]

We all send you our love & hope you'll come & see us when we are in our new abode –

44 Finborough Road[3]
West Brompton =

We must be there by the 7th & my chicks – my pretty buds – are in a high state of excitement to think they will be near the Casella [~~children~~] girls who are

[p. 4]

their chief "chums" & good friends –
I shall be nearer Mama & that's a great comfort to both of us I think –
Hoping you are quite well now with every good wish
Yours always
with grateful affection
Ellen Terry

CLAREMONT

Incomplete letter.

1. Edith Craig (1869–1947), daughter of ET and Edward Godwin, whom ET often refers to as 'Edie' although the alternative spelling 'Edy' is also used, creating some confusion with other women in their circle.
2. Should.
3. ET entered 44 Finborough Road as the address on her marriage certificate in 1877 (Holroyd, *A Strange Eventful History*, p. 81).

23. To [Sir William Harcourt], [1877?]

221 Camden Road
N.W. Thursday

I too was glad – really glad to see your kind calm face with the old peace-full smile upon it as in the old-young days – imagination wants to work + I seemed to hear the quiet grand voice again – Strange – the long ago seemed <(when I looked at you)> only yesterday — & what time has made appear like shadow to me became real & living once more – You will, I am

[p. 2]

quite sure be glad to know that I have had much happiness since we met. Such days & <flower days> as make up our life eternal & grow, as the years go on to such a big size as quite to crush out the dark & weedy corners – I live in the thoughts of these days – tho' their continuance is prevented – Hate itself must die even the hatred of ones [*sic*] own evil mindedness with all it's [*sic*] untruth & icy-heartedness – Enfin! – forgive me –

[p. 3]

I'm talking & taking up your time.

Your little boy! I wondered looking at you, how he was & if all had gone well with both of you –

Why I suppose he's almost a man now! You looked exactly the same as you looked on a certain evening in (I fancy in February) then you stood by the fire-place in a certain big studio & said a few wise words to a poor

[p. 4]

– almost child then – but that's a long while ago –

I'm thinner now, am I not? Well "it's better to wear out than rust out".

Fare-well – with all affectionate wishes I am

Yours very sincerely
Ellen Terry –

BOD, MS Harcourt dep. 246, ff. 171–2

24. To unidentified, [1877?]

3 Cambridge Gardens
Notting Hill =

I'm staying at my Mother's & the girls take up my time or I shd have written before in answer to your little kind letter –

All I wanted to ask you that day you called was not to mention anywhere what I told you in regard to Mr Minto & my self – for the marriage may never take place

[p. 2]

– all sorts of things might happen to prevent it – may have happened – Mr Minto may have discovered that I have a bad temper – or – or – all sorts of things – at all events be kind enough not to speak of us together –

So many thanks for the song ! – It's lovely – & if I could sing, I'd sing that song ~~song~~ ravishingly ! –

[p. 3]

but I can't sing –
Alas !

Excuse this ill written scrawl but I'm just starting for home & my young brother is shaking the table

With best regards
Very sincerely yours
Ellen Terry =

CLAREMONT

2 'OUR LADY OF THE LYCEUM' (1878–80)

25. To Stephen Coleridge,[1] 19 June 1878

Private=

~~33 Longridge Road,~~
~~South Kensington~~
Court Theatre
19 June 78

Dear Sir

I have put off from day to day my most unpleasant task & have made bad worse I fear.

My good husband[2] tells me I must send you back the beautiful Turners!

Might is Right! he is a big man – I am a

[p. 1]

– little one! and – I return the Turners –

Will you be kind enough to accept my best thanks for what I had long coveted & been too poor to buy. My husband is so generally right, that it wd not become me to pick & choose as

[p. 2]

to when my judgement was better than his –

I feel very ungrateful
& rather shamefaced –
& a little cross –
& terribly sorry to seem so ungracious –

Believe me

Truly yours
E. Wardell.

Will you accept "Olivia's"[3] photograph & be kind enough to take no further notice of her or her letter.

GARRICK, Vol. I/1

The headed notepaper for 33 Longridge Road, South Kensington, is embellished with a crest, consisting of a lion within a crown with the motto 'Prisca fides' ('old-fashioned fidelity'; Latin). Annotated by Stephen Coleridge: 'This is the first letter I preserved from Ellen Terry. "The Turner Gallery" which I sent her in return for a photograph still adorns my library; she has in later years frequently begged to have it back again, but I am adamant!'

1. Stephen Coleridge (1854–1936), barrister and son of Lord Chief Justice John Duke Coleridge, was an author and campaigner against cruelty to children and animals. He was one of the founders of the London Society for the Prevention of Cruelty to Children in 1884, president of the League for the Prohibition of Cruel Sports and activist in the anti-vivisection campaigns of Frances Power Cobbe. He was an admiring fan of ET and became a close friend, confidant, legal and financial adviser and mentor in the period 1878–1911. He acted as her adviser on legal and business matters until some time after her third marriage in 1907 to James Carew. Coleridge accumulated a large collection of correspondence from ET, some of which he later annotated and of which he published twenty-six letters, with ET's written permission, in *THET*.
2. ET married Charles Wardell (1839–85), an actor whose stage name was Charles Kelly, in 1877. Originally a soldier with the 66th regiment and active in the Crimean War, Wardell was the son of a Northumberland vicar. ET met Wardell in 1874 when he was a co-performer in Charles Reade's plays in London and on tour. She praised his acting in *New Men and Old Acres*, *Dora* and *Much Ado About Nothing*. They separated in 1881. Wardell died in 1885. Christopher St John and Edith Craig noted in their revised and posthumous publication of ET's autobiography that Wardell had 'had a violent and jealous temper' (*Memoirs*, p. 117).
3. ET performed the role of Olivia in the adaptation of Oliver Goldsmith's novel *The Vicar of Wakefield* (1766) by W. G. Wills for the first time on 30 March 1878 at the Court Theatre opposite William Terriss; and later with Henry Irving at the Lyceum Theatre on 27 May 1885. Willam Terriss (1847–97) first appeared on stage in 1867 but became famous in the role of Squire Thornhill opposite ET in *Olivia* in 1878. He joined Henry Irving's Lyceum company in 1880. His most memorable work was in melodrama at the Adelphi Theatre, the site of his murder in 16 December 1897. See *ODNB*

26. To Mr Hipkins, 9 July [1878]

July 9th, 33 Longridge Road

Dear Mr Hipkins

What can you think of me! –

It was kind of you to think of me at all, when the pretty piano was "on view", & very ungrateful am I not to have written to say thank you before now – I write this in pencil as I am in bed where I pass most of these bright summer days, being just able to get through with my

[p. 2]

work at night[1] – existing not living, most people wd call it – but "I was born in a merry hour"[2] I suppose, for I'm jolly enough =

I'm very sorry I cd not come, for 'twould have been a treat =

With kind regards & many thanks Yours sincerely

Ellen Wardell

[p. 3]

I go away each Saturday night <till mon-eve> into the country somewhere, & take in enough fresh air to last for a week –

Do you know Surley Hall on the "sweet Thames" about 2 miles from Windsor? Let me recommend it – quite an ideal Inn & the place !!! --- ------

I hope you & Mrs Huffer[?] liked the play – I looked

[p. 4]

but could not find either of you –

E.W

BL, Add. MS 41636, f. 142.

Envelope extant; postmarked 'JY 10 78'; addressed to Mr Hipkins Esquire, 9 [illeg.] Street, Soho.

1. During this period ET was performing Olivia at the Court Theatre. See n. 3 to letter 25, above.
2. William Shakespeare, *Much Ado About Nothing*, II.i.333.

27. To Stephen Coleridge, [10 July 1878]

Tuesday

I've let you talk great nonsense to me & time spent so, is ill spent – but "non-sense" should be laughed at shouldn't it? – & I've laughed – "Out of doubt I was born in a merry hour"[1] – but I can laugh no longer for I think you looked sad last night =

Here is Griffith Gaunt[2]

[p. 2]

sweet boy – dear Epic[3] – come to beg pardon for a featherheaded woman & to say she's sorry – *sorry*. Excuse her – forgive her – & forget her =

ET[4] =

GARRICK, Vol. I/2

Envelope extant; postmarked 'JY 10 1878', London; addressed to 'The Hon. Stephen Coleridge, 1 Sussex Square, W='. Annotated by Coleridge 'the 10th of July 1878 ='.

1. Shakespeare, *Much Ado About Nothing*, II.i.332–3.
2. Unidentified.
3. Epictetus, Stoic philosopher of the first century, a former slave, who recommended restraint, self-abnegation and loving one's enemies.
4. ET signs her initials in a distinctive way, superimposing the two letters.

28. To Stephen Coleridge, 1 August [1878]

August 1st = The Rectory
Aug 1st Winlaton=

Mine can only be a homely little letter (on child's scribbling-paper) & it may be that one who sings of Portugal, Spain, & Africa as if they were so many villages will not condescend to listen to my small piping.[1] However, I'll run the risk of this being thrown on one side unread & will tell you where I am & what I'm doing – I'm staying with my Father in law.[2] At this particular moment I'm resting on an old stone wall which seperates [*sic*] the Rectory garden from the <u>prettiest</u> Churchyard! – & am writing in pencil to a sunny lad far over the sea – From where I sit I command the old fashioned garden with it's [*sic*] thickets of sweet smelling flowers – roses, lilies,

[p. 2]

honeysuckle, jessamine, sweet-peas, and close pinks, which seem to spring up of themselves—all this is bathed in sun warmth whilst I am sheltered by a huge yew tree –

From here too I can see into the comfortable old parlour (right away into the round mirror which has hung with it's [*sic*] slender chains in the same place for over 60 years, the servants tell me) & hear through the open window the laughter of my brat 8 years old who is teasing the merry old Rector – This all on my left –

To my right, the Church Tower "Ivy clad" –"O rest in the Lord" is being played upon the organ inside, & two little white headed children staring with big round eyes at <u>me,</u>

[p. 3]

resting on my wall –
The sun is shining to make all golden, & and my heart shines too, for this is a sweet most peaceful spot. I'm well in health—a letter's in my lap from my little boy Edward (6) telling me he's well & happy – another in my pocket from my man that he loves me – altogether, with peace all around I doubt if I'd change places with—<u>even</u> <u>you</u>! Tho' "to see other men's lands" was once my heart's

desire—but now I'm getting old I find more satisfaction in every day & close about me – How much I wish you could

[p. 4]

be with me here this moment[.] Your fresh fair face would "go" with the place so –

There's a little wood the other side of the Church Oh! The cool shadow & the smell of the ferns, (which "muffle the feet of the old oaks and elms") – it's delicious!

Yes – I wish you were here – we'd read together – here's a nice mixture—this little wood – a sweet companion—a book to ones [*sic*] taste—sitting in the ferns hand in hand in cool shadow looking out on golden sunshine, peace all around one, and

[p. 5]

peace in one's (twos!!) heart – Pretty boy, I'm very happy—even without you – still you see you are in my thoughts, or how shd I be ~~writing~~ talking to you in pencil at this moment –

Evening –

I finished work in Manchester[3] the God-forsaken hole!) [*sic*] 4 days ago & have been resting here since with my little girl. We stay two weeks, & then go into Yorkshire for a week, to my brother[4] —then back again home to ugly but dear London ("dear" from association) to my husband who has been there

[p. 6]

all this time working – I'm wanted to do Dora at the Haymarket Theatre the week after next, but I feel I must rest 'till Xmas when I have to play "Ophelia" to Irving's "Hamlet" at the Lyceum[5] –

I've a very small mind, & it cannot quite follow you, in your wonderful rushings about—but very distinctly can it in the fact of Cyprus being an unhealthy place & I apprehend all sorts of danger for you.

Little dear, take care of yourself "praise be blessed" you're not a coward, but—prudence – just think how dear you are to very many – & if the knowledge

[p. 7]

will only make you more prudent, know that you are dear, in a sense, to "Livie" too. Be prudent=

I don't think I shall see you when you come back—I'm very serious – I shall not, if I can help it, & I think we can all help what we want to help. If you feel it's wrong to have deceived Boo about that little matter of the name – (so it is, but 'twas only for sport! –) – think what I've got on my conscience – Yes – I shall tell

Boo when I return to town, all about you I think – Your letter made me laugh. You very naughty boy to tell ~~[illeg.]~~ such fibs about someone taking the Bey of Tunis to be the Bay of Tunis. That won't do Sir – when I read it I simply shouted! – Farewell for the present.[6]

[p. 8]

GARRICK, Vol. I/3

Unsigned letter, reproduced in *THET*, pp. 11–15. Coleridge's note to this letter reads: 'This moving letter was sent out to me when I was travelling in the East in 1878. I was then twenty-four years old.' The original letter is annotated by Coleridge: 'This most beautiful letter was sent out to me when I was at Cyprus, where it reached me struck down with fever and gave me unspeakable comfort and happiness. S.C.'

1. Stephen Coleridge describes his travels in his autobiography, *Memories with Portraits* (London: John Lane, 1913). In 1878, after having graduated from Trinity, Cambridge, he travelled to Egypt by sea. Having landed at Larnaca with the first troops who occupied Cyprus for the English government, he contracted fever (p. 7).
2. Charles Wardell's father was a vicar in County Durham and had been a friend of Sir Walter Scott; *Memoirs*, p. 115.
3. ET had been on tour in August.
4. ET's brother lived in Yorkshire.
5. ET played in Charles Reade's adaptation of Tennyson's *Dora* on 23 August 1878 at the Prince of Wales Theatre, Liverpool, and on 30 December 1878 as Ophelia in *Hamlet* at the Lyceum Theatre.
6. At the end of the letter, ET draws a decorative cross.

29. To Stephen Coleridge, [7 August 1878]

Oh! my pretty beads!! They look so delicious by day light – fit to eat – you can't eat yr beads & have 'em or I'd try![1] – Did you expect to hear from me before, my Epic[2] dear? –

I've nothing to tell you, & I thought only lovers wrote, when they'd nothing to tell

[p. 2]

& we are not lovers –tho' I'm very loving. I cd find it in my heart to love every <pretty> thing I meet – & cd kiss any little street child if only it's [*sic*] face were clean – & pretty – I thought we were to write – you and I – when you were far away, & I was in dirty dear old Manchester[3] hard at work & sighing for <fresh> green woods & pastures new. Now you foolish shepherd you've misunderstood – I go

[p. 3]

to [*]"Proof"[*] on Thursday, not to "Olivia".[4] I've a box, & go with "Boo", & my brother-in-law & his wife – & I start for L'pool either Friday or Saturday.[5]

These lines in a grand scurry as I'm tired, tired, tired !! & have to act, & pack, & do everything for myself, for & because folk have brains that want blistering I do think. Read between the lines all nice

[p. 4]

& sweet things that I've not got time to write – & now to --------
Oh! Blasphemous ! ! ![6]
Yours always
W – of the Wisp
E. Wardell.[7]

GARRICK, Vol. I/5

Envelope extant; marked '*Not* to be forwarded' addressed to 'The Hon Stephen Coleridge, 1 Sussex Square'; postmarked '7 AUG 1878', London. The decorative notepaper depicts a young girl with flowing hair, annotated by ET, 'Isn't this a lovely female?!' This letter is reproduced in *THET*, p. 27. Coleridge's note states, 'This is an undated letter of this period. I had sent her some amber beads in a necklace.' The original letter is annotated by SC: 'She let me give her an amber necklace. She still has them and wears them 34 years later.'

1. An allusion to the phrase 'have your cake and eat it'.
2. See n. 3 to letter 27, above.
3. At this time ET was on tour in the north of England.
4. See n. 2 to letter 25, above.
5. ET appeared at the Prince of Wales Theatre in Liverpool in W. G. Wills's adaptation of Tennyson's *Dora* on 23 August 1878. Stephen Coleridge omits '& my brother-in-law & his wife' (*THET*, p. 27).
6. Coleridge omits '& now to – Oh! Blasphemous ! ! !' (*THET*, p. 27).
7. See n. 3 to letter 25, above. Two pencil sketches of a female face in profile, one showing the full face with eyes closed and the other focusing on the mouth and chin only, are located next to her signature and are probably self-portraits.

30. To unidentified man, 17 September 1878

Winlaton Rectory[1]
Blaydon-on-Tyne
Sep = 17 = 78=

Sir/ I beg your forgiveness for the long delay in answering your letter, but at first I was ill – scarcely able to get thro' with my work & then I had to send to London for the Photographs – I send them with this –

Wish best wishes for the success of your kind undertaking believe me
Yours faithfully
Ellen Terry.

FOLGER, Y.c.434 (117)

1. The rectory in County Durham of ET's father-in-law.

31. To Stephen Coleridge, 2 October [1878]

Wath on Dearne
Yorkshire
October 2

I send you scraps[1] I wrote some time ago to you & now I write to tell you I'm going back home to London town the day after to-morrow – I send this with the promised Photo = to Sussex[2] but surely it can remain there 'till you return to the smoky[3] —at all events I shall put "not to be forwarded"—for you can't want to hear from me—not at present. <I can not give you news.> Your letters to me are a very different matter. Think how interesting not to say instructive (!) they ought be [*sic*]—and are—considering "you see what you see."

Yes, isn't it wonderful that beautiful places, don't make the people beautifuller <– in mind and body too>. The beauty of Durham Cathedral which I saw

[p. 2]

the other day, for instance. I never did see such ugly folk as the Durham.
I think they are all sense less.

Dear pretty youth will you be glad to hear I am much better. I fear I shall be wanted in London for work sooner than Xmas, but I mean to make my holiday as long as possible.[4]

There are a lot of people down ~~stairs~~ to night & I am being bothered to come down ~~stairs~~ when I'd [made] up [*sic*] my mind for a quiet chat with you – I must go.

You'll not get this for a long time, I suppose, & will of course have concluded you are quite forgotten by me. Not quite. It's not easy to put from ones [*sic*] thoughts such a bright affectionate boy –

[p. 3]

Remember "Beauty, Good, & Knowledge, are three sisters and never can be sundered without tears"[5] (– Don't know who says it—who does? By the way? Do you know?)

You are beautiful –good—and wise < knowing!!!>, – *?* Keep so =

Boo[6] tells me you have sent me some little lace things! Ta Sir. Do they come from Malta?

I must go down – but not to dance. I've promised I wouldn't!!!

You must not write to Boo = nor to me when your return.[7]

I shall have forgotten you by then & it will be better so. You are "wise" but you have yet to learn it's "dangerous to play with edges [*sic*] tools"[8] =

Yours always affectionately,

E.W. Your friend
not yr enemy.

GARRICK, Vol. I/4

Reproduced in *THET*, pp. 17–19. This letter has been presumed to be a continuation of the letter dated 1 August [1878] from Winlaton Rectory – 'the scraps' enclosed – but it is dated several months later. The chronological sequence has been preserved.

1. A reference to ET's letter to Coleridge of 1 August 1878 (letter 28 above).
2. ET draws a square to refer to the address. The published version omits 'Sussex' here.
3. London.
4. She had been on tour in August.
5. Alfred, Lord Tennyson, 'To —'.
6. Stephen Coleridge notes that this was 'The pet name of the gracious old lady with whom she always lived'.
7. He was travelling abroad; see notes to letter 28, above.
8. The last sentence is omitted from the published version of this letter.

32. To Stephen Coleridge, [5 October 1878]

HOME ! ! Saturday

Welcome home[1] you too !

I've only been in the house 2 hours, & find from Boo that you've returned. Praise be blest you're safe.[2]

Now this from Boo & me. You are *not* to "call upon her on Monday", nor upon any other day – Now be a good boy & do not ~~not~~ write,[3] or you will bring dreadful trouble upon

[p. 2]

poor all of us. We will let you know when we are going to some Theatre, &, if you will care to do so, you shall come to greet us. I am glad you're safe.

With affection I am yours

E.W.

I ask Boo if I shall send her love! – Silence gives consent. So I send it = (She is sorry you're not "C.S." – Was it your suggestion or mine?

I only posted my other letter to you today at Kings X.[4]

GARRICK, Vol. I/7

Envelope extant; postmarked '5 OCT 1878', London; addressed to 'The Hon Stephen Coleridge, 1 Sussex Square'. Coleridge annotated the original: '"Boo" in this & all the letters stands for Mrs Rumball, a dear old thing who lived always with her through all other comings & goings & kept the house for her for many long years. Her husband at this time was nightly drunk & might have made himself offensive.' The letter is annotated 'the 5th October 1878'.

This letter was reproduced in *THET*, p. 21. Coleridge omitted most of the letter, reproducing only the first two sentences. Coleridge's note states that: 'I got home from my Mediterranean wanderings in the autumn of 1878, and received this letter at once. With Ophelia she began her long reign with Irving at the Lyceum. She had before established her fame at the Old Court Theatre, now long disappeared, where she played *New Men and Old Acres*, and afterwards Wills's *Olivia*. Her rendering of her parts in these two plays was surpassingly touching and beautiful. She was a vision of loveliness and led all London captive. Irving had become lessee of the Lyceum in 1878 and at once invited Ellen Terry to join him there, and so began what I suppose is acknowledged to be the most splendid era in the history of the English stage' (*THET*, p. 21).

1. He was travelling abroad at this time; see notes to letter 28, above.
2. ET had good cause to be worried about Coleridge's safety since he arrived at the same time as the English troops who occupied Cyprus.
3. The double negative and scoring through of the last 'not' here renders ambiguous what would otherwise be a firm instruction.
4. King's Cross, London.

33. To [Stephen Coleridge], [7 October 1878]

Monday

Poor boy! – I intend running round to see you this evening – some time after 8. Cannot help it – to think of your being ill![1] I am so sorry.

Your sincerely yours

E.R.[2]

I shall only be able to stay half an hour and then I shall be called for.

GARRICK, Vol. I/8

Envelope extant; postmarked 'OC 7 78', West Brompton; addressed to 'The Hon Stephen Coleridge, 1 Sussex Square'. This is annotated by Coleridge: 'This & the next letter were no doubt written ~~[illeg.]~~ by Boo. E. R. stands for Elizabeth Rumball.' It is also annotated 'the 7th of October 1878 – I was ill. S.C.'

1. See p. 7.
2. Elizabeth Rumball; see note 2 to letter 1, above.

34. To [Stephen Coleridge], [10 October 1878]

Haste

We are engaged each other night my dear Stephen – Do you leave town Saturday or Sunday?

Are you better? – a little stronger![1]

Yours always affecly

E.R!![2]

GARRICK, Vol. I/9

Probably written by Elizabeth Rumball on behalf of ET; envelope extant; postmarked 'OC 10 78', West Brompton; addressed to 'The Hon Stephen Coleridge, 1 Sussex Square, W'.

1. See notes to letter 28, above.
2. Elizabeth Rumball; see note 2 to letter 1, above.

35. To Stephen Coleridge, [16 October 1878]

33 Longridge Road

Wednesday =

Dear Epic[1] –

Boo has been miserable for some time since, & her "ways are ways of melancholy" so I've packed the poor old dear off to the sea for a bit, to get braced.

We went (Boo & I, with our little governess & a pretty young friend) to the Olympic last eve to see my pretty sister[2] – I wd not let Boo tell you, & 'twas fortunate I didn't – such a lot of folk in front I knew, who

[p. 2]

wd have asked who you were.[3]

~~We are~~ I am glad to know you're better[4] – go on & prosper.

I'm ill – are you sorry? – oh! this London, this London it'll kill poor

Livie.

GARRICK, Vol. I/10

Envelope extant; postmarked 'OC 16 78', London; addressed to 'The Hon Stephen Coleridge, 1 Sussex Square, W'. Annotated by Coleridge: 'I can not now at this long distance of time recall the origin of this nick name of "Epic" for me! S.C.' Also annotated 'the 16th of October 1878'.

1. See n. 3 to letter 27, above.
2. See n. 4 to letter 1, above. Kate Terry acted with Charles Albert Fechter and with Charles Kean, joining Kean in *King John* for a command performance for Queen Victoria at Windsor Castle. In 1866 she performed with Henry Irving in *The Two Lives of Mary Leigh* at the Prince's Theatre, Manchester.

3. This demonstrates ET's awareness of public perception and the risks of her being seen in public, as a married woman, with men other than her husband.
4. See notes to letter 28, above.

36. To Stephen Coleridge, [December 1878]

~~33 Longridge Road~~
~~South Kensington~~

Lyceum Theatre

Dear little Stephen – How glad I am you're back safe once more & well enough to go to the play house. So the white flowers came from you! I had a pale bunch of flowers the same night, & a great bunch of violets bigger than your pretty little noddle – Did you send those, too? – Come to the stage door any night you like, a little before

[p. 2]

11 o'clock & send your card directly in to me, then I'll see <that> you don't wait about in the bitter night air, but will come straight to you & we'll chat in the Hall[1] for a while. Boo shall come with me one night for she'd dearly love to see ~~her~~ our bright boy. Where's my Table Sir? I'm in an 'urry[2] – just going on the Stage. I'm so unsatisfactory to myself in Ophelia.[3] I imagine her so delicate & feel myself old & frumpish in the part. Write here & tell me if you're well.

ET.

GARRICK, Vol. I/6

Envelope postmarked 'OCT 5 78', London. The original is annotated by Coleridge: 'With "Ophelia" she began her long reign with Irving at the Lyceum – I have been in her dressing room when she came off & have found the front of her dress all wet with her tears. There never was such an Ophelia & never will be.' This letter was reproduced in *THET*, p. 23. Coleridge's note states that, 'Hamlet was produced with Ellen Terry as Ophelia towards the end of 1878. The subjoined letter was written soon after its production' (*THET*, p. 23). The associated letter is thought to be dated 5 October 1878; see letter 32, above.

1. Coleridge edited the letter, introducing some stylistic changes. In the published text it reads 'wait about in the Hall' (*THET*, p. 23); Coleridge omitted 'in the bitter night air, but will come straight to you & we'll chat'.
2. Coleridge replaced 'in a 'urry' with 'in a bustle' (*THET*, p. 23).
3. ET performed Ophelia in *Hamlet* from 30 December 1878, the opening production in Henry Irving's management at the Lyceum Theatre. Although an experienced performer, ET was anxious about Irving's refusal to rehearse her part (see L. Irving, *Henry Irving: The Actor and His World* (London: Faber & Faber, 1951), p. 312). This production was costly, at £4,000, but it sold out and ran for 100 nights. The reference to this production helps to date this letter and confirms that Coleridge incorrectly dated it as October 1878.

37. To Stephen Coleridge, [6 January 1879]

Poor little Stephen

I have been so busy – too busy to write & tell you how sorry sorry I am to know you ill & far away from home. I've found time to think it tho', many & many a time – poor little boy. Boo[1] & I talk often of you & we both fear for you. Why do you work so? "What's to come in stern measure".[2] True work is happiness – pleasure – (I find most satisfaction in work.) but Oh! do not throw yourself away. Rest – give your delicate body more <rest> at heart & don't rush about so.

I'm anxious about you. When you come back let me know by a white flower to the Lyceum.

Ever your affectionate
"Livie".[3]

GARRICK, Vol. I/11

Envelope extant; postmarked 'JA 6 79'; addressed to 'The Hon Stephen Coleridge, 1 Sussex Square, W' and marked 'Private. To be forwarded'. Coleridge annotated the original: 'I went out again to Cyprus & was struck down again with fever – and once again received this exquisite note of sympathy from the most adorable woman of her time. S.C.' Reproduced in *THET*, p. 29. Coleridge's note states, 'Early in 1879 I had to go off again to the East, and was struck down with fever in a miserable place in Cyprus. There I received the following note.' In his autobiography he refers to these travels; see n. 1 to letter 28, above.

1. Mrs Elizabeth Rumball
2. Unidentified.
3. See n. 3 to letter 25, above.

38. To Mrs Lewis, 23 May 1879

33. Longridge Road,
South Kensington.
May 23rd 79 =

My dear Mrs Lewis[1]

How dreadful! I <mis>took the date on your card, & thought it was next Saturday.

Thank you for your invitation. We shd like to come very much but my careful husband[2] thinks that Hamlet & The Lady of Lyons will about

[p. 2]

finish me (both in one day!)[3] & that if I go out anywhere afterwards I shan't wake up in time to catch the early train to Brighton on Sunday <where my chil-

dren have gone with a fine thing in whooping coughs>.[4] – So please "excuse" us, & with kind regards to Mr Lewis. Believe me always

most sincerely yours
Ellen Terry Wardell.

[p. 3]

How much I wish when you & your husband come to the play house, you'd come some other night than the 1st of a new play.

The acting is ~~nearly~~ always bad at first

[p. 4]

but I think it gets better about the 8th night.

SMA, ET-Z2,206

Headed notepaper with crest 'Prisca fides' ('old-fashioned fidelity'; Latin).

1. Probably Elizabeth Lewis (1845–1931), who was the daughter of Ferdinand Eberstadt of Mannheim. On 10 February 1867 she married George Lewis (1833–1911), a lawyer who achieved great publicity from his part in the cases of Charles Bravo in 1876 and Louis Staunton in 1877 and was a trusted adviser to the Prince of Wales. He was knighted in 1892. See *ODNB*.
2. Charles Wardell; see n. 2 to letter 25, above.
3. ET had performed for the first time in *Hamlet* on 30 December 1878 and in *The Lady of Lyons* on 17 April 1879, both at the Lyceum Theatre.
4. This addition is linked to the word 'Brighton' with an arrow.

39. To [Mr and Mrs Tom Taylor], September [1879]

Prince of Wales Theatre
Liverpool = Sep

I'm sure that the best friends I have, will be glad to hear that our little speculation – this 7 weeks tour – has proved successful,[1] so I write to tell them so – & to say too, that altho' I've not written before, I've thought with great affection of you all & wondered if you were all well & happy as usual – Edie came from London (quite alone!)[2] yesterday to go on with us to

[p. 2]

Newcastle on Saturday – & dear old George[3] is with us as "Acting Manager," so we're quite a little family party – the Comyn Carrs joined us at Glasgow where we produced Alice's version of "Frou Frou" – "Butterfly"[4] –

It was a very great success – at the end of the 3rd Act I thought the people were going mad, they seemed to like it so much = I was more glad for Alices' [*sic*] sake than anything, for 'twas her first venture = We did most excellent business in Glasgow – Birmingham – Buxton & Leicester =

[p. 3]

Preston was queer – still it paid us very well –
Here (L'pool) "New Men & Old Acres"[5] continues [to be] the favourite tho' last night we did Dora & Charlie[6] was as good as ever in it = You see he has not very good parts in the other plays, & he doesn't much like it = George sends his love – he has not been well but is much better now – & it's a great comfort to me to have him with us = he is such a good fellow & does his work so very well – & then it does him good to be able to earn a little money without much fatigue – My work at the Lyceum was hard but this is much

[p. 4]

harder. We have had to rehearse nearly every day since we've been from London

Mr Kemble[7] (who played Bunter very well, & Butterfly's father) has had to leave us to go to the Prince of Wales' –
Next Saturday there is a morning performance, and another at night, & then afterwards we travel all night to Newcastle = but I'm wonderfully well only tired – tired =

The news from home is all good news – they all seem well, & poor Polly better =

CLAREMONT

1. ET went on tour with Charles Wardell from August to October 1879 (*Memoirs*, pp. 125–7). ET mentions visiting Edinburgh, Buxton and Leeds.
2. ET's daughter, Edith Craig, was nearly ten years old. The journey from London to Liverpool would have taken several hours.
3. George Terry (1850–1928), ET's brother, who was her business manager on tour in 1879; see *Memoirs*, p. 125.
4. Alice Laura Comyns Carr (1850–1927), née Vansittart Strettell, married Joseph William Comyns Carr (1849–1916) on 15 December 1873. She adapted *Frou Frou* from *Butterfly* by Meilhac and Halevy. She also designed ET's costumes, including those for Lady Macbeth and Queen Katharine in *Henry VIII*. ET recalled 'No one was ever cleverer in the pursuit of theatrically effective materials than Mrs Comyns Carr' (*Memoirs*, p. 240). Her husband was an author and theatre manager. He was manager and co-founder of the Grosvenor Gallery in 1877, from which he resigned in 1886. In 1887 he and Charles Halle founded, built and opened the New Gallery in Regent Street which was to promote the work of the Pre-Raphaelites. In 1897 Carr was to adapt *Madame Sans-Gene* by Victorien Sardou and Emile Moreau for Irving.
5. Tom Taylor's play, *New Men and Old Acres*.
6. Charles Wardell; see n. 2 to letter 25, above.

7. Henry Kemble (1848–1907), grandson of the actor Charles Kemble, first acted at the Theatre Royal, Dublin, then later with the Bancrofts at the Haymarket; he acted alongside ET and Charles Kelly on tour in 1880. See *ODNB*.

40. To unidentified, [1879]

Haste

Tuesday

My dear friend – Send me your word where & I'll come to you anywhere tomorrow morning after 10 = I am so sorry you are still an invalid[?] = Didn't you get my letter at Pye-Pye Lodge – this morning? I wrote yesterday I am in amazing lodgings at 107 Bath Row – will you come there, or shall I come to you – & where – Tuesday – tomorrow you say = Do get well = Stop & see the last act & then come round for one moment – Yrs

E.T

Henriette Maria[1]

UCLA

1. ET performed as Henrietta Maria in *Charles I* by W. G. Wills on 27 June 1879 at Lyceum Theatre. It was a play sympathetic to the monarchy, ending before the execution; see R. Manvell, *Ellen Terry* (London: Heinemann, 1968), p. 369.

41. To Mrs Holtz, 2 January 1880

Jan 2nd/80

My Dear Mrs Holtz[1]

I hope it's not too late to say I accept with much pleasure your kind invitation for my children on Saturday. They are delighted !!

Sincerely yours

Ellen Wardell =

FOLGER, Y.c.434 (28)

1. Mrs Holtz may have been a family friend. In her autobiography, Kate Terry Gielgud, daughter of ET's sister Kate, briefly mentions a friend named Dolly Holtz; see K. T. Gielgud, *An Autobiography* (London: Max Reinhardt, 1953), p. 55.

42. To [Stephen Coleridge], [May 1880]

Thursday

Oh! I am so glad you've written – here's the box – I thought you'd write, & so reserved it – I began to write <to you> about a week ago, & then the very stupid & unkind thought (I see now it was stupid & unkind) crossed my mind, "he'll think it's just because of the 20th I write at last" – & then I could not go on. Now I'm ill and weak & worried by business & other things, & have no time to write long to you. Are you both well – all well I mean –

[p. 2]

I forgot Johnny Master – Is it too late to send the child – wife – mother any pictures? A bundle has collected for her – But I seem so rough I didn't thank her (or you) you know for hers – I don't answer letters sometimes & then I get too much ashamed, & hide behind the thought which scarce sounds (but is) honest (as daily papers are read) that people will forget me – Will you write me here – The theatre – "Ellen Terry" – & tell me if you & Mrs Coleridge are coming in this box on the 20.[1] if you're not <you yourselves coming>[2] I'll ask you to send it back to me, as there's not another & I cd desire there were. With affectionate wishes for the happiness of you & yours I am ever yours

E. Wardell –

GARRICK, Vol. I/12

Written on the back page and inside a play bill for the Lyceum Theatre production of *The Merchant of Venice* and *Iolanthe* on Thursday, 20 May 1880. Coleridge's annotation: 'From April 1879 when I married & left for South America until our return early in 1880 I received no letters from ET being most of the time travelling from place to place'.

1. Her benefit performance on Thursday, 20 May at the Lyceum Theatre
2. ET draws a decorative cross to indicate this insertion.

43. To Stephen Coleridge, [14 May 1880]

Wednesday Night

(So nervous about tomorrow.)

Dear Stephen – I sent off such a dirty copy <to you> of Wills' hash of the pretty german tale[1] – I think it dreadful stuff myself, but I hope you'll think it will "come out well" in the acting – I wish your wife wd throw me a flower & just pencil down on a bit of paper (wrapped round the stalk) whether she likes me in the part or no. Will she? Will you ask her? I'm very very nervous, & shall get no sleep for anxiety to night= Dear old Boo will be in the stalls just under you with my husband & my little woman (Edie[2] – the pip of my heart.) Greeting to you & yours.

"Livy"[3] – E.Wardell

GARRICK, Vol. I/13

Written on the back of a play bill for her benefit performance. Envelope extant; postmarked 'MY 14 80'; addressed to 'The Hon Stephen Coleridge, 1 Sussex Square'. Coleridge's annotation: 'Written on back of playbill for Lyceum Theatre play May 20th performance of *The Merchant of Venice* with ET as Portia and Irving as Shylock – plus *Iolanthe* – Irving as Count Tristan, Terry as Iolanthe'.

1. An adaptation by W. G. Wills of *Faust*, commissioned by Henry Irving. ET was to perform the part of Margaret in the Lyceum production on 19 December 1885.
2. Probably her daughter Edith Craig.
3. Olivia; see n. 2 to letter 25, above.

44. To Stephen Coleridge, [14 May 1880]

Grosvenor Gallery Library
Limited
New Bond Street

I'll send you a book of Iolanthe[1] this evening. Meanwhile please don't "pay at the box office" for the ticket I sent, or 'twill muddle accounts =

Yours sincerely ever
<& ever tired>[2] *Olivia*

GARRICK, Vol. I/14

On headed notepaper for Grosvenor Gallery Library Limited, New Bond Street'. Coleridge's annotation: '14 May 1880'. Reproduced in *THET*, p. 31. Coleridge's note states, 'On the 20th of May 1880 at her benefit *Iolanthe* was produced for the first time. As I happened at that time to be the dramatic critic of one of the London daily papers, I asked her to let me see the play as written by Wills before going to the theatre – and received this note.'

1. ET acted in the title role of *Iolanthe* adapted by W. G. Wills form Henrik Herz's poem 'King Rene's Daughter' on Thursday, 20 May 1880 at the Lyceum Theatre for her second benefit performance. F. J. Furnivall, of the Shakespearian Society, wrote to Henry Irving objecting to the replacement of the final act of *The Merchant of Venice* with *Iolanthe*; see Irving, *Henry Irving*, p. 357.
2. Coleridge alters the signature in the published version to read 'Your ever tired' (*THET*, p. 31). In the original, '& ever tired' appears to have been added by ET after she had signed the letter.

45. To Stephen Coleridge, [24 May 1880]

Sunday Hampton Court

No flower!
No message!!
& I *did* look for it so – Plenty of bouquets (mayhap one from her!?) but not a line – I was so

[p. 2]

disappointed – will you tell her so – ?

I acted frightfully that night[1] – but was better on Friday & best on Saturday. & now I am so tired & have come here for some fresh air. We have a cottage here (just

[p. 3]

a labourers [*sic*] cottage)[2] & I always come from Sat: to Monday =
Why did you reject my present of a private box?
Boo sends her love =
Always yours

Livy=

GARRICK, Vol. I/15

Envelope extant; postmarked '24 MY 80', Kingston and Hampton Court; addressed to 'The Hon Stephen Coleridge, 1 Sussex Square, London W'. Coleridge annotated the original: 'My memory now affords no explanation of this letter. S.C.' Reproduced in *THET*, p. 25. Coleridge omits '(mayhap one from her!?)' and 'will you tell her so – ?', which alters the meaning. Coleridge's version implies that she was waiting for communication from him.

1. Probably ET's benefit performance on 20 May 1880 at the Lyceum Theatre where she played Portia in *The Merchant of Venice* and the title role in *Iolanthe*. The production was controversial, criticized by Dr Furnivall for the cuts which had been made to *The Merchant of Venice*; see n. 1 to letter 44, above.
2. Rose Cottage, Hampton Court Road, ET's second home from 1876. Coleridge's note states that 'The little cottage at Hampton Court was in the row between the gate into Bushey Park and the corner where the road turns down to the bridge. Its windows at the back looked out into Bushey Park though there was no access to it. The deer would sometimes come under the windows to be fed. It was a very quiet restful little place then before the advent of the motor car and its horn' (*THET*, p. 25).

46. To Lady Pollock, 24 December 1880

24. Dec . 80

Sweet Lady Pollock[1] –

Your kind letter of remembrance of me! Thanks. Thanks. If you cd see how ill I am,[1] you'd "excuse" more now than my sending you my love & affectionate wishes. ~~For~~ I'm very sorry you've been ill & am very very glad you are better.

Yours Yours
E.Wardell=

UCLA

1. Lady Pollock (d. 1935), née Georgina Harriet Deffell, married Sir Frederick Pollock in 1873. Sir Frederick Pollock was a distinguished barrister who had become professor of jurisprudence at Oxford University in 1883 (see *ODNB*). The Pollocks were supporters of Henry Irving and were prepared to subsidize the Bancrofts' production of *The Merchant of Venice* in 1875, in which ET had performed as Portia, which relaunched her career. Lady Pollock also brought ET to Henry Irving's notice as a potential leading lady for the Lyceum Theatre. See *Memoirs*, pp. 88, 146.
2. ET stayed periodically in a Miss Pollock's private nursing home at 50 Weymouth Street, London. She may also have stayed in her other home at 92 King's Road, Brighton.

47. To Miss Mary, [*c.* 1880]

Friday

33 Longridge Road
South Kensington

My dear Miss Mary

I'm so sorry! We can't come. A stupid photographer is coming to "do" me "at home" on that very day & so we shall not have the pleasure of seeing you

[p. 2]

After all this year.
Edie[1] is so sorry too – & says I'm to tell you so.

Does this weather blight you? It does me.

With kindest regards to your kind mama

Yours very sincerely
Ellen Terry – Wardell.

PML, LHMS Misc Ray 188735 MA 4500

1. Edith Craig.

48. To Mr Hills, [1880?]

221. Camden Road. N.W.
Friday night

Dear Mr Hills I always loved you, but now –

Words are weak –

Oh! That bottle! You must have known I had a headache – that bottle cured me. How very kind of you & thoughtfull [*sic*]. I thank you, & thank you. If there is anything I at times wd like to be extravagant

[p. 2]

in (!grammar!!) & wont afford myself – it is Eau de Cologne !! Can you wonder at my weakness? I'm so good ~~I~~ Portia (I never do such things) didn't ~~wink~~ close one eye at the wrong man, & that it was you in the stalls after all.

Do you I wonder

[p. 3]

ever see the good Dr Quain now? If you shd hear he was the inclination & the time to go theatre –visiting & wd care to see The Merchant, if you, like <~~him~~> our kind Friend, wd tell me so, I'd send him a "box" –

I hope you are very well indeed. Wish

[p. 4]

my bestest thanks for your delicious present

I am dear Doctor-learned-in-~~the-law~~- ladies-tastes –

Yours sincerely

Ellen Terry.

FOLGER

The date has been inferred from the address of the letter.

49. To Mrs Hill, 9 March [1880?]

Margate – 1 – Fort Paragon

22 Barkston Gardens
Earls Court SW

9-March.

My dear Mrs Hill –

How exceedingly kind to write (with difficulty) such a dear letter to me = I don't look much when I'm writing & so writing is not as difficult to me as reading but I'm too ill at present to do anything much – It's kind of you to want to know about my health [.] I think I am mending & that's the best that can be said –

[p. 2]

One lesson I've learned lately is not to wrestle with *The*Influenza – but to "give in" unconditionally & to go to bed –

That second night of Richard III[1] was an event to remember – I was here in this horrid Margate far too ill to think of going up to town – About a quarter before <ten o'clock> I cd scarcely endure – I knew they were coming to the fight & oh, how I was dreading lest the dear gentlemen[2] shd hurt his knee again! But of course he didn't – much too splendid a darling fellow to be clumsy

[p. 3]

& then the good Bram[3] sent me telegraphs all the evening for he knew how I shd be feeling[.] Yes. he is a king of men to of course they loved to have him back again –

I've not see him for three weeks & it seems an age – but he never forgets to let me know how things are going on – The affairs of the Theatre which is so dear to both of us –

Dear Mrs Hill I wonder what your comfort is now

[p. 4]

your eyes are a trouble? = People read to me – & I'm obliged to learn my parts that way – & it is very difficult –

Have you read (or heard) Stevenson's Weir of Hermiston If not I'd like – love to send it to you –

I must scribble no more= but again thank you thank you for your sweet letter –

With affectionate remembrances – & to Mr Hill yours always

Ellen Terry=

FOLGER

1. ET first performed in *Richard III* at the Lyceum Theatre on 25 July 1879.
2. Henry Irving.
3. Bram Stoker.

50. To Mrs Wigan, [1880?]

44 Finborough Road
Fulham Road

My dear Mrs Wigan is as kind as ever I see, & I should be more than ungrateful after so gracious, & kind a letter, were I not to take heart of grace & work with fresh energy & hope, towards the ideal in our Art which she first taught me to see.

With sincerest thanks for your letter & affectionate regard

Yours always
Ellen Terry

V&A Enthoven

Annotated 'To the Wigans, 1st Princesses [Theatre] April 28th 1856'.

51. To Mrs Wigan, [1880?]

Sweet Mrs Wigan

How are you I wonder? So sorry you are seeing me to night – I'm ill & am acting this difficult part worse than usual. I can do nothing with it. If only I cd have been some years with you, I might have made an actress – Too late now

[p. 2]

~~I've~~ I have not learned enough & fear I am grooved now

Are you very well & nice – & kind as usual I wonder! "You wos very good to me you wos" – I am and always shall be gratefully & affectionately

Yours
E. T.

Pen won't work

V&A Enthoven

3 *THE CUP* (1881–2)

52. To [Mr Chute], 8 January 1881

Jan 8. 81.

Dear Sir[1]

I thank you for the Photograph you sent me, of a lady I knew many years ago as "Janie Denman" & who appears not to have altered in the least as far as the face goes

[p. 2]

tho', the child & the widow's cap tell of change – of joy & of sorrow =

When you see, or shd you write to Mrs _____ "Janie Denman"! will you kindly thank her for me for her kindly

[p. 3]

remembrance of "Ellen Terry" & tell her I remember as if it were yesterday the singing of "Ruth" — & the dear old Mrs Denman who held my hand in hers – I shd be very glad to know how she – Mrs Denman – is.

[p. 4]

Pardon this long letter
& believe me

Truly Yours
Ellen Terry

I am wondering it is Mr Chute of Bristol who has forwarded me this Photograph?

SMA, ET-Z2,288

1. Mr J. H. Chute ran a stock company in Bristol which ET had joined in 1861; see *Memoirs*, p. 36.

53. To Stephen Coleridge, 9 January [1881]

Dear Stephen

I was so glad to see your handwriting. Nelly says she would like you to go on Tuesday or Wednesday to see "The Cup"[1] and half an hour after The Cup she wd

[p. 2]

see you at the Stage Door. She tells me to tell you that she is not "puffed up by the news paper notices about Camma" that she is pretty fair but not

[p. 3]

Excellent.

Wishing you every good wish for the New Year
Very sincerely yours
Boo[2]
January 9th

GARRICK, Vol. I/16

Envelope extant; postmarked 'JA 10 81', London SW; marked 'private'; addressed to 'The Honble Stephen Coleridge, 1 Sussex Square'.

1. ET performed as Camma in *The Cup* by Alfred, Lord Tennyson (1809–92), which opened at the Lyceum Theatre on 3 January 1881. Tennyson followed William Wordsworth as poet laureate and ventured into poetic drama on numerous occasions with varying success, the most notable productions being those by Irving's Lyceum company.
2. Elizabeth Rumball writes here on behalf of ET. Although ET preferred to write her own letters she would sometimes employ secretaries in order to maintain her correspondence.

54. To Stephen Coleridge, [17 January 1881]

33 Longridge Road

Dear Stephen

Be patient – I've been ill, & scarce able to get thro' my work.

Yours
Ellen Terry

GARRICK, Vol. I/17

Envelope extant; postmarked 'JA 17 81', West Brompton; addressed to 'The Hon Stephen Coleridge, 1 Sussex Square'.

55. To Stephen Coleridge, [25 January 1881]

<u>Monday</u> =
~~Belgrave Mansions~~
~~Grosvenor Gardens, SW~~

Dear Stephen

I've read it = ! ! & wd much like to have half an hours [*sic*] talk about it with you before I send it off to Manchester to be printed (for £5!) I think it <u>very beautiful</u> – & very cleverly managed (you see ~~I know~~ I know the <u>old</u> play very well).[1]

[p. 2]

For an <u>acting</u> play, 2 or 3 little things <altered> wd (we wont say <u>improve</u> it, but –) make it more acceptable to a manager & the players –

There [*sic*] are all talking & playing here, & I cant write. Write me a line & say what day (Thursday or Friday?)

[p. 3]

you cd come – just half an hour wd <u>do</u> us. I'm very busy & a good deal worried & very vague I know

but I am yours
always affectionately
<u>Ellen Terry.</u>

[p. 4]

I thought your child (your <u>charge)</u> looks <u>younger</u> & <u>paler</u> than on the Hamlet night = I saw the grand old gentleman & the children from the stage box – He must have been surprised to find himself in a theatre[.] Scarcely his "line" I shd think. I never acted worse!! & it vexed me awful!

'cos you all were there[2] =

GARRICK, Vol. I/18

Headed notepaper for Belgrave Mansions, Grosvenor Gardens. Envelope extant; postmarked 'JA 25 81', London SW; addressed to 'The Hon Stephen Coleridge, 1 Sussex Square'. Coleridge's annotation: 'This refers to an adaptation of Don Carlos. S.C.' Later annotation: 'Of course this letter was all kindness of heart. I know now quite certainly that the play was & is hopeless for the stage. SC 1913.' Also annotated 'the 25th January 1881'.

1. Stephen Coleridge adapted *Don Carlos*, probably by Frederick Schiller.
2. ET had been acting at the Lyceum Theatre in Tennyson's *The Cup* since 3 January 1881.

56. To [Stephen Coleridge], [27 January 1881]

Wednesday =

"On such a night" I'm counselled not to go home, so will seek shelter with a lovely friend (not Miss Codrington)[1] for I have a terrible cold, & fear my voice leaving me.[2] So please don't come tomorrow but on Friday if possible – if not, on Sunday evening = at home with the children.

[p. 2]

Forgive me – putting you off, but "my voice is my fortune Sir" —

Coward! Not you! I was thinking of Donna Carlos & doing her afore the looking glass[3] =

I hope you'll come on Sunday?

Yours
Olivia grown old =

GARRICK, Vol. I/19

Envelope extant; postmarked 'JA 27 81', London; addressed to 'The Honble Stephen Coleridge, 1 Sussex Square'. ET annotated the envelope: 'Here is the box for Friday night. I do hope I shall act well = & that you & yours are well.' And on reverse, 'Don't think very much of 2nd + speech'.

1. Possibly related to the distinguished military family of Codrington, notably of Sir Edward Codrington (1770–1851), naval commander who fought at Trafalgar, and his sons, Sir Henry Codrington (1808–77), naval commander during the Crimean War and admiral of the fleet in 1877, and Sir William Codrington (1804–84), army commander in the Crimean War and later governor of Gibraltar.
2. ET had problems with loss of voice periodically which affected her performance and sometimes required her to take time off work.
3. Stephen Coleridge's play *Don Carlos*. See notes to letter 55, above.

57. To [Stephen Coleridge], [3 February 1881]

Here is the box for Friday night = I do hope I shall act well = & that you & yours are well.

Livie –

[p. 2]

Don't think very much of yr[1] speech.

GARRICK, Vol. I/20

Envelope extant; postmarked 'FE 3 81', London WC; addressed to 'The Hon Stephen Coleridge, 1 Sussex Square = W'.

1. ET has drawn a cross.

58. To Stephen Coleridge, [10 February 1881]

Thursday

Dear Stephen

I've written for a box for the Court for Saturday eve, & will send it on to you, & hope to join you about 10 o'clock = Please give my love to the child wife – She's a beautiful young thing & too good for you[1] –

No – thats [*sic*] only my fooling – for I think you very good = I'll bring the Tennyson hortygraf[2] on Saturday.[3] *THE* play has gone to the printers[4] =

Yours affecly

Livie[5]

What beautiful arms your child has!

GARRICK, Vol. I/20

Envelope extant; postmarked 'FE 10 81', London SW; addressed to 'The Honble Stephen Coleridge, 1 Sussex Square'. Annotated by Coleridge 'the 10th February 1881'.

1. Geraldine Beatrix Coleridge (d. 1910), née Lushington, known as Gill. She married Stephen Coleridge in 1879. She was the daughter and co-heir of Charles Manners Lushington, of Norton Court, Kent, and niece of Stafford Northcote, first Earl of Iddesleigh. See *ODNB*.
2. Autograph.
3. ET had performed in Tennyson's play *The Cup* opening at the Lyceum Theatre on 3 January 1881.
4. Probably Coleridge's play, *Don Carlos*. See notes to letter 55, above.
5. See n. 3 to letter 25, above.

59. To Ellen Terry, 24 March 1881

38 Albemarle St
March 24 81
2 P.M.

My darling,

Will you please give the enclosed to "Wisdom"[1] & make him deduct the enormous amount he spent in tea & silence for a "youth", & the enormouser [*sic*] amount for the youth's entrance to the gallery of female octopuses & waists. I'm so ashamed of myself – I didn't say goodbye to anyone last night –

[p. 2]

but oh, I was so wretched – ask them to forgive me.

We are going in a few minutes, but its [*sic*] not the Scotch side of London is it. [?] If you are well shall I see you on Sunday? If you go will you 'tellewag'[2] & tell me. Do go. I forgot my book last night, do you think "Boo" would roll it up

& send it me? What a nuisance I am. Please give Edie & Ted[3] a hug & a kiss from me. I am so glad I didn't know it was 'goodbye' last time I saw them. I've such lots to say to you – but no. I cant [*sic*] bear to write any more

Your most loving Eden[4]

[p. 3]

Here's a precious lot of stamps Stephen! You are "Wisdom" – & I send 'em to you. Turn round this minute & give that sweet little wife of yours a kiss – *2*– one for me –

Nell

GARRICK, Vol. I/21

Envelope extant; postmarked 'MR 25 81', London NW; addressed to 'The Hon Stephen Coleridge, 1 Sussex Square, W'. Coleridge's annotation: 'This letter, to Ellen Terry, was sent to Coleridge by ET who added a [signed] note of her own at the end'.

1. Stephen Coleridge.
2. Telegraph.
3. ET's children, Edith Craig and Edward Gordon Craig.
4. Robertson Ramsay, according to ET's annotation. His letter ends here and is followed by ET's note addressed to Stephen Coleridge.

60. To unidentified, [21] June 1881

Royal Lyceum Theatre
Strand

Tuesday 22. June
1881

You dear – I was on my way to you this afternoon, on the chance of finding you at home, when my eyes (from which I've been suffering lately – the gas – & a long <working> season –) became so painful I was obliged to turn back home,[1] & I lay

[p. 2]

*my garden is *about* 6 x 2ft !!!

like a log in the garden = in my Hammock 'till it was time to go to the Theatre[.] I want to see you very much indeed & as I know Henry Irving won't let me go long, without more long rehearsals I write, to thank you for your dear kind letter & also to ask you to ask,

[p. 3]

me to luncheon – (I suppose you are sure to be engaged next Friday or Saturday!?) what can H.I. be made of? We had a 5 hour rehearsal of Hamlet[2] last

Friday & he was as fresh as flowers in the evening & Dorincourt was more like Thistle downy than ever – Poor old Camma was a rag – & Letty was nowhere! – Sunday is the

[p. 4]

only day I find time to breathe in – off we go (the chicks & I) to my country estate at Hampton Court[3] =

Now you know – & so do I – that you'll forgive me & that you will ask me to luncheon some day soon –

And you will give my love (bound in silver) to Mr Skirrow & you will believe me, spite of <my> not knowing how to write, your loving & appreciative

Desdemon[4]

HARV

Headed notepaper.

1. This may refer to 33 Longridge Road, where ET was living at this time.
2. With ET as Ophelia and Henry Irving in the title role, *Hamlet* was performed for the first time at the Lyceum Theatre on 30 December 1878.
3. Rose Cottage. This is an ironic reference, describing in grandiose terms the property she refers to elsewhere in this volume in humble terms, as a 'labourer's cottage'. See letter 45 above.
4. ET signs herself in the name of her role in *Othello*, which was first performed at the Lyceum Theatre on 2 May 1881

61. To Stephen Coleridge, [29 July 1881]

Stephen[1] dear I hope you too will be able to go to I.C. They say it's done so well: I've just been sent a box & had had another sent by the German folk (courteous!) already – In hopes that you'll both be able to come

[p. 2]

(& how about Babs?) I send one of the boxes. I shall go myself in the other with Miss Codrington[2] & Mrs. Dasent[3] (her sister) & Johnstone Robertson:[4] We'll change & change about! Shall us? Ask Gill & give her my blessing & a kiss.[5]

May all the saints have you in their keeping =

GARRICK, Vol. I/22

Unsigned letter; envelope extant; postmarked 'JY 29 81'; addressed to 'The Hon Stephen Coleridge, Judges Chambers, Liverpool ='.

1. Ellen Terry has drawn a square around the name 'Stephen'.
2. See n. 1 to letter 56, above.

3. Possibly a relative of Sir George Webbe Dasent (1817–96), scholar of Scandinavian studies, trained as a barrister and assistant editor of *The Times* (1845–70).
4. Sir Johnston Forbes-Robertson (1853–1937) made his debut on the stage in 1874. He was one of the leading actors in London and became manager at the London Lyceum in 1897. He married Gertrude Elliott (1874–1950) in 1900.
5. Coleridge's wife; see n. 1 to letter 58, above.

62. To Stephen Coleridge, 29 [no month] 1881

Willow Bank
Moss Side
Manchester

Friday. 29. 81–

Dear Stephen

I'm intending starting tomorrow from Liverpool for Falmouth by 12 from south side Trafalgar Dock. I get into Liverpool by 10 – 15 & *if*you are not very busy wd be enchanted by a glimpse of yr dear young face either at the station or the

[p. 2]

Adelphi Hotel[1] (I shall drive there straight from station & have a "clean up" & some milk –) I hope you are missing yr Gill very very much – half as much as she is missing you will do! When I get to The Beacon Crag (& rest) I'm going to write her a volume for oh! doesn't she miss the

[p. 3]

peace & rest of your arm on hers – your lips – your voice — not that I think my volume will console her but I shall speak of you in it & oh! It will seem such a "nice" letter –

I'm with friends & they're wanting me to put this in the post & come along. I'm so tired dear old Stephen & hours seems days till I get to my Crag & my Beacon (Edie=)[2]

[p. 4]

I've lost your address – but think I remember it –

Yours ever & ever
Nin-com-poop=

Manchester & L'pool !! Aren't they 'ateful 'oles? I hope your Father & you keep well in spite of their 'atefulness.

GARRICK, Vol. I/23

Headed notepaper for 'Willow Bank, Moss Side, Manchester'. Coleridge's annotation: 'I was on circuit as Marshall with my father at Liverpool where I received this letter. I saw her off from Liverpool.' Bound in series before the 17 August 1881 letter, below.

1. The Adelphi Hotel, Liverpool, is located near the railway station.
2. Probably her daughter, Edith Craig.

63. To Stephen Coleridge, 17 August 1881

33 Longridge Rd
South Kensington

17 August 81=

Dearest old Stephen

Don't say the fifteen thousand has fallen ~~through~~ through! You say "it hasn't come off" – what do you mean?

I've this minute got the play & yr letter.

[p. 2]

I wd not speak alone to Blount (Cecil) about it – Daniel Fosque – Hermann Vezin[1] is even on the look out for good things & you like him don't you? Do you know him? Will you ask him down

[p. 3]

whilst I'm with you for a day – for a talk – for some practical advice & help – ?

I must catch the post –

Love to you both

All I mean !

Nell =

GARRICK, Vol. I/24

Headed notepaper for '33 Longridge Road, South Kensington', inscribed 'Prisca Fides' ('old-fashioned fidelity'; Latin); envelope extant; postmarked 'AU 17 81', Porthleven; addressed to 'The Hon Stephen Coleridge, Halliford, Walton on Thames'.

1. Hermann Vezin (1829–1910) managed the Surrey Theatre then Sadler's Wells. He became a renowned and versatile Shakespearean actor. He acted as Dr Primrose opposite ET in the first production at Royal Court 1878; his last appearance on stage was in 1909.

64. To Stephen Coleridge, 4 October 1881

2 Hume Street =Dublin

Dear little S.S (that means Stupid Stephen)
You surely don't believe that stupid tale about Merivale![1] Oh! Lord Lord! – I know him well (Hermann Merivale I mean) & his goodwork [*sic*] & know how finished most of it is = & "Rome was not" finished in a day, surely. Most like the truth would turn out to be that he plans the whole thing in a day – but really Stephen

[p. 2]

a straight – strait – ?? jacket won't hold you if you "go on" in this fashion — How lucky it is you write! You can get rid of so much force so – better put it into more plays tho' & do be patienter dearie boy, or you'll upset the nerves (in time) of the goodest little devotedest girl (gurl !!!!!!!) who breathes but to serve (& save) you[.] Don't look so sorrowfully! You'll fret your body

[p. 3]

to a bone & your poor brain to a husk, & ------ Impudence – but forgive me – I love you, & your letters make me very sad sometimes – Let "Love, & joy, & smiling Spring" (it's September but no matter)—
"Inspire your little soul to sing."[2]
Don't be sad dear =
I'm writing a line to Merivale to ask him something =
I had a frightening letter from home the other day
one of the maids (fat

[p. 4]

blooming Martha) had gone away ill, & I was told, "not to be frightened"! I did it on the spot of course, & blundered over my Portia[3] at night worser [*sic*] than ever – but I've since heard the children, Boo, & Co are quite well so I'm easier – I tell you this because I think sweet Gill & your boy should not go there for a week – tho' I feel sure alls [*sic*] well. When I shall trouble you to read a few letters for me (C's & mine in re: (!) the legal seperation [*sic*].[4] I'll send 'em you during the week = I'm well but very tired = letters from home my chiefest pleasure =
You're a dear for your letters – I'll answer questions next time. Best love to you & Gill

ET[5]

GARRICK, Vol. I/25
Envelope extant; postmarked 'OC 4 81', Dublin; addressed to 'The Hon Stephen Coleridge, c/o The Rev Charles Noel-Hill, Church Stretton Rectory, Shropshire'. Coleridge's annota-

tion: 'The allusion at the end of this letter is to my part in arranging her legal separation from her drunken husband Wardell. We had to buy him off with £100 a month, afterwards reduced to £60. This was before the Jackson case, when a husband could claim legal possession of his wife's body. So it had to be done. With her money so paid him monthly by for years, he kept a mistress!' Also annotated '4th Oct 1881'.

1. Herman Charles Merivale (1839–1906), educated at Balliol College, Oxford, had worked as a barrister and civil servant (as permanent under secretary of the India Office). He was also a novelist and dramatist; his plays included *All For Her*, a dramatization of Charles Dickens's *A Tale of Two Cities*, co-authored with J. Palgrave Simpson (produced on 18 October 1875), and his own adaptation of Sir Walter Scott's *Bride of Lammermoor* under the title *Ravenswood* (produced at the Lyceum Theatre on 20 September 1890). See *ODNB*.
2. ET appears to have used underlining here to mark the stresses in this quotation from Samuel Rogers, 'Epitaph on a Robin Redbreast' (1806), ll. 11–12.
3. ET first performed as Portia in *The Merchant of Venice* on 1 November 1879 at the Lyceum Theatre.
4. ET separated from her second husband, Charles Wardell (Kelly) in 1881. She took advice from Stephen Coleridge on this matter. See letter 65, below.
5. ET signs using her initials, one superimposed on the other.

65. To Stephen Coleridge, 26 October 1881

Bath Hotel, Glasgow
Oct 26 81

Stephen dear I'm "beside myself" for want, of time, & of people to help me do what I have to do =

Thank you for your pet letters – I hear too, just this minute from Boo that dear Gill is at home (I hope so!) & that she seems comfy =

Will you be kind & send these letters I enclose to Mr. Fisher[1] – I ought to have sent them to him so long ago =

[p. 2]

If you remember, Mr. F said, there was no need for Mr. K's signature[2] – Smith[3] says there is – ask F to settle it quickly – he has the papers = I fear I shall have to give up the hope of Mrs. W. the first[4] being alive – for New Zealand wd be a wild goose chase =

It's shameful troubling you so in this business =

=

Now ha'done with "Business!" Your lines are lovely – that I know at (all) a glance – tho' my brain works so slowly & dully

[p. 3]

that I must study everything before taking it in altogether. Thank you for sending 'em to me – it was kind & like Stephen – It was so like *me* to intend answering yr questions about Rochester & then not not [*sic*] do so. I pray you to go on writing it – Of course you'll alter "Jane" – for me.[5] I knew you would if it were possible when we first spoke of it –

Oh! Stephen – I've been

[p. 4]

writing all the morning to Boo (& some business letters) & I cannot go on with this = I'm afraid I shall break down on this tour = (Don't tell Boo.)
I'll write again

Your loving tired
Livie

~~I so ad~~
I'm so glad about Tanner & his picture =
Tell him so –

GARRICK, Vol. I/26

Coleridge's annotation: 'Mr Fisher was the lawyer I employed for the business of the separation. "Mr K" is her husband Wardell who acted as "Charles Kelly". I was adapting *Jane Eyre* for the stage. It was no good. I know that now. (1913). "Tanner" was our nickname for Edward Matthew Hale the artist who I had commissioned to paint her portrait for me. I gave him forty guineas for it. It hangs in my dining room. S.C.'

1. Mr Fisher, apparently a solicitor advising ET on her legal separation from her second husband, Charles Wardell.
2. Charles Wardell's stage name was Kelly; see n. 2 to letter 25, above.
3. Probably a solicitor.
4. Charles Wardell's first wife may still have been alive in New Zealand. In that event, his marriage to ET would not have been legally recognized.
5. Coleridge sought advice from ET on his own literary writings. His adaptation of *Jane Eyre* seems never to have been produced.

66. To Stephen Coleridge, 21 December 1881

Tuesday

33 Longridge Road
South Kensington

Dear ~~Art Critic~~ Heart

I've just seen The Lady Gill[1] – & she did – Oh! Yes, she did look as if she'd like to get out o'that big yellow carriage & go plodding thro' the mud with me – You're a

[p. 2]

dear boy, & if you can spare me your time tomorrow & will fetch me at some time 'tween 12 & 1 – I will go with you to Mr Fisher[2] & be very glad =

Yours to a cinder

Eleanora=

Half a sheet !!

"Thrift. Thrift, Horatio".[3]

GARRICK, Vol. I/27

Headed notepaper inscribed 'Prisca Fides' ('old-fashioned fidelity'; Latin); envelope extant; postmarked 'DE 21 83', London SW; addressed to 'The Hon Stephen Coleridge, 1 Sussex Square'. Coleridge's annotation: '21 Dec 1881' and 'At this time my dear wife was sometimes lent my father's carriage to drive about in. S.C.'

1. Geraldine Coleridge.
2. See letter 65, above. This probably relates to her arrangements to separate from her husband, Charles Wardell.
3. *Hamlet*, I.ii.180.

67. To Bram Stoker and family, [3 November 1881]

To/The Stoker family in general but
Bram[1] in particular! :

Dear Bram

Mrs Rumball tells me you'll bring Ted[2] with you to Edinburgh when you come[.] It's very kind, & I can't tell you how glad I am & thankful to you, but I beg you to think – he is only a little child & may trouble you[.] Your good nature runs in front of you – of all the Stokers – & if on

[p. 2]

second thoughts you think it will bother you to bring the boy just don't do it, & I shall be as glad as ever to see you your dear old kind sunny face – Tell Flo[3] I've learnt to miss it dreadfully on this Tour = Be quick & come, you funny old Sun beam for we all

[p. 3]

want you dreadfully. Oh! my beautiful little Flo, I've such fun about Loveday[4] to tell you when we meet – You'll laugh so = I can see you now quite plainly holding the little chin in, & looking out of them eyes – George[5] dear I was real [illeg] bad, I mean when I first came to Glasgow & H.I.[6] sent me a Dr Moore (an Irishman!) to put my throat to rights – & I think it right to send you the presentation = my voice got suddenly

[p. 4]

thick as thick! not sore-only tired = will you send me the prescriptions back please George= I think it was right to see Dr Moore H-I sent him you see & [H-I] can't be wrong. (Ask Bram !) The dear fellow (H-I = not B!) has a bad cold, but he is superior to such a trifle. In my life I never saw such a feat as H.I. acting Hamlet at Belfast[7] –

The proportion of stage to Auditorium (the Lord knows how it's spelt!)[8] to this, to this! scarcely

[p. 5]

any gas – the acoustics of the place – *too too* & – oh! but I could go on for ever mentioning the defects of the place – & he has never "with all appliances, & means to boot" acted so well at the Lyceum as he did that wonderful night = I shall never forget that 19th Oct – I've heard of "acting in a Barn"[;] Henry's acting wd shine brightly through a sewer. I believe some of H's velvet friends

[p. 6]

(? friends!) are doing their best to keep him from getting well again[.] He was really ill two or 3 nights ago = Really I think you'll all be ill too if I don't ~~shut up~~ close this epistle!!!

I trust Noel you are taking care of your child-Mother[9] = Remember she is a porcelain mama= – very rare – very fine –

[p. 7]

"well made – well wrought"
Farewell all my dears
This is from your loving

Nell =

FOLGER, Y.c.434 (55b)

Envelope extant; postmarked 'NO 3 81', Glasgow; addressed to 'Bram Stoker Esquire, 27 Cheyne Walk, Chelsea, London'.

1. Bram Stoker (1847–1912) was something of a polymath; trained in law, he worked as a civil servant before devoting himself to Henry Irving and acting as business manager of the Lyceum Theatre from 1878 to 1905. He is more widely known as the author of the highly influential novel *Dracula* (1897).
2. Edward Gordon Craig was in his ninth year.
3. Florence Anne Lemon Stoker (1858–1935), née Balcombe, married Bram Stoker on 4 December 1878; see *ODNB*.
4. H. J. Loveday was stage manager of the Lyceum Theatre.
5. George Stoker, Bram Stoker's brother, was a doctor.

6. Henry Irving (1838–1905), the stage name of John Henry Brodribb, actor-manager at the Lyceum Theatre from 1878 to 1902, later the first Knight from the acting profession.
7. Henry Irving performed as *Hamlet* in Belfast at the Ulster Hall in October 1881.
8. ET draws two squares of differing sizes to indicate the relative proportions of the auditoria.
9. Bram Stoker's son, born in 1879, was named Noel. ET referred to young wives as 'child-mother', possibly signifying the woman's youthfulness as well as the fact of her being a mother of children; see her reference to Gill as Stephen Coleridge's 'child-mother', letter 74, below.

68. To Kate Terry Lewis, [December? 1881]

Hampton Court
Sunday.

Dear Kitty[1]

Thank you much for asking us all but we won't come thank you dear = Charlie[2] is away & I have forwarded him your letter, so he may see your "honorable intentions"= I'm down here without a soul to speak to!! To get perfect quiet & to try what I can do with "Camma"[3] = My poor head troubled me so the last 2 ~~days~~ months that I forgot everything from hour to hour & began to simply abhor everybody= I'm better but back again today, for going up last evening to see "Agamemnon"[4] excited me very much =

I wonder did you see it? A boy in it (who played Cassandra) was extraordinarily clever = I wd not have missed the whole thing on any account. I'm thinking that perhaps it might do poor old George[5] good to come and stay here a bit quietly with me, or with Mother[6] – or with Mother & me! Directly after Xmas.

Of course you know I'm very fond of

[p. 2]

the country, but it does seem to me quite beautiful here tho' it's winter= For me it's just a 10 minutes longer journey to the Lyceum, than from Kensington.

I like Tennyson's Play even better now than I did – I hear Daddy doesn't think much of it – We'll see!!

I hope you're all very well –

Give my love to all at C-G[7]= Just writing this scribble has dazed me –

Yours affecly

Nell=

SMA, ET-Z2,208

Handwritten copy of letter; annotated '1881'. Note at the end in the same hand as the rest of the letter: 'Written to her sister Kate Lewis in reply to Xmas invitation C.G. – Cambridge Gardens, her parent's home. K.T.G.' (Kate Terry Gielgud).

1. See n. 4 to letter 1, above.
2. Presumably Charles Wardell, ET's husband; see n. 2 to letter 25, above.
3. ET performed Camma in *The Cup* by Alfred, Lord Tennyson, on 3 August 1881.
4. *Agamemnon* was produced in Oxford in 1880. ET and Henry Irving went to see the production; see R. Foulkes, *Lewis Carroll and the Victorian Stage* (London: Ashgate, 2005), p. 42.
5. Possibly George Lewis, Kate's husband; or George Terry, their brother.
6. Sarah Terry; see n. 3 to letter 1, above.
7. Probably Cambridge Gardens.

69. To Florence Menzies, December 1881

London – Dec=81

From Ellen Terry to
Florence Menzies =
=
"Common Report is a common liar" =
=
"Where Ignorance is bliss, 'twere folly to be wise"[1] =
=
Remember, you have not

[p. 2]

seen me!

Take my thanks for your letter, & resting in your "ignorance" of me believe that "Distance lends enchantment to the view"[2] of yours gratefully, for warm words & feeling.

Ellen Terry =

PML, LHMS Misc Ray 188736 MA 4500

1. Thomas Gray, 'Ode on a Distant Prospect of Eton College' (1747), ll. 99–100.
2. Thomas Campbell, 'The Pleasures of Hope' (1799), I.7.

70. To Stephen Coleridge, [14 January 1882]

Friday night

Thanks Stephen dear for troubling about that blessed parcel – I was annoyed tho' that you had been told anything about it! Your letter was the 1st I knew of it – I roared at the lines on Oscar![1]

Epictetus[2] – yes. You have my copy, I think my friend, of his little handbook! I can't find it & fancy I lent it to Gill. Don't trouble pleease [*sic*] about it.

Dr George Thomson[3] (<u>of Oldham</u>) writes that he consents to be the trustee in this settlement business but he says – "I shd like to know precisely what it means" – I propose

[p. 2]

my solicitor shd inform him by letter = "precisely what it involves to the Trustee" = What shall I do?//Flossy[4] is staying with me & all my people are in & out so I think I shall have to fly <u>back</u> to Brighton again for quiet & <u>study</u>.[5] I'm not well, tho' <u>Boo</u> is <u>much</u> <u>better</u> = <u>Rochester</u>!! Well Henry[6] has not read it yet = Of course <u>I</u> say go on with it – yes indeed – you know what delight I take in your work but <u>I</u> am nobody whilst <u>I</u> —,[7] is somebody[.] My wits – my wits — Can't write more than that I love you –

<u>Nell</u> =

GARRICK, Vol. II/5

Envelope extant; postmarked 'JA 14 82', Earls Court; addressed to 'The Hon Stephen Coleridge, 1 Sussex Square', marked 'Please forward'. Coleridge's annotation: 'The allusion to "Rochester" in this letter refers to an attempt of mine to dramatise *Jane Eyre*. Nothing of course ever came of it.' This letter is bound out of chronological sequence in the Garrick Club volumes.

1. The allusion is not clear but ET is said to have left a gift expressing her sympathy for Oscar Wilde in 1892; see Manvell, *Ellen Terry*, p. 232.
2. See n. 3 to letter 27, above.
3. Probably a matter relating to the separation from Charles Wardell. Henry Irving wrote to Coleridge regarding contact with Dr Thomson to ensure that the matter was resolved favourably for ET.
4. Florence Terry (1855–96), ET's younger sister, had acted in her youth in various parts, including Nerissa opposite ET as Portia in *The Merchant of Venice* and as Olivia in a tour of the play. She retired from the stage in 1882 on her marriage to William Morris.
5. ET may have stayed at Miss Pollock's nursing home at Brighton; see n. 2 to letter 46, above.
6. Henry Irving.
7. Henry Irving. ET puns on the first person pronoun and use of Irving's initial.

71. To Stephen Coleridge, [14 February 1882]

Stephen's Valentine
That young thing Boo! (With<u>out</u> her glasses)

GARRICK, Vol. I/unnumbered

ET has sketched the head in profile and shoulders of Elizabeth Rumball and provided this caption. A separate envelope is addressed to 'The dear boy Stephen with love from his valentine Boo' and has been annotated by ET: 'A shameless hussy I think =At her time of life='. This letter is bound in sequence before the letter of 15 February 1882 below.

72. To Stephen Coleridge, 15 February [1882]

Stephen dear – I have no rehearsal tomorrow & when I have seen The Doctor at 11.30 <to 12> I mean to make my way to Mr. Fisher[1] on the chance as there's no time for an appointment of seeing him & you – Manage it for me if possible = I shall leave George St. Hanover [Square][2] at about

[p. 2]

12 – 'twould be awfully nice (for *me*) if you could turn up there – !! but if you cant – if you're not there I shall drive straight to 10 Jewry Chambers & I'm *sure* you will contrive to be there =

I'm told your Babs doesn't look quite himself – I am sorry – he was well enough at Hampton Court – how about a couple of weeks there for him? the pretty sweet –

Give my love to your poor angel & believe me yours ever gratefully

For love

Nell

Tuesday night.

The 15th of February

GARRICK, Vol. I/28

Envelope extant; postmarked 'FEB 15 82', London. Annotated 'the 15th of February 1882'.

1. Mr Fisher was involved in giving advice to ET on her legal separation from Charles Wardell.
2. ET has drawn a square instead of writing it.

73. To Arthur J. Bright, 10 March 1882

Lyceum Theatre – March 10 82

Pray accept my thanks for the comfort of your letter – it comes well in such a needy time, overpowered as I feel by a sense of utter failure.[1] (And I meant so well!!) That you should have percieved [*sic*] so clearly my intentions, strikes me as quite wonderful & un-explainable – but indeed I can say nothing of my own words to thank you for yours – my failure can't spoil my love of the dear work – Oh the exquisite story! Do you remember Leigh Hunt's lines about Hero and Leander?[2]

> " I never think of poor Leander's fate –
> And how he swam & how his bride sat late
> And watched the dreadful dawning of the light –
> So might they both have lived & both have died
> The story's heart, for me, still beats against its side'[3] –

So I feel about Romeo & Juliet –
I'm ill & sad – & you will "excuse" this ill written scrawl & again read my good "intentions" & thanks & thanks between the lines.
Your words are grateful comforting – oh! dear! that's like Epp's [*sic*] Cocoa[4] (& I don't mean it!!) I'd ~~write~~ tear this up and write again but can not – I'm so tired – At least no more, but thanks and ever thanks –

Sincerely yours
Ellen Terry

SMA, ET-Z2,061a

Typed copy; envelope extant; postmarked 10 March 1882, Earls Court; addressed to Arthur J. G. Bright Esq., The Glen, Forest Hill

1. ET appeared as Juliet in *Romeo and Juliet* for the first time on 8 March 1882 at the Lyceum Theatre. Perhaps the ending of her second marriage the previous year and the performance of Juliet at the age of 35 may have contributed to the pressures she experienced in trying to make a success of it.
2. James Henry Leigh Hunt (1784–1859), poet and editor of the *Examiner* from 1808 to 1821, during which time he published the poetry of Shelley and Keats. He was a significant promoter of writers.
3. Leigh Hunt, *Hero and Leander* (1819), I.21–5.
4. The Epps family were famous cocoa manufacturers. ET may have known Laura Epps, who married the artist Laurence Alma Tadema in 1871.

74. To Stephen Coleridge, 14 March 1882

March.14.82.

33 Longridge Road
South Kensington

Dear Stephen. I had noted the — "*from * my lawyer", & approved so much the precise way it was put,[1] for many little delicate reasons I thought it wd make it so much better for Mr Carter !!!

[p. 2]

However — will this do? – I still have said Lawyer*s* further on – it don't matter does it? – 'twill give Clavering a chance I think of behaving quietly if there's still *others* behind somewhere –

[p. 3]

Thanks for your telegram = Mary takes your bonny boy home in a cab, & the dear boy this note = he looks splendid !!

My bestest
love to the child-mother.[2]
Nell:

GARRICK, Vol. I/29

Headed notepaper for '33 Longridge Road, South Kensington'; the inscription 'Prisca Fides' ('old-fashioned fidelity'; Latin) has been scored out several times. Coleridge's annotation: 'The negotiations still proceed re. the separation'.

1. ET is appreciative of the draft correspondence provided by Coleridge who was giving advice to her during her separation from Charles Wardell.
2. Geraldine Coleridge.

75. To [Dr Louis Borchard], 15 April 1882

Saturday. April 15 = 82

Dear old friend

How kind of you to think of Juliet's woes,[1] & to send her the lozenges. Did you say 8 a'day I wonder!! 'eavens!! I shall want no other food! I'm very grateful to you – That sounds very stiff – besides, hasn't somebody said, Gratitude may be defined as a lively expectation of future favours![2] = I wrote my little buds (that's Edie & Ted)[3] yesterday they were to

[p. 2]

come up to town on Wednesday to meet a good friend of their old Mummy's, & I know there is excitement in their little hearts this morning at looking forward to the event=

Farewell dear Dr Borchard – (Please don't [illeg] make yr wife laugh at me!) yours affectionately Ellen Terry =

FOLGER, Y.c.434 (1)

Envelope extant; postmarked '15 AP 82', Earls Court SW; addressed to 'Dr Louis Borchard, Barton Arcade, Manchester'.

1. ET suffered from difficulties with her voice while she was performing Juliet in *Romeo and Juliet*, which had opened at the Lyceum Theatre on 8 March 1882.
2. From François de Marsillac, duc de La Rochefoucauld, *Reflections: or Sentences and Moral Maxims* (1665), maxim 298.
3. Edith Craig and Edward Gordon Craig, in their thirteenth and tenth years respectively.

76. To William Gladstone, 20 June [1882]

33. Longridge Road
Earls Court = S.W
Tuesday-June20=

My dear Mr Gladstone[1]

Mr Irving tells me you think of coming very soon to see "Romeo & Juliet"[2] –

Now on the 24 – (next Saturday) The event of the season takes place! My "benefit" at the Lyceum – & if it should but chance that you are not engaged for that

[p. 2]

evening it would make me very proud & happy if you would come ~~that~~ & beam upon us, as you always do when you are at a theatre =

I should feel prouder of your presence than of any other Englishman & would carefully secure you the most

[p. 3]

comfortable box in the house:
I hope you will be able to come –
Yours with great respect & devotion
faithfully Ellen Terry =

BL, Add. MS 44475, f.305

1. Mr William Ewart Gladstone (1809–98) had a long and distinguished parliamentary career as a Tory, becoming leader of the House of Commons in 1865 and prime minister in 1868–74 and 1880; he resigned from parliament in March 1894. He sometimes sat watching plays at the Lyceum Theatre from the wings; *Memoirs*, p. 43. See also *ODNB*.
2. See n. 1 to letter 73, above.

77. To Janet Achurch, 30 November 1882

Dear Janet[1]

I have written to Miss De Gray[2] commending a "young pretty & very clever" Miss Janet to her notice – When I hear from her I'll send her letter on to you – Meanwhile

[p. 2]

<Something> is sure to be going on if you'll join merrily in whatever it may be –

With love yours sincerely
Ellen Terry =
in haste

33-Longridge Rd
Earls Court Nov-30-82

FOLGER, Y.c.434 (1–140)

1. Janet Achurch (1864–1916) had her stage debut in 1883 and became known for her performances in the plays of Henrik Ibsen, notably as Nora in *The Doll's House* at the Novelty Theatre in 1889, and produced *Little Eyolf*, in which she performed alongside Stella Campbell and Elizabeth Robins. She was commended by George Bernard Shaw in *Our Theatre in the Nineties*. This letter demonstrates that ET played a part in recommending her for work in the period before her first appearance on the stage. Janet Achurch married Charles Charrington. In 1897 Edith Craig joined Charles Charrington's company, playing Prossy in George Bernard Shaw's *Candida* and Mrs Linden in Ibsen's *A Doll's House*.
2. Possibly Ellen Washton Knox, who performed under the name Marie de Grey in drama and burlesque in England and in 1878–9 in India. She married on 22 July 1882 and retired from the theatre on 18 September 1895.

78. To Dr Meadows, 6 [no month] 1882

33 Longridge Road
Monday 6 – 82

My dear Dr Meadows

Here are the 2 stalls for Wednesday evening –
I will come & report myself to you if you please on Friday or Saturday next[.] at present I feel rather shattery,[1] which is not to be wondered at I think with the prospect in front, of being sat upon by every critic

[p. 2]

in London –

Yours most gratefully & sincerely
Ellen Terry =

FALES, MSS 177:16b

1. When mentioning her emotional state here she accentuates the meaning by underlining the word with a wavy line.

4 THE LYCEUM COMPANY IN THE UNITED STATES (1883–4)

79. To Stephen Coleridge, [4 January 1883]

33 Longridge Road
Tuesday –

My dearest Stephen

Never being able to thank you enough for your very constant care for us all, it seems to me I take refuge in silence & never express my gratitude at all!! Oh! dear Dear I don't feel as bad as I seem.// About Ted [1]– will you come here soon, when you return on the 10th, for I fancy the

[p. 2]

journey to Tunbridge will be unnecessary – Fancy your rushing down there for me! Let me speak with you instead of writing about this – As to the place for Ted, I think I would sooner not choose whether it shd be Brighton, Tunbridge Wells – Dover, or Rochester if you wd be so kind as to decide for me –
I wonder what Gill[2] thinks

[p. 3]

of my not writing! As usual, she "goes to the wall" whilst I have answered during the last fortnight heaps & heaps of letters from people I care nothing or very little for! = At least I hope you've all been awfully happy down in that beautiful Devonshire – I know if you and Don are happy & well our little

[p. 4]

angel is content. Give her a tender little kiss for me & say I think we have found a charming lodging for her – Dolly found it, & I went to see it – I want you when you come back to meet a lady – (a friend of ours of about 8 years –) Boo thinks she is just *the* party to go to America[3] with me – ~~Her~~ &she wants to go! Since her husband died just 3 years ago, & her only daughter marries in March next

[p. 5]

& she has a son in New York! I find it difficult to live with people if I don't love 'em – &, away from Edie Ted & Boo, I can count up the people I love on my fingers, & there's a finger left!!! & that's shameful isn't it =

Tell Gill it has been dreadfully sad with us all about Mother lately[4] – It is a pity to see her = so

[p. 6]

helpless & gentle now she is ill – On New Years Day we all went to her, & she was like a little child so pleased with our cards & little gifts = but she could speak scarce a word, & it made my heart ache intensely. Edie & Ted were so dear – grieved to see me grieved =

"Commodore B" was in front 2 or 3 nights ago – alone –

[p. 7]

I fancy he looked rather shocked when I laughed at him, so I was discreeter in the next scene, & looked at another man!!

Dear Henry[5] is – ever the same! "Gentle & he's kind, You'll never never find, A better dog than poor Dog Tray"[6] (Robson's old song=)

He'd send his love to you both if he knew I was writing, but he doesn't, so I send it for him with mine, to my darling little

[p. 8]

boy & girl friends & their toy-boy =

We are all pretty well here –Boo much better, & we all look forward to Gill coming near us, & being with us nearly always = The chicks are "really having jolly holidays" they say – They & I (& sometimes Booey) <or Dolly> – go out driving & walking together every day, & I get up ever so early now they are at home, & read to them & they to me – in fact we have a rare old time together. Here's a lot about self – Forgive & love me –

Nell =

GARRICK, Vol. I/31

Envelope extant; postmarked 'JA 4 83', London W; addressed to 'The Hon. Stephen Coleridge, Heath Court, Ottery St Mary, Devonshire'. Coleridge's annotation: 'I arranged to send Ted [Edward Gordon Craig], her son, to school with my old friend Wilkinson (now alas long dead) at Tunbridge, & had been down to see him about it. – "Commodore B" was Burrows, a friend of my brother's & of mine who I had introduced her to on some occasion now forgotten, his nickname was "the Commodore" He was really a school inspector.'

This letter is reproduced in *THET*, p. 33, where Coleridge notes that 'This is an undated letter written somewhere about 1881 or 1882'. Coleridge omits, as usual, the salutation, in this case, 'My dearest Stephen'. Unusually he omits most of the letter, from the third sentence about Edward Gordon Craig until the penultimate paragraph, beginning again with 'Dear Henry'. He also omits 'to my darling little boy' until 'with us nearly always'.

1. ET was looking for a school for her son, Edward Gordon Craig.
2. Geraldine Coleridge, Stephen's wife.
3. The first Lyceum tour to America took place in October 1883. ET was making early preparations for this.
4. See n. 3 to letter 1, above.
5. Henry Irving.
6. Stephen Collins Foster (1826–64), composer of the song 'Old Dog Tray (1853); other songs included; 'Camptown Races' (1850) and 'Oh! Susanna' (1848). See *American National Biography*, gen. ed. J. A. Garraty and M. C. Carnes, 24 vols (New York: Oxford University Press, 1999).

80. To [Stephen Coleridge], [January 1883?]

Dear Old Stephen
Heres a proof of my attachment! Correct it & send it back to your

Ellen

GARRICK, Vol. II/1
Bound at the beginning of Volume II in the Garrick Club series.

81. To Stephen Coleridge, [12 January 1883]

Very well – Then under those circumstances I will fetch something from the Lyceum tomorrow & will leave there for home at 1.30, or 1.45 o'clock, so if you are in the city & can call we might come along here together – eh?

Yr loving old Nell =

GARRICK, Vol. II/2
Envelope extant; postmarked 12 January 1883, London SW; addressed to 'The Honble Stephen Coleridge, 1 Sussex Square, W'.

82. To Stephen Coleridge, 19 January 1883

19 Jan 83 =

Your Darling Stephen
I could never tell you how your letter to my boy touched me –

GARRICK, Vol. II/3
Unsigned letter; envelope extant; postmarked 'JA 19 83', London SW; addressed to 'The Honble Stephen Coleridge, Dolgelley, Wales=', redirected to 'Camarvon'.

1. Coleridge had written to Edward Gordon Craig about a church window which Gordon Craig had possibly broken. Gordon Craig had replied, thanking him for his advice. ET sought Coleridge's guidance of her son and he seems to have acted in the capacity of guardian at this time.

83. To Rev. E. Wilkinson, 1 February 1883

1 Feb – 83
33 Longridge Road
Earls Court – S. W

My dear Mr Wilkinson[1]

I hope most earnestly that you have not found Ted[2] to be either a bad, or hopelessly dull, boy. It makes me very happy to realize he is with you – Stephen's friend[3] – the gentleman I had the

[p. 2]

pleasure of meeting here on Tuesday 23.Jan.
Ted's letters make me quite comfortable about him – He quite appreciates his master, & his lessons – altho' mingling with so many boys seems rather to appall him! & I gather he would wish life were all master & lessons

[p. 3]

& no boys!

I would not have troubled you with this letter, except that I am sure you will kindly pardon my desire to know that Ted my boy does not give very much trouble.

Believe me

Yours most sincerely
Ellen Terry=

FOLGER, Y.c.434 (57)

1. Rev. E. Wilkinson of Southfield Park, Tunbridge Wells, was a teacher.
2. Edward Gordon Craig.
3. Stephen Coleridge; see Coleridge's notes to letter 79, above.

84. To Stephen Coleridge, 2 April 1883

33 L.Rd.[1] April 2. 83.

Dearest Stephen,

£40 enclosed, & more thanks than I can write or tell = When I see you next you shall tell me how much more money I owe you already –

Every day this precious week I am engaged either to rehearse ~~of~~ or to "sit" to somebody[2] – however

[p. 2]

this week sees the end of that sort of thing – the sitting business = I rather fancy I must be home Friday & if you'd come then I shd be very glad –

I'm glad to hear a good acct of the wing-less one & of you all – Boo is fairly well, the chicks quite well, & I very far from well.

With truest affection

Your Nell.

GARRICK, Vol. II/6

1. 33 Longridge Road, where ET lived from 1878 to *c.* August 1888 when she moved to 22 Barkston Gardens.
2. At this time ET was sitting for a painting by the artist Louise Jane Jopling (1843–1933), née Goode. Her portrait *Ellen Terry as Portia* was exhibited at the Grosvenor Gallery in 1883; see *ODNB*.

85. To [Mrs C. Gladstone], 26 April 1883

33 Longridge Road
South Kensington
26-April.83–

Miss Ellen Terry very deeply regrets that she is so far from well, as to be obliged to forgo the pleasure of accepting Mrs Gladstone's kind invitation for the evening of the 28th[1]

BL, Add. MS 46044, f. 63

Headed notepaper for '33 Longridge Road, South Kensington', with the crest and motto 'Prisca Fides' ('old-fashioned fidelity'; Latin) crossed out.

1. See n. 1 to letter 76, above.

86. To Stephen Coleridge, [April 1883?]

Lyceum Theatre

My dear –
Mr Pinches address is –

Edward Pinches[1]
3 Garden Court
Temple E.C.

Tell little Gill the only night now I can a pass ~~for~~ for any where in this theatre will be 31 May Thursday. Shall I send her 2 D.C.[2] seats for that night? I'm dreadful bad <to night> dear Stephie

Love to you all – Livie –

[p. 2]

Thanks Thanks about the papers & all – all[3]

GARRICK, Vol. II/7

Bound in sequence implying it is dated the end of April 1883.

1. Edward Pinches was the son of Henry Irving's headmaster; Irving, *Henry Irving*, p. 484.
2. Dress circle.
3. Possibly a reference to his work for her regarding her legal separation from Charles Wardell.

87. To Bertha Bramley, 9 May 1883

"Suspicions amongst thoughts, are like bats
amongst birds, they ever fly by twilight"[1] =

My dear Bertha[2]

Yes – the misgiving did occur – (in the night – the only time I have to think –) but there was no bitterness, for "'twould be so natural," I found myself saying out loud! Your letter is as a bit of you to me this morning

[p. 1]

& I'm very glad to get it – much gladder than I can say with this cold pen & ink = so "excuse" more than an outbreaking of my heart & brain, most lovingly towards you.

Who shd be at my workhouse last night but old Matthew

[p. 2]

Arnold[3] ("**Old/"!**?/?? –) – & – family – Co! = a lot of 'em. They spoke of the young Ethel,[4] & Mr Irving[5] & I both advised she shd, at first, read with Mrs Stirling.[6] Between you & me that, "reading with Mrs Stirling" is rather expensive – but a dozen lessons wd greatly benefit any body who thinks to speak one day in public, but 'twould be

[p. 3]

be [*sic*] as well I think to arrange for only a dozen lessons in the beginning – Mrs S. is a clever kind old soul, but, she flatters her pupils – oh! that's not your experience of her by the way! is it?

This scrawl in great haste – I'm just off to rehearsal –

Your affect

Nell =

May 9. 83 =

SMA, ET-Z2,010

1. The first sentence of Francis Bacon, 'Of Suspicion', *Essayes* (1597).
2. Bertha Bramley, ET's long-standing friend, with whom she had a long correspondence.
3. Matthew Arnold (1822–88), poet and author.
4. Ethel Arnold, niece of Matthew Arnold (see *ODNB*).
5. Henry Irving.
6. Mrs Mary Anne Stirling (1813–95), known as Fanny, had her stage debut in 1829, notable in her performances as Peg Woffington in *Masks and Faces* by Tom Taylor in 1852. She was well known and respected for her work in comedy, in the plays of Sheridan and as the nurse in *Romeo and Juliet*, a role which she had played alongside ET as Juliet at the Lyceum Theatre in March 1882. After retirement in 1870, she gave readings and taught students. Mrs Stirling was seventy years old at the time of ET's letter; see *ODNB*.

88. To Stephen Coleridge, 14 May 1883

33 Longridge Road,
South Kensington.

My dear Stephen

Would you mind going to the lawyers in the city for me, & bringing me all my papers as I want to go through them & settle what to take with me to America[1] & what I can leave with you.

Yours affect'ly

Ellen Terry.

To the Honble Stephen Coleridge
1 Sussex Square =
W=

14 May – 83 –

GARRICK, Vol. II/8
Headed notepaper for '33 Longridge Road, South Kensington'; the inscription 'Prisca Fides' ('old-fashioned fidelity'; Latin) has been scored out; envelope extant; postmarked 'MY 22 83', London WC; addressed to 'The Hon. Stephen Coleridge, 1 Sussex Square, W'. Coleridge's annotation: 'This formal letter was of course meant to be shewn as my authority for getting her papers'.

1. The Lyceum Company's first production was *Charles I* in New York on 29 October 1883. ET was starting her preparations for this trip in good time. It was to last for several months.

89. To [Mrs Skirrow?], 22 June 1883

Friday 22 – June 83

Dear old thing

I have written to my boy[1] to tell him you may look in upon him tomorrow – I know you will if you can for the sight of a kind face he has seen at home would make him very happy.

[p. 2]

In case you go his address is —
Edward Wardell[2]
C/o Rev. E. Wilkinson[3]
Southfield Park
Tunbridge Wells =
– Wonder if you liked the Play[4] the other night? Wasn't I good to consent

[p. 3]

to make myself up such a dreadful old guy! ? I looked at you again & again, but you didn't seem to notice –
My dear, if you & Mr Skirrow are really bent upon giving me something by which to remember you (Oh! ye Gods !!) – well there is a thing I want

[p. 4]

Love – (that's the only thing I really *do* want in the world.) – & an umbrella!! one to keep me warm – the other to keep me *dry* !!!

Your loving old
Nell=

FOLGER, Y.c.434 (118)

1. Edward Gordon Craig.
2. Gordon Craig had assumed his stepfather's name, Wardell.
3. See Coleridge's notes to letter 79, above.
4. ET performed in *Robert Macaire* on 14 June 1883 at the Lyceum Theatre.

90. To [G. F. Watts], 1 July 1883

July 1.83.

It is impossible for me to stay away since you say you desire me to come.[1] For what can I see in your request but an expression of your life, of beautiful gentle goodness.[2]

When you wrote to me last Easter twelvemonth you forbade me saying anything in answer only "yes", but in truth your words made me dizzy with exquisite waves of feeling

[p. 2]

& gratitude & joy. It is impossible for me to get[3] <a spare quarter of an hour in the days until July 29[4] is over my work being incessant>[5]

May I come directly after? Enclosed is the name & address so you may send the picture & I am vexed [?] & perplexed to think I can say nothing while the whole wish is so great to desire [?] some words that could thank you & bless you.
Nelly.
Read between the lines of mine how sacredly I shall hold your letter =

SMA, ET-Z1,498

1. Some of the letters from G. F. Watts to ET have survived and a few are undated; see the AHRC Ellen Terry and Edith Craig Archive database catalogue of the National Trust's Ellen Terry and Edith Craig archive at http://www.ellenterryarchive.hull.ac.uk.
2. Since their separation, Watts had committed himself to a life of work and retirement from public life.
3. At the top of page two ET has repeated part of her second sentence.
4. ET had been acting in *Robert Macaire* since June at the Lyceum Theatre.
5. This addition appears at the top of the page, with a line drawn through it directing the reader to insert it after 'get'. There is no clear reason for this insertion since the text is repetitive. Visually it links with the last line of her letter, alerting the reader to scrutinize the text.

91. To Stephen Coleridge, [1883?]

Oh! Goodness! (I mean Stephen)

There is no supper!! For I've not eaten for many days – likewise I have my Mother here (Box 3.) H.I. goes out to sup, so theres [*sic*] none here – but what say you to tea – & –toast – & – what-can-be-snatched from the larder at home? Come & try at least, for – for a wonder –I'm fairly

[p. 2]

well to night = I hoped little Gill wd turn up this morning

Beatrix

~~To Miss Ellen Terry~~

To the Hon Stephen Coleridge

GARRICK, Vol. II/9

Coleridge's annotation: 'I had sent a note round to her dressing room at the Lyceum & this pencil note came back to me in the stalls. It is written on the unused sheet of my own letter –'.

92. To Stephen Coleridge, [1883?]

Shall send carriage round for you to Globe – if they will sing out ~~Mrs Ward~~ "Miss Terry's carriage" – then you'll call round <u>here</u> for me wont you & I'll take you home –

So tired – <u>Wonder</u> have you been to Tunbridge Wells?

[p. 2]

To the Honble Stephen Coleridge

To be called for =

GARRICK, Vol. II/10

Coleridge's annotation: 'I went to Tunbridge Wells to arrange with my old friend Wilkinson who kept a school there, to take her round there – he agreed and we went there for a short time. Wilkinson has now long been dead (1913).'

93. To Stephen Coleridge, 1 July 1883

<u>Sunday</u> – 1 July –

Do you know my dear old Stephen I quite forget whether it was Monday or Tuesday arranged you'd come here! Make it Monday (tomorrow) <u>if it's possi-</u>

ble[.] Hope poor Gillyflower[1] has recovered from that precious play![2] Tell her, I have not!

Your tired – old –

Livie[3] =

GARRICK, Vol. II/11

Envelope extant; postmarked 'JY 2 83', London; addressed to 'The Honble Stephen Coleridge, 1 Sussex Square'.

1. Geraldine Coleridge.
2. Possibly *Robert Macaire*, which ET had been performing at the Lyceum Theatre since 14 June.
3. ET signs herself in the name of Olivia.

94. To Stephen Coleridge, [9 July 1883]

"There was a star ------

A friend in need, is a friend indeed! Thanks dear friend.

E.T.

GARRICK, Vol. II/12

Envelope extant; postmarked 'JU 9 83', Earls Court; addressed to 'The Honble Stephen Coleridge, 1 Sussex Square'. Coleridge's annotation: 'Nellie telegraphed me asking for a quotation to be put under photographs of her sold by Window & Grove I telegraphed back! – "There was a star danced and under that was I born".

95. To Bram Stoker, 12 July 1883

12 – July – 83.

Dear Bram

See my brother (Mr George Terry)[1] for a few moments if you please – Mr Irving[2] asked me about him, & wd wish me to send him to you, or to see him himself if he had time Yours ever

Ellen Terry –

CLAREMONT

Envelope extant; addressed to 'Bram Stoker Esq, Lyceum Theatre' and marked '(Ellen Terry=)'.

1. George Terry (1850–1928), one of ET's brothers. George worked for a time in theatre management; see P. M. Hartnoll (ed.), *The Concise Oxford Companion to the Theatre* (Oxford: Oxford University Press, 1972).
2. Henry Irving.

96. To Stephen Coleridge, 16 July 1883

16 July 1883 – Bed. Home –
~~LYCEUM THEATRE~~

Dear dear Stephen

I pray you not to blame the Commodore.[1] Really 'twas my fault since he understood (& naturally expected) I should write –

Why Stephen my little dear friend[2] I require such very hard hits to be hurt by any

[p. 2]

outside the wee circle of folk I love, it's only when my perfect faith in that small ring is shaken that I can suffer – that wd go nigh to kill me, so don't you or the Gillyflower[3] or

[p. 3]

a few others I know, try experiments[.] The Commodore is merely just, & I can't complain even if I would – & I don't want to –

// Thank you for getting those priceless letters of C.K's = Mr Carter had other papers

[p. 4]

but I can't remember what papers, & I rather wished he (Mr C) shd not think I had forgotten.[4]

I will come for a day or three to Woodham – Thank you, thank you = & 'will write to my little Gill very soon about it.[5]

Your loving "dead-beat"

Nell =

GARRICK, Vol. II/13

Headed notepaper for 'Lyceum Theatre'. Envelope extant; postmarked 'JY 16 83', Earls Court; addressed to 'The Honble Stephen Coleridge, Judges House, Winchester', redirected to Dorchester. Coleridge's annotation: '"The Commodore" was the nickname of E. Burrows, a friend of my brother Bernard's. He put some indignity upon her, the nature of which I now have forgotten.' This letter is reproduced in *THET*, p. 35, where Coleridge notes that, 'A friend of mine, whom, at his request, I was instrumental to bring into her presence, put some indignity upon her the nature of which I have now long forgotten. This letter alludes to the matter.'

1. In his publication, Coleridge anonymized the man referred to here and below as 'Mr —'.
2. Coleridge edited this endearment in the published version, rendering it possibly less intimately as 'Why my dear friend'.

3. This phrase is removed by Coleridge in the published version, consistent with his practice to omit from his publication any references by ET to his wife.
4. Coleridge omits this entire sentence from the published version. 'C. K.' refers to ET's second husband, Charles Wardell (Kelly), from whom she had separated.
5. The last phrase is omitted by Coleridge, removing reference to his wife from the published version.

97. To Bertha Bramley, 30 July [1883]

No time dear Bertha to send you more than thanks & love & every kind thought my heart can wish, it wishes you –

Nell =

33 – Longridge Rd July 30 –
(just starting for Hertfordshire)

SMA, ET-Z2,011

98. To [Elizabeth Rumball], [3 October 1883]

'Ask Stephen to pay the *<u>full £40</u>* at once & also Whiteleys bill enclosed <u>at once</u>.

GARRICK, Vol. II/unnumbered
Note written on back of an envelope addressed to 'Mrs Rumball, Childwall Abbey, near Liverpool'; postmarked 'OC 3 83', Liverpool. Coleridge's annotation: 'For a great many years ET regularly paid her salary into a special account my bankers & I paid all her bills for her & her rent, & wages, and house bills, and everything for her and generally managed all her affairs'.

99. To Elizabeth Rumball, 9 October 1883

Adelphi Hotel. October 9 – 1883
Liverpool
Only a little line dearest old Booie[1] to tell you that considering all things sweet Nellie is wonderfully well. Her poor little heart nearly broke when she drove away from you all,[2] but she picked up very soon, and rested a good bit in the train – and has been very happy all day to day – but

[p. 2]

I am very very glad I was with her all the time for I think if she had been alone she would have broken down dreadfully. It is needless to tell you how happy I am with her for you know it.
Much love dear Booie
Yours Gill.[3]

[p. 3]

Dear Booey – poor Booey – We are all fairly right, & little Gill is of course a great comfort. I'll write from Queenstown[4] – the two darlings how are they? Take very nearly

[p. 4]

All my love with you 3 = A letter came <u>for me I know</u>, & was taken back, & then out on here – no news – Only love & love.

<u>Nelly</u> =

Tuesday

SMA, 5.148

1. Elizabeth Rumball.
2. ET left from Liverpool for the Lyceum Tour of the United States and Canada on 11 October 1883, leaving her two children at home in the United Kingdom.
3. Gill, possibly Geraldine Coleridge, writes the first two pages of the letter and ET writes pages 3 and 4.
4. ET planned to put a letter in the post at Queenstown (now Cobh, Ireland) en route to the United States.

100. To Mrs George R. Shaw, 16 December 1883

Tremont House
Dec 16 = 83 =

My dear Mrs Shaw

Calling in at the Theatre last night on my way home, I obtained Mr Irving's most amiable permission to stay away from rehearsal tomorrow morning: So I shall hope

[p. 2]

to be with you about 1 o'clock –? 1-30? 2-o'clock?

It gave me great pleasure to see your face in the crowd last night, I seemed to <u>know it</u>, as you came up & before you said a word –

[p. 3]

Sincerely yours
Ellen Terry=
33 Longridge Road – Earls Court

HARV
Envelope extant; addressed to 'Mrs George R. Shaw, 158 or 138 Mount Vernon St' and marked 'By hand'.

101. To Stephen Coleridge, 22 [no month] [1883]

Sunday 22

My dearest Stephen

I'll dictate to Boo[1] – for I'm anxious your care for me shd not seem unappreciated, & I'm frightfully fatigued[2] – Your long letter to Fisher[3] was very funny & clever & it made me laugh, but dear Stephen forgive me, I have not posted it = In your letter to me you say you ~~humbly~~ "humbly advise" me "not" to worry Henry"[4]

[p. 2]

in this matter, it has not worried him, but I have told him, since I am sure he would be hurt at not being consulted. ~~in~~ He begs you to omit one part of your letter (the part I have marked) if you send it at all. H.I's advice[5] <to me> is – "Write yourself to C.K[6] and propose yourself what

[p. 3]

Stephen proposes." This I think would be good, but I wish to tell you first, and also to ask you to write me a few words (that I may copy) to C.K. (Don't laugh, Stephen) I am astounded at this fresh proof of Mr Kelly's impudence & degradation

[p. 4]

and also at the fresh outbreak of vanity which induces him to make a second time Ducks & Drakes of his (?) money in ventureing [*sic*] upon management ~~before the~~ of a company before he has learned to manage himself. It is very kind of him, is it not, to agree

[p. 5]

about the lease of Longridge Road. I ~~I suppose I~~
I am too tired to think for another minute so good-bye

dear Stephen and forgive all the trouble I cause you.

Your Boo
for Nelly

GARRICK, Vol. II/14

Coleridge's annotation: 'Her drunken husband started touring the country as a "manager"! and of course lost large sums of money which Nellie had to pay for him. We had great difficulty with him continually.'

1. Elizabeth Rumball.
2. Handwritten by Elizabeth Rumball from here onwards.
3. See n. 1 to letter 65, above.
4. Henry Irving.
5. Henry Irving.
6. Charles Wardell (Kelly), ET's second husband, from whom she was separating at this time.

102. To [Bertha Bramley], [1884]

Monday

33. Longridge Rd

Oh! it's lovely to see the handwriting of so many I care very much for! How to send a sign back to them all? That's the difficulty, seeing as how Time flies & I have a good six months [*sic*] work to do in 6 weeks –!! So you know

[p. 2]

Madame de Strueve [?] in Washington – ! The Basilisks!!! not to speak of <you> to me –

Oh! it has all been lovely – lovely! & best of all the coming home & finding all well – & all loving –

I'll tell you some day, but now this pencilled scrawl to tell

[p. 3]

you my train for Seven Oaks starts in an hour – not a word do I know of Viola (my next work) & I'm off away from friends to study in quiet the words & the play – just Boo with me & that is all – so – not next week but when the work at the

[p. 4]

Lyceum begins – the week after next – *then* do try to come to me – or I'll come to you – of course –

How I do hope you are well & happy – & the good Father (Lear) & all you love. I love you & am

Yours faithfully
Nell =

One friend missing:
Charles Reade[1] –

SMA, ET-Z2,016
The date of the letter is inferred from the reference to her forthcoming new role as Viola. ET first performed Viola in *Twelfth Night* at the Lyceum Theatre on 8 July 1884.

1. See n. 1 to letter 14, above. Reade died on 11 April 1884, so ET may be referring to his illness or recent death.

103. To Charles Dodgson, 26 May 1884

The Crown Hotel
Seven Oaks =

May 26 = 84 =

Dear Mr Dodgson[1]
Your letter was forward-ed [*sic*] me to this place – The rest remains behind – the book you so kindly say you have sent me – "Rhyme & Reason", I guess ("I guess"!!) & if so I'm very glad

[p. 2]
& thank you very heartily = Yes – "like Christine Nielson" I'm quite spoiled by the Americans, but then I was spoiled before I went to America by ~~injudicious friends~~ dear delightful sweet people, friends, who will I hope to continue to do so till the end of the chapter =

[p. 3]
I am very sorry for the little girl (22)'s sake that there will be no performance at the Lyceum, either Friday evening, or Saturday morning – We begin work there next Saturday evening – that evening will be witness to such a scene of "spoiling", as would make ones [*sic*] enemies shiver!!!

Only I don't <think> I – for one –

[p. 4]
have any enemies!

Polly[2] is much better thank you – she is wretchedly thin but looks robust compared with the Polly of a year ago = Floss[3] (& her infant) makes progress marvellously – I can never quite believe in it's [*sic*] being actually Flossie's baby, but at least I have brought the wee thing a Perambulator, from New York which does

[p. 5]

credit to that wonderful place – my taste (!!) – &, I hope, to the baby!

Dear Mr Dodgson I hope you are very well & happy – I am <at> this lovely country place with Mrs Rumball & ~~The~~ my two little anchors[4] & we are all desperately happy – We all send our love Yours faithfully

Ellen Terry =

FALES, 5:453 XV-294 47/09

1. Charles Lutwidge Dodgson (1832–98) was a mathematician, a don at Christ Church, Oxford University, a photographer and an author, publishing under the name Lewis Carroll. He published *Rhyme? and Reason?* in 1883.
2. Marion Terry, ET's sister.
3. Florence Terry; see n. 4 to letter 70, above.
4. Her children, Edith Craig and Edward Gordon Craig.

104. To Bertha Bramley, 18 July 1884

18. July 84. 33. Longridge Rd

S.W.

Oh! Bertha my dear Bertha I did want you by my side the other day – You are strong & clever & courageous (*) & I have spoken but to very few & ------ I did wish for you

* "Me thinks most men are but poor hearted, else
Should we so dote on courage were it commoner"[1]

[p. 2]

so much = so much = However, all's well now for it's so difficult for me to be unhappy long together – ("God tempers the wind[2] – etc & c –)!!

Here's your letter – & here am I – in bed since Tuesday with rheumatism in every joint of my anatomy

[p. 3]

& a vaccinated arm to boot, which has set my blood on fire – As I have to play "a mother" every evening until further notice 'tis somewhat unfortunate, but better a poisoned arm than no arm at all –! I intended

[p. 4]

driving (?) going to Eltham Sunday next to see some friends & now fear 'twill be impossible – If it be possible to go & I find myself in Eltham, wd you like me to come to you for an hour, or wd you rather I did not come –? If not surely I shall see you before I start for America[3] (my dear America) early

[p. 5]

in September?

I saw Edgar the other day in St James' St looking just the same as years ago, kind & simple, & a glad-to-see-one-sort of look on his face –

Mrs Coleridge is sitting with me & tells me

[p. 6]

rudely to "shut up" – end up, for your cheeks are very red" & since she has marvellous command over me (!) & is such a giant I must do as she bids me –

[p. 7]

I hope you are as happy as I can wish you, & as well – you & all your dear ones – I am most faithfully

Yours

Nell =

SMA, ET-Z2,012

1. Alfred, Lord Tennyson, *Queen Mary* (1875), II.ii.
2. Laurence Sterne, *A Sentimental Journey* (1768), 'Maria'.
3. The Lyceum Company left for its second tour to the United States and Canada in the autumn.

105. To unidentified, 23 July 1884

23. July 84. 33. L. Rd[1]

Oh! I do wish I do wish I could come to you on Sunday but if I'm well enough to go anywhere I'm engaged that day.

This week the Doctor Mackenzie[2] forbids me speaking, & an apology for

[p. 2]

loss of voice is given for me each night in front of curtain at the Lyceum –

I do think this week must see an end to the "woes which tread upon another's heels so fast they follow" & then next week

[p. 3]

I do so much hope you'll be coming to town & will come this way. Edie & Ted[3] will be home then too – their holidays – that always makes me well –

Yes – they wd have morning performances but I'm not well enough –

If you could come some

[p. 4]

night "next week" to our play, it wd please me to send you a box, & you perhaps wd come to my room for a little while –

I am your faithful

Nell =

I'm wishing all the time I cd come on Sunday. Will you have this new photograph?

SMA, ET-Z2,013

1. 33 Longridge Road, ET's home from the time of her marriage to Charles Wardell to autumn 1888.
2. Dr Alexander Mackenzie treated ET for some time.
3. Edith Craig and Edward Gordon Craig.

106. To Stephen Coleridge, [October 1884?]

Here is the paper.

I was asleep & they wd not disturb my rest =

Gill is none the worse I hope for last night's dull entertainment.[1]

Do send me the paper you spoke of that tells of the plans of our great painter-sculptor.[2] – here's

[p. 2]

a bright day for him I thank the Lord = I always do—, for him—when the Sun shines – I wish I could have made his sun – shine, but I was so ignorant,[3] so young, & he was so impatient.

Don't think, dear, but that he hates me—if he can hate he must hate me

[p. 3]

but to "revenge is no valour but to bear"[4]—I'm not half awake[5] & here's a pretty rambling servant. Let's go, Gill & I, to Oak Lodge to luncheon next Sunday week after church I cant bear going to church but I do want to hear Mr Eyton – I kiss you both

Your loving but ill

Nell =

GARRICK, Vol. III/3

Coleridge reproduced this letter in *THET*, p. 37. His note states, 'The following letter contains one of the very few allusion to the past that find place in her letters. I had the inestimable privilege of the friendship of the great painter, and was able at once to reassure her and tell her that no shade of ill-will, but rather a deep and abiding kindliness towards her, continually occupied his mind, and I quoted to her a few lines from one of his letters to me thus. "Nothing has weakened my deep interest; please let me have a line to tell me that your most important friendship is unbroken—and that all is well."' The published letter is not a direct transcript of the original. The original is bound in the volume in the sequence of letters in October 1884. Coleridge's annotation: 'This letter contains one of her very few allusions to Watts & her life with him'.

1. This sentence was omitted in the published version.
2. G. F. Watts, with whom Coleridge was friends. He features in Coleridge's books, *Memories with Portraits* (London: John Lane, 1913) and *Famous Victorians I have Known* (London: Simpkin, Marshall Ltd, and Cardiff Western Mail Ltd, 1928).
3. This word is not underlined in the published version.
4. Shakespeare, *Timon of Athens*, III.v.39.
5. The rest of the letter from here was omitted in the published version.

107. To Elizabeth Winter, 28 November 1884

Victoria Hotel
Nov.28. Midnight

My dear Mrs Winter[1]

Hamlet – I mean Mr Irving[2] –, asks me to ask you, to be so sweet & kind as to come to dinner on Sunday with him – the dinner hour is – Mercy!! I don't know!!! but sure sure 'twill be 7-30 or 8 – & you cd come here first perhaps, for a dull ten

[p. 2]

minutes & we cd go in together

The place of meeting is Delmonico's — & I will put on a white dress & you'll put on a pretty one (with a bit of pink somewhere, for that colour becomes you) & you will come, wont you, & we'll all be Lords & Ladys – [*sic*]

Madam! I love your husband – & I love the

[p. 3]

remembrance of a Sunday in last year which I spent on Staten Island.

Love to my sweetheart Sir Arthur & the rest of the Lamb kins –

Faithfully yours
Ellen Terry=

This is an invitation to a dinner !!!
P.S= I think a good many people are coming on Sunday

FOLGER, Y.c.434 (59)

Annotation, presumably by William Winter: 'Ellen Terry. The letter was addressed to my wife. Irving wrote to me. We went to the dinner – which was very pleasant. – W.W.'

1. Elizabeth Winter, wife of American critic William Winter (see n. 1 to letter 128, below).
2. Henry Irving played *Hamlet* on the American tour in Boston (25 October), New York (2 December) and Philadelphia (8, 18–20 December).

5 MORTALITY (1885–6)

108. To [Queen Palmer], 28 February [1885]

28 Feb = = Boston. Sat. Midnight

Yes. I will let you know if there be any little or big thing you can do for me – & I thank you – I thank you – About Ted[1]– It is too far my dear Queen[2] from the lad's work, for he play-acts each

[p. 2]

night – but he & I will I hope, see something of you & the little Elsie, who is liker [*sic*] to Edie[3] than anything I know. I'm dead beat – for poor old H. I.[4] – has been ill – unable to act – & I am head nurse, & bottle-washer!! & "Boss of the Show" into the bargain – &, I was not "born to rule"

[p. 3]

Oh! I hope you're well, & happy – I'm not – not well I mean – I'm always pretty happy – it's the best philosophy I think to mean to be! Now I know that "Gracie" who went

[p. 4]

with ~~Elifrida~~ (Elsie I mean) to our play is Mrs Parish's's's child! – didn't take that in before –

I am very much Yours

Eleanora

In tearing haste –

[p. 5]

sick of all I have to do & the utter want of time & power to do it all –

Thank you for yr letter & as you say, "When you are well away from it"(!!) I will come to the mote & see Tante,[5] & the chicks I suppose! May you have sunshine on your path all the way to Switzerland & back again & on to Heaven – where I hope to ~~meet~~ "have the pleasure" of meeting you a few seasons hence

– perhaps there'll be <a> little more time there – fewer perplexities – & a few old friends!! Your loving Nell.

SMA, SCB6-A19

Envelope extant, annotated 'Letters to Mother from Miss Ellen Terry. Elsa='

1. Edward Gordon Craig.
2. Mary 'Queen' Palmer (1850–94), née Lincoln Mellen, was an opera singer from a New York family before her marriage to General Palmer, with whom she travelled in Europe before settling on a vast estate in Colorado Springs. In poor health, she moved to England in 1882. Her daughter was Elsa, sometimes referred to by ET as 'Elsie'. See P. F. Skolout, 'Queen Palmer', *Cheyenne Edition*, 9 June 1995, pp. 17–18.
3. Edith Craig.
4. Henry Irving.
5. Nannie Held, known as 'Tante', was a long-standing friend and companion.

109. To [Edith Craig], 17 March 1885

New York March. 17. 85

Here's a sweet letter from one of Ted's American friends[.][1] Mrs Flint is a pupil of Moscheles[2] & condescended to teach Ted – she taught him music & learned to love him[.] All my friends love him & they are all ready to love *you* for yourself alone whenever you come out here: Bright America! 'Twould break my heart if I thought I shd never come again. [p. 2]

To day I lunched (!) at a beautiful home on Murray Hill (so called for Lindley Murray was born there) – at a Mrs Parke Godwin's = She is the daughter of William Cullen Bryant[3] the Poet – & her husband is very like dear Mr Tom Taylor –

Very odd what you tell me about the Lawrence Barretts[4] going to stay near you! Gertrude has been seriously ill, but is now better. I don't like your

[p. 3]

dogs [*sic*] head, as well as a little sketch you once made of Fussie[5] & Charlie but the flower was very pretty. I think it is a very difficult way to learn drawing – by letter – still, Mrs Malleson[6] is sure to do her best for you, & I am very grateful to her for being so ingenious & even yet some day, something better may be contrived – meanwhile observe all angles in natural objects, & proportion, note too

[p. 4]

The unequal balance in flower-life & shell – all will be of use to you should you one day for instance play Lady Macbeth! I'll explain "because – why! When we meet, my little noodlemus – Please study Jessica (M of V=)[7] next (what a come down) & get done with, the only, to my mind, *Cat* in Shakespere= It is a very effective "part" tho' played properly, & "looked" as you could look it – Poor Ted has a little cruel pain in his little stom-tack, & I must go & make a fuss of him & rub it!!

Your own Mummy =

SMA, ET-Z2,356

1. Edward Gordon Craig, who was in his thirteenth year.
2. Ignaz Moscheles (1794–1870), composer from Czechoslovakia, who produced many works especially for the piano. See *ODNB*.
3. William Cullen Bryant (1794–1878), an American lawyer and a poet with a transatlantic reputation. He campaigned for the abolition of slavery and wrote for the *New York Evening Post*. See J. D. Hart (ed.), *The Oxford Companion to American Literature*, 5th edn (New York: Oxford University Press, 1983).
4. Lawrence Barrett (1838–91), American actor and director known for his performance in *Julius Caesar* alongside Edwin Booth, whose Booth's Theatre in New York he managed in 1871. In 1884 Barrett took over the management of Irving's Lyceum Theatre in London while Irving was on tour in the United States. See Hartnoll (ed.), *The Concise Oxford Companion to the Theatre*.
5. Fussie was ET's dog, later given to Henry Irving.
6. Elizabeth Malleson (1828–1916) was an educationist and campaigner for women's suffrage and the extension of education to women and working-class men. She taught Edith Craig at her home at Dixton Manor, Winchombe, Gloucestershire, preparing ET's daughter for the entrance examination for Girton College, Cambridge University, which was ultimately unsuccessful. See *ODNB*.
7. *The Merchant of Venice* was first performed by Henry Irving at the Lyceum Theatre on 1 November 1879. Edith Craig performed the role of Jessica in 1895 at the Lyceum Theatre.

110. To Augustin Daly, 27 March 1885

Victoria Hotel March 27.85

My dear Mr Daly[1] =

The days fly by &, although I have tried, I find I cannot make the time in which to get to you – so I write instead to thank you exceedingly for your letter & kind proposal which a hundred stupid ~~things~~ reasons prevent me accepting – The hundred reasons would take up precious time, but one good reasons is, I am quite quite ill – & another <is>, want of

[p. 2]

time (just now) for any– thing – but to be ill! – & pack for home, & say goodbye to friends –

I thank you sincerely for your intended kindness – I beg you to excuse this hurried scrawl & to believe me Yours cordially

Ellen Terry=

I hope to see <you> in England very very soon –

FOLGER, Y.c.5076 (2b)

1. John Augustin Daly (1838–99), American manager, dramatist and critic who managed the Fifth Avenue Theatre in New York from 1869–73 and later founded Daly's Theatre, for which Ada Rehan played. The company successfully toured in London in 1884, 1886 and 1890 after which he formed theatres in London and New York. See Hartnoll (ed.), *The Concise Oxford Companion to the Theatre*. The 'proposal' mentioned here may have been to enlist ET in his company.

111. To unidentified, 15 April 1885

Guion Mail Steamer Arizona,
Near Queenstown. 15 April 1885.

Dear Old Girls –

First give "Pet" a kiss for me, & then hold your 2 selves in readiness to meet us at Euston[1] by the train leaving Liverpool at 12, & arriving Euston 5 o'clock = Henry[2] ("That dear man") is coming back with Ted & me to Longridge Road for some dinner, & I'm sure you won't mind being "dropped" at the corner of your road unceremoniously, for he (The "D–M")[3] doesn't want to see anybody but just you two children at first & then Booie[.][4]

[p. 2]

We have had a perfect journey, & are very well & very happy to be back home again[5] =

Boo will send a shanderadau – a carriage – *a vehicle* round for you in time to meet us, & we'll all come along together –

SMA, ET-Z2,065

Headed notepaper; unsigned.

1. ET and Henry Irving were returning from the second tour of the United States.
2. Henry Irving
3. 'That dear man', or Henry Irving, referred to earlier in the sentence.
4. Elizabeth Rumball.
5. ET has scribbled some curved lines at this point between the two halves of this page of the letter.

112. To George Coleman, 23 May [1885]

Saturday. May 23.

Dear Mr Georgie Coleman

I'd like to come on the 31st, but I dine out that day & *too* much gaiety is not for the likes o' me! – & so "excuse me", & ask me another day some day – Please =

// Private

I've £20 hanging about to offer to the Charles Reade[1] memorial & don't know who to send it to!! Tell me, like a kind

[p. 2]

little friend – I never give anything to anybody without doing it in his dear name so my little memorial to him has been built some time ago – ~~I loved him so~~ – I love him so –

= Do you know, not a word of thanks have I sent Mr Molloy for his Peg Woffington!![2] It was beautifully done, wasn't it? =

Yours ever
Ellen Terry =

SMA, ET-Z2,150a

Annotated '1885'.

1. Charles Reade had died on 11 April 1884. See *ODNB*.
2. Joseph Fitzgerald Molloy, author of *The Life And Adventures of Peg Woffington* (1884). Charles Reade and Tom Taylor co-wrote a play, *Masks and Faces*, about Margaret (Peg) Woffington (*c.* 1720–60), an actor whose successful career included performances opposite David Garrick, with whom she had a close relationship. See *ODNB*.

113. To Lady Pollock, 4 June 1885

33 Longridge Road.

June 4. 85 =

Dear Lady Pollock,[1]

Yes – yes – yes – !! With delight I will come to you on the 12th –

Thanks for your letter – you spoil me – but I like to be spoiled! It was very good of Sir Frederick to write – will he take my thanks, in the gentle "care of" my true friend S.P = ?

Ever affectionately yours
Ellen Terry

UCLA

1. See n. 1 to letter 46, above.

114. To unidentified, 8 June 1885

My poor dear friend

Lady Gordon[1] has told me the bad news about your eyes – That I grieve about it you know nevertheless I send this line to tell you I love you much more because of the troubles & to thank you for your message & for thinking of me (at such a time!) & my work =

[p. 2]

Be quick & get well & come back home – I always miss your face & gentle ways when you are away from our fresh work – you will love the Vicar[2] when you see him I promise you! When the Curtain went down on the first night of "Olivia", he said, "And now for Faust"!!! & has been working at it ever since,[3] although the crowds each night at the Lyceum

[p. 3]

speak most plainly that for months at least to come no Faust will be wanted – !

God bless your dear eyes –

Yours ever affecly
Ellen Terry =

33 Longridge Road –
Earls Court–
Monday 8-June-85=

P.S. Will you remember me to your husband & say I'm so sorry for him too in this trouble =

FOLGER, Y.c.434 (22a)

1. Presumably Lady Caroline Duff Gordon, who had known G. F. Watts from the time when she had taken over Casa Feroni in Florence from Lord and Lady Holland with Watts already installed; see Holroyd, *A Strange Eventful History*, p. 27. Lady Gordon was Edward Gordon Craig's godmother, explaining the origin of his middle name; E. G. Craig, *Ellen Terry and Her Secret Self* (London: Sampson Low, Marston, 1931), p. 77.
2. Henry Irving became known as 'the vicar' following his performance in this role in *Olivia*, which was first shown at the Lyceum Theatre on 27 May 1885.
3. Irving performed in *Faust* at the Lyceum Theatre for the first time on 19 December 1885.

115. To Stephen Coleridge, [1885?]

On my way to the Doctor. Just came in to look upon you all. I can't speak. (I mean I must not.) Henry[1] is all right now but it might have cost him an eye! I came up yesterday for to be treated by Mackenzie. Thanks for Gill's dear little letter.

Love – Nell.

GARRICK, Vol. III/4

Coleridge's annotation: 'I think the allusion to Irving relates to his falling in *Faust* from a moveable ascent & striking his head on a table.'

1. Henry Irving.

116. To Stephen Coleridge, [17 June 1885]

Thanks dear Stephen for the boat – it was lovely – but I was wretchedly ill &, except the little while in the boat I had to leave Floss[1] & the rest & go away & lie down. I've a fit of melancholy

[p. 2]

upon me which I cannot conjour – How are you all? Don't forget you & Gill[2] said you'd come with me to Normans [*sic*] matinee on Monday – I enclose the voucher for box for I am known by sight at that theatre –

[p. 3]

going to lie down – cheer up – I will too if I can – meanwhile dear old Booie[3] flourishes = & Edie[4] writes she is safely at school – Why should I repine?
Oh! I am your
loving old Livie=

GARRICK, Vol. III/5

Envelope extant; postmarked 'JU 17 85', London SW; addressed to 'The Hon Stephen Coleridge, 12 Ovington Gardens, SW'; Coleridge's annotation: 'I sometimes lent her my boat on the river which I kept at Halliford at the Red Lion.'

1. Probably Florence Terry, ET's sister.
2. Geraldine Coleridge.
3. Elizabeth Rumball.
4. Edith Craig was at school at Elizabeth Malleson's house; see n. 6 to letter 109, above.

117. To Stephen Coleridge, [29 July 1885]

Wednesday =

Dear old boy – all right – don't come – as to being "mobbed" that's rubbish – more likely robbed, as one might be at the Theatre or Church – <(now you are roaring!!)> I think Henry[1] is coming now, so perhaps it's as well = I hope he won't tho', for it will spoil the fun to have "the Govenor [*sic*]" as Norman calls him.

I'm excited, for Edie comes home today, Ted tomorrow.[2]

Love to you all – all

Nell =

GARRICK, Vol. III/6

Envelope extant; postmarked 'JY 29 85', Earls Court SW; addressed to 'The Honble Stephen Coleridge, The Cottage, Addlestone, Surrey'.

1. Henry Irving.
2. Her children, Edith Craig and Edward Gordon Craig.

118. To unidentified, 15 September [1885]

33 Longridge Road. 15 Sep.

My dear friends

Your kindness shames me – how good of you to send to me again – for I must seem to you quite quite ungrateful[.]

I must tell you I had thought of driving over in hopes of seeing you & thanking you for

[p. 2]

your kindness, last Sunday – but, "Man proposes" – (he proposes too often!) & Sunday morning found me too ill after the previous night's excitement to do anything at all but stay quietly at home with the children =

I hope you are all quite well – We had a

[p. 3]

splendid time in America[1] – & enjoyed ourselves very very much were half killed by kindness & in fact did everything but rest. & so I'm tired, but not ill = Edith[2] was a great success with my friends over there. & that gave me great delight – There is little doubt but that Mr Irving[3] & I will have

[p. 4]

to go over there again before another 2 years are passed – Margaret[4] with spectacles & crutches wd be a fine sight! – I do hope the gout is better – Dear old

Mr Toole[5] has been through a terrible time with it, but he is almost free from it now –

Won't you come & see Faust some day? The best box in the

[p. 5]

house shall be Juliet's if she wd care to come – no seats are to be had. But my box <u>always is</u> for any of you if you will come. & the private door near at hand is convenient & saves stairs & labour.

Mother[6] is away at the Sea. I saw her just before she went away. Flossy[7] was with me yesterday – the dear little thing – Marion[8] is in Venice – (lucky girl) & my children go back to school on Monday next – With best regards affectionately & gratefully yours

<u>Ellen Terry =</u>

UCLA, 2843

1. The Lyceum company toured the United States in the autumn of 1884 and 1887.
2. Edith Craig.
3. Henry Irving.
4. ET played Margaret in *Faust*.
5. J. L. Toole (1830–1906), actor and manager, who married Lydia Thompson, actor. He performed alongside Marie Wilton and Henry Irving, acting for years at the Adelphi Theatre and then managing his own theatre, where he produced J. M. Barrie's first play, *Walker, London* (1892). Toole left the stage in 1895 as a result of ill health. See *ODNB*.
6. Sarah Terry (see n. 3 to letter 1, above) was in her sixty-eighth year.
7. Florence Terry, ETs sister.
8. Marion Terry, ET's sister.

119. To Albert Fleming,[1] 26 September [1885]

Sunday . Sep 26 =

One day, just before I started for America this last time, I returned from a drive & found your card & a lovely book – The card was for me I knew, but what about the book? Why, I thought you must have surely left <u>England</u> if not the land of the living, for spite of my letters & orders (!) of linen, not a word had

[p. 2]

you Sir vouchsafed me!

Unkind not to say <u>rude</u>!! Oh, never mind but I want the linen if you please, for I have gotten myself (or rather a friend of mine who is staying with me) a new Sewing Machine – I suppose you dont [*sic*] approve of sewing machines? but – oh, I do work it so nicely, you cant [*sic*] think, & it's so <u>quick</u>, & so serviceable some of the people I do things for – Anyhow I have it & I want to make up linen

[p. 3]

I have told you how much I want & I shall not tell you again, unless you confess you have forgotten all about me & my wants, & have lost my "order"!
Won't you come & see our Faust again when next you are in town? & let me know – so I can introduce you & Mr Irving –

I hope you are very well – I am fairly so – the visit to America did not rest me much, for

[p. 4]

friends there nearly killed me with too much cherishing. It was intensely interesting to me the taking Edith[2] there – my girl – she was delighted = (& delightful they say!) I hope you have had a lovely time in the country this summer, with not too many friends – for it's so horrid, I think, to feel a little glad when they are all gone, & that comes from having too many = I hope your Mother is well (Lady Gordon told me of her, & of how fond of her you are) & that all the dear work people are working away to heart's content – With very kind remembrances

Yours faithfully
Ellen Terry

SMA, ET-Z2,322

1. Albert Fleming was a long-standing friend of ET who taught her how to spin for her role of Margaret in *Faust*. He had apparently followed Ruskin's advice in reviving the arts of spinning and weaving. See *Memoirs*, p. 186. Albert Fleming, or 'Daffy' as he was known to ET, often sent her linen as well as daffodils from his home in the lake district.
2. Edith Craig.

120. To Miss Perrott, 9 October 1885

Dear Miss Perrott

I thought our play[1] went very dully last night, & I played wretchedly, except in one act – however I'm glad you were pleased & thank you for your note =

I send you my distinguished autograph! With pleasure

Yours very [illeg]
Ellen Terry.

[p. 2]

Believe me
Very truly yours
Ellen Terry =
Lyceum Theatre.
London =
October 9. 1885 =
"Remember me"!
Hamlet =

SMA, ET-Z2,223b

1. ET performed in *Olivia* at this time.

121. To Bertha Bramley, 15 October 1885

15 Oct. 85 =

Dear Dear Bertha You are a "darling" & you are so funny your letter made me laugh spite of my neuralgia – Tell your sweet Aunt she shall have any photograph she may desire & "it does me proud" to send it to her – I enclose of <one> the good "Vicar,"[1] feeling sure she will care to have that! – I'm still in bed, feeling pretty bad –

Still, I want that question settled, as to whether you are a Darling or not!! I know! Ask your husband = you lucky girl to know beforehand what he will say.

With love to The Firs

Your Nell –

SMA, ET-Z2,018

1. Henry Irving as the Vicar in *Olivia*.

122. To Mrs Nixon, 29 October 1885

Lyceum Theatre) Octbr – 29th
London
England

Dear Mrs Nixon

The Doll[1] shall be dressed, & forwarded to you as soon as possible. I think Letitia Hardy[2] would be popular in America if they have not forgotten her – will you kindly note that I have only received your letter today, & this is

[p. 2]

29th of Octbr. I should be much obliged if you will send me the address of the lady in S. Louis who is making the quilt – – she wrote to me, & I lost her letter. With best wishes for your noble scheme

Believe me
yrs truly

signed.

Ellen Terry

(Excuse a dictated letter –)[3]

FOLGER, Y.c.434 (44b)

Dictated; signed. Annotated '1885'.

1. The doll may have been made for a charity event.
2. ET performed in the role of Letitia Hardy in *The Belle's Strategem*, first seen at the Lyceum Theatre on 16 April 1881.
3. ET signs this dictated letter and adds the apology at the end in her own hand.

123. To Elsie Palmer,[1] October 1885

Oct. 85 – London –

My little Elsie. What a lovely seat that must be! I wish I could see it – this cannot be a letter to match yours, to me = it is only just a line of love, & thanks for remembering me & writing. I remember you, but I cannot write because I am ever ever at work & I think <that> writing (to people one loves) is pleasant play – & I cannot make the time = The feather was quite beautiful, & I'll always keep it – Ted[2] is at school away from me, but we had lovely holidays together – he, & Edie[3] & I – & now we are all at work, & all seperated .. [*sic*] to come together again, I pray God, at Christmas =

I am playing a very pretty part now – "Olivia Primrose" in "The Vicar of Wakefield" – & dear Mr Irving plays my father, & *is* the Vicar – & an adorable Vicar too – *You* give a kiss for me to your darling pet little Mother, since I cant [*sic*] do it for myself. With best love Your old friend Portia Viola Ophelia Olivia[4]

SMA, SCB6-A5

1. Daughter of ET's friend Queen Palmer; see n. 2 to letter 108, above.
2. Edward Gordon Craig.
3. Edith Craig.
4. ET signs herself with multiple names, listing the significant roles she had played to date: Portia in *The Merchant of Venice*; Viola in *Twelfth Night*; Ophelia in *Hamlet* and Olivia in her current role in the play of the same name.

124. To Elsie Palmer, 6 November [1885]

6. Nov. New York

Sweetest Elsa I wish I cd come with Katie & stay awhile with you & D & M = She will bring you my love & a wee bookie & will tell you of all our doings = I shall hope (until we leave America in May)[1] to see you all yet before we leave = Nanny Held[2] – The good Tante – comes to me for 6 or 8 weeks beginning on the 1st December = & I'm hoping the change

[p. 2]

may do her good = I'm sending you a few photographs & you can but tear 'em up if you can't care for them – I miss Helen very much indeed from New York, but Katie has been very good to me = I'd like to have a little word from you when you "get used" to having Katie with you & can spare time[.]
Much love to the pets D & M, & kind remembrances to yr Father – Darling Elsa I am yr loving old friend.

Ellen Terry=

SMA, SCB6-A21

Envelope extant; postmarked 'MAR 10', New York; addressed to 'Mrs Palmer, The Dakota, 72nd St and 8th Avenue, New York'.

1. ET was in Canada and the United States on the Lyceum Company's second tour from 30 September 1884.
2. See n. 5 to letter 109, above.

125. To [Geraldine Coleridge], [23 November 1885]

Monday morn – Oak Lodge

I'm not going to play Olivia[1] any more darling – impossible to do the two & I quite broke down Thursday night. So I shall just rehearse. (enough too!!) & leave Olivia to little Miss E.[2] Tell dear Stephen I thought it wd not be the same if Boo[3] wrote, & it was only this

[p. 2]

dreadful being-ill business, which stopped me day after day from writing to him[4] to thank him from my heart for his letter to Ted[5] – a lovely letter – just word-right –
I'm better darling but frightfully weak[.] Dear love to you all. Now not another sign from me my pet till after Faust[6] is out – my hands are full. I was too ill to stop Gilbert[7] but I don't think he will regret going. Your own old Nell.

GARRICK, Vol. III/7

Envelope extant; postmarked 'NO 23 85', Earls Court SW; addressed to 'The Honble Stephen Coleridge 12 Ovington Gardens, SW'; Coleridge's annotation: 'I fear my letters to "Ted" were not much use!'

1. ET performed in *Olivia* for the first time at the Lyceum Theatre on 27 May 1885.
2. Miss Winifred Emery, ET's understudy at the Lyceum Theatre.
3. Elizabeth Rumball.
4. This implies that the letter may be addressed to Stephen Coleridge's wife, Geraldine.
5. Edward Gordon Craig.
6. ET performed in *Faust* at the Lyceum Theatre from 19 December 1885.
7. Gilbert Coleridge, Stephen's brother, who was to be assistant master of the Crown Office from 1892 to 1921; see *ODNB*.

126. To Joe Evans, [5 December 1885]

J. Evans[1] Esqre
36 . East 31st Street

Will Miss Tabert [*sic*] & you & the others come ~~with me~~ tomorrow night to stage box to see The Bells. & me –

Ellen Terry =

NYPClub

Telegram; envelope extant and annotated '1884'.

1. Joe Evans, an American artist, was a close friend of ET and gave Edith Craig art lessons. He met ET after having illustrated a commemorative book presented to her by a group of fans from the Star Theatre, New York. This group included Robert Taber, who later was to act with Henry Irving in *Peter the Great* in England. ET mentions Evans as part of the group to whom Henry Irving read *Coriolanus* in August 1895 at Winchelsea; *Memoirs*, pp. 204, 269.

127. To Albert Fleming, 28 December 1885

33 Longridge Road
Earls Court = 28 Dec 85

Dear M[r] Fleming

You are quite right – Margaret[1] should spin – but the poor thing who plays the 'part' was taken very ill & banished to Brighton[2] just when she was wanted for rehearsals on the stage of the Lyceum Theatre, & 10 days preparation was insufficient for learning the mere words & business alone! To learn to spin was 'out of the question'[.]

[p. 2]

~~She~~ I am still far from well, but if only you will kindly tell me of somebody who will teach me[3] to turn that lovely, *dreadful* little wheel I will try to learn so very willingly ___.

Many thanks for your letter. I did "fasten a string to the Bobbin – passed it through the eye of the nozzle, united it to the flax" on my distaff & then ___ "went ahead"! The wheel flew round – my heart thumped – the cord came off the wheel –

[p. 3]

the flax broke – Mr Irving[4] laughed (!) I got fearfully nervous – forgot my words in my agitation & ___ (very sorry now!) laughed too!! = Please tell me of a master or a mistress & my girl,[5] a "nice old-fashioned ~~people~~ person, shall learn to spin, & teach her Mother, who will tell Margaret all about it = ~~& the~~

Later on I will ask you to send me some linen

SMA, ET-Z2,297

1. ET performed Margaret in *Faust* for the first time on 19 December 1885.
2. ET may have stayed at Miss Pollock's Brighton nursing home; see n. 2 to letter 46, above.
3. Fleming taught ET to spin; see n. 1 to letter 119, above.
4. Henry Irving.
5. Edith Craig.

128. To [William Winter],[1] [1885]

Sunday =

Will you, if you can, tell me whether Mrs Willie Winter will be able to come tonight?

A word yes or no on the enclosed card & the "favour of your autograph will oblige" –

Yours ever
Ellen Terry =

FOLGER, Y.c.434 (86)
Annotated '1885'.

1. William Winter (1836–1917), drama critic for the *Albion* in 1861 and then the *Tribune* in New York from 1865 to 1909, was widely read and influential, and, like Clement Scott, critical of Ibsen. See Hartnoll (ed.), *The Concise Oxford Companion to the Theatre*.

129. To unidentified, 8 January 1886

33 Longridge Road
Earls Court = Jan.8.86 =

Dear Sir

Will you accept my appreciative, although tardy, thanks for your most interesting gift =
Poor Goldsmith![1] Was there ever written ~~a~~ more fascinating~~ly told~~ any tale! Many many thanks for the dainty little books =

Sincerely yours
Ellen Terry =

HARV

1. ET performed in *Olivia*, adapted by W. G. Wills from Oliver Goldsmith's novel *The Vicar of Wakefield*.

130. To Elise Ennions, [26 January 1886]

Dear little Elise. I have been quite ill – just contriving however to get through with my work, for Duty's sake & Mr Irvings, [*sic*] – but my voice – has almost gone – just from fatigue & cold. Just a line or two to give you thanks for making those pretty frames for me! They were very pretty – I think I liked the Banjo one, best. Your lovely delightful Mother came to me in Philadelphia with yr brother – a dear fellow – *After they were* gone I was able to read a letter which had only reached me that same morning so much of her time, or I wd have treated her better, & quite differently – However she is one of the angelic beings who wd always excuse her mortal friends, & think there might be a possible reason, where one did not show itself, for shortcomings in others –

This vague, & lengthy epistle shall close – for the slightest thing tires me to death – & there's much I wd write if I could – but I cannot – yet – God bless you & yours – Pray remember me to yr Father & Mother & to Hamilton when you write

Yrs very affect
Margaret. E.T.[1]

SMA, ET-Z2,193

Envelope extant; postmarked '26 JA 1886', Boston, MA; addressed to 'Miss Elise Ennions, (c/o Mrs. W. Crow.), 603 Garrison Avenue, St. Louis, Mississippi'; torn into four separate pieces.

1. ET played Margaret in *Faust*.

131. To Austin Brereton, 22 February 1886

22-Feb-86=

Dear Mr Brereton[1] = Here's Margaret (isn't she a nice big one?)[2]
I can't tell you how much I enjoyed the play (Faust) the other night – It was just delightful – I felt so excited = Here am I without a scrap of voice this morning, else feeling so mighty well! Why don't you put these Fogs to flight? Yours ever E.T.

HARV

1. Austin Brereton (1862–1922), a journalist and author of *The Life of Henry Irving* (London: Longmans Green & Co., 1908).
2. ET probably encloses a photograph of herself in the role of Margaret in *Faust*.

132. To Bertha Bramley, 23 February 1886

23rd Feb – 86 –

Dearest Bertha – I think I must have destroyed your letter in which you say I may come to you "a fortnight from today" – & fearing the "fortnight from today" *may* be next Sunday the 28th, I send this line to tell you I'm engaged for that day, but not for the Sunday after, & sd[1] like to come then if you can have me –

[p. 2]

I've been away – at Bournemouth – not being able to do my work makes me anxious & fearful – Suppose my voice never comes back! – I shall probably have a visit paid me by "Joe" Carr[2] to day, & get some news of your fairy-tale = it's surely time I heard, – you heard – something about it = I hope all is well with you & all the lucky loved ones –

[p. 3]

& that the weaning business was well got through with, Babs being none the worse –

Poor little Bertha having to give up her cosset – (Cossett?) lamb.

Berthas' loving
Nell –

SMA, ET-Z2,020

1. Should.
2. Joe Comyns Carr; see n. 4 to letter 39, above.

133. To Sir John Everett Millais, 30 March 1886

33 Longridge Road
Earls Court – Tuesday

Dear Sir John Millais[1]

Of course I will lend you the dress (here it is –) or anything in the world that I possess, that could be of the very smallest service to you.

The dress was away in Scotland being cleaned for storing or I should <have> sent it to you before –

Yours sincerely
Ellen Terry =

March 30 86 –

PML, LHMS Misc English 116008 MA 1485 K713

1. Sir J. E. Millais (1829–96), artist, created a baron by Gladstone in 1885. He was involved with the Grosvenor Gallery in early 1886 when a large exhibition of his work was shown there. Millais was at the centre of the Pre-Raphaelite Brotherhood, which had formed after a discussion at his house in Gower Street in 1848. Some of his most famous paintings are *Isabella* (1849), *Christ in the Carpenter's Shop* (1850) and *Ophelia* (1852). In 1883 he painted a portrait of Henry Irving.

134. To Albert Fleming, 30 March 1886

33 Longridge Road
Earls Court – 30 Mar

86

Dear Mr Fleming

Thanks for your delightful letter – I do envy you going down to the Daffodil Woods! Pray dont [*sic*] trouble about the book – I don't – I'd like to have it back some day because perhaps you'll bring it

Don't I wish you were

[p. 2]

indeed the Lord Chamberlain if you'd promise to make those righteous laws for the public & me ("me most especially"!)

Please I want some linen – not fine – for sheets! – I wish you'd send me some – ~~old~~ body's address,* that I can send the money to, & get the linen from! –

Very sincerely yours
Margaret[1] =

* at your leisure

SMA, ET-Z2,298

1. ET performed Margaret in *Faust*.

135. To [Albert Fleming], [Easter 1886]

Sunday.

Isn't Easter a beautiful time to you? I love it the best time of the whole year. I'm in London – & *yet* all is quite beautiful – How – *how* must it be with you – with all the flowers around! Easter in Daffy-Land!!.[1] I have been exceedingly busy & shd before this have thanked you for the Daffys you sent me but I do now – (& I did then!) Was not it a Good Friday? You don't mind me telling you, but I acted quite nicely last night – the beautiful time, & a few days [*sic*] rest, accounts for it for I've not played Margaret[2] well but one other time – I send you back the precious bits of delicious linen[3] – (– feel as if I could eat it, when I touch it –) = Wishing you health & Love & fine weather Ever sincerely yours

~~E.T.~~ Margaret.

SMA, ET-Z2,301

1. Albert Fleming lived in the north-west and was called 'Daffy' by ET, referring to his daffodils, which he sent her every year.
2. ET performed Margaret in *Faust* on 19 December 1885 at the Lyceum Theatre.
3. Albert Fleming taught ET to spin and sent her linen.

136. To [Albert Fleming], 15 April 1886

Will I have some Daffodils ? you ask –

Won't I? – if you will send a basket of the fairy things to me I'll love them, & care for them & be most grateful to you & to them –

Your prose is poetry dear Sir. Do you write verse?

Ever yours sincerely

Ellen Terry =

Oh! The linen!! I'm so sorry

[p. 2]

– I shd have sent it back to you before – but I have been quite ill again –

Come Sunshine or Death I think —

I wish you & your guests good weather & a good time.

E.T.

Thursday 15th April = 86

SMA, ET-Z2,300

137. To Stephen Coleridge, 24 June [1886]

24 June –

None of your larks Sir about my "benefit" – only to hold yourselves in readiness to be all there that evening, or never more be pedagogue[1] of mine!! Glad you've come back

[p. 2]

to town – you *may* see me within the next month – ! I do hope Ted is going to get on in the new state of affairs[.][2] I think he will – He came here from Sat to Monday last & we all thought him much improved – I expect to see Johnnie a little Hercules now those tonsils are gone –

Love to all of you but most of all to my little Gill.[3]

Your loving

Nell.

[p. 3]

Blow the 18/!!

I'll "do" with a little less hair on the stage, & pay the 18/- out of my poor little nest egg –

Hope you're all well – I positively don't feel terrible bad, but I have a tooth out tomorrow!!

GARRICK, Vol. III/8

Envelope extant; postmarked 'JU 24 86', London SW; addressed to 'The Honble Stephen Coleridge, 12 Ovington Gardens, SW'. This letter is bound out of sequence in the Garrick Club volume.

1. ET is for once explicit about her perception of their relationship, in which she casts herself in the role of mentor.
2. Edward Gordon Craig.
3. Geraldine Coleridge.

138. To Queen Palmer, [17 July 1886]

Saturday

In greatest haste my sweet dear Queen to tell you I am far too ill to act – I leave in an hours [*sic*] time for the Sea (Thank God for the Sea!) – & returning on Thursday will play "Peggy"[1] (Tell Nannie Held[2] my name is Peggy)

SMA, SCB6-A8

Envelope extant; postmarked 17 July 1886, Earls Court SW; addressed to 'Mrs Palmer c/o Mrs [illeg.]. The Vicarage, Kings Langley'.

1. This is likely to refer to Margaret in *Faust*.
2. See n. 5 to letter 109, above.

139. To Joe Evans, [18 July 1886]

<u>Sunday</u>

Dear "Mr Joe" Evans

I was desperately ill yesterday – to day I look 10 years, & <u>feel</u> 20 years younger. I was to act next Monday but found it impossible – The Doctors have sent me here until Wednesday evening next – <u>I never was in Margate before</u>

[p. 2]

my mind's eye pictured a ghastly hole, with people in it whose business in life seems to be to make night & day hideous –
but instead here is a very quiet lodging[,] a fair cook , & <u>out</u> o'doors -----
---- so beautiful, so beautiful, I cannot

[p. 3]

tell how beautiful! but this line is to ask you if you wont [*sic*] come down tomorrow (when you get this) evening & stay a day & night with us – we [illeg.] (my dear sweet pretty Aunt & I –) we, would take care of you , & be so pleased to see you, for

[p. 4]

I despair of ever seeing you in old Smokey – I could not <u>live</u> in any place but London but at this time of the year it kills me – <u>Do come</u> – we have luncheon 2 – supper (or dinner) at 9 , & keep on driving, or walking – anyhow <u>resting</u> – all the rest of the time –

[p. 5]

in fact we are very busy – come & help us to do nothing – A telegram to me here --------------

26 Ethelbert Crescent
Cliftonville – Margate,

– & I will get a bed for you in this house or the next, just for one night, & I'm <u>sure</u> it will do you good to come –

[p. 6]

My brother is here to day he was ill, & is better already

– I go back to my work next Saturday evening = Expecting to hear Yea, or Nay, at once Yours ever sincerely

Ellen Terry =

The beautiful flowers & dear little card – (a picture!) was – were duly appreciated believe me.

E. T.

NYPClub

140. To Queen Palmer, [22 July 1886]

33.L.Rd Thursday.

Dear – Thank you for your letters – I came back from the Sea last night late – & shall be at rehearsal to day & tomorrow, altho' not acting at night = You must not come on Friday or Saturday for as I have to speak on Sat – the Doctor forbids

[p. 2]

an unnecessary word (any word but the work would till Sunday is passed. & many friends have written just saying as you do, about Friday & Sat –)

So I *did* see Tante! I thought 'twas very like her, but not Tante! Quite ill & prostrated on Saturday, the sea made a nice – new person of me, by Tuesday morning – unrecognisable!! May not write more now –

Take my love & may it keep you cool this blazing sunny weather.

Nell.

SMA, SCB6-A14

Envelope extant; postmarked 'JY 22 86', London W; addressed to 'Mrs Palmer, Kings Langley, Herts ='.

141. To Stephen Coleridge, [24 July 1886]

Saturday Evening

Dearest old Stephen –

Your letter (which I have this moment read) is so earnest that I feel you mean it most kindly to me & seriously,[1] altho' I couldn't help smiling when I began to read it (it seemed to me so much ado about nothing) still I know you're serious, & I'll be serious too. I love you very much[2] – if now at the last minute (for we start next Sunday) I were to alter my plans of going to America with my daughter[3] it would spoil all my best friend's[4] pleasure in his holiday – just too when he has been so extra kind & has been sparing me from my work for two whole weeks – Edie's pleasure would be dashed, & so wd mine – I've paid for my 2 Berths on board ship, my friends

[p. 2]

in America are looking out for me, their pleasure wd be spoilt & all this, for what – ? Just to please my dear old ~~old~~ Stephen's whim – for it can be nothing else – he never even mentioned it to me before today!! – Believe me Stephen not one other intimate friend of mine thinks as you do about the trifling matter – One, (a lady) spoke to me about it – <long ago>, but ended up by saying "Edie!! Why, I didn't know *she* was going – Of course, that's entirely different." And added – "how silly you must have thought me"! I hope you will not trouble your mind now

[p. 3]

any more in the affair –

Edie is here to day & she & I are ~~beging to have~~ beginning to have a good time together –

– Just now I'm off to my work & altho' the new part "Peggy"[5] is only 12 lines[.] I'm quite
nervous & excited – SO farewell.

With much love (tho' you are a "trying" friend

Yours affec'ly

Nell=

Mr Irving by the way never tried to "persuade me" to go to America. I told him I was going with Edie – Didn't I tell you that?

GARRICK, Vol. III/9

Envelope extant; postmarked 'JY 24 86', London SW; addressed to 'The Honble Stephen Coleridge, The Cottage, Addlestone, Surrey'. Coleridge's annotation: 'This letter is in answer to one I wrote to her because I learnt that the company were going over to America in one ship, & she & Irving going together in another. I thought this was needlessly inviting the wagging of scandalous tongues, so I said so – at this time Edie was only a child.'

1. Several illegible characters are scored out here.
2. Possibly six or seven illegible words heavily scored out here.
3. Her daughter, Edith Craig, aged seventeen, accompanied her on this Lyceum tour of the United States.
4. ET specifically designates Henry Irving her 'best friend' here.
5. ET performed in the role of Margaret in *Faust*.

142. To Queen Palmer, [27 July 1886]

In bed – Tuesday –

Dearest Queen –

The only way I can think of to see you, <which I very very much desire> for a little while before flying away on Sunday is this way – Could you endure to see "Faust" twice –? to stay at Alice's[1] two whole days & we'd get luncheon at The Grange one of the days, & I'd see you at the Theatre too in the evening – I'll keep my box

[p. 2]

free for Thursday, <(you have it for Wednesday)> & anyhow perhaps dear old Nannie[2] will use it one night – the night you don't want it – <I enclose ticket for box> You I hear are so much better in health – I rejoice – rejoice = I am really ill & am just dragging myself thro' this week fearing a break-down again – ~~strickt~~ strict orders are that I dont talk at all during the day.

[p. 3]

– but I'd like to listen to you. & to hear good of Olive wd come as music to my ears – I'm full of sorrow & puzzlement about her for I believe she must be terribly ill – & to hear ~~at all~~ of Sara – Angela Sara – I shd think the best woman in all America, & my dearly beloved old darling Angel.

----- Cant sit up to write. have been at it the whole morning –

Elsie – dare you take

[p. 4]

her to Faust? Wont it be too much excitement? Come first yr self – & then you know Thursdays [*sic*] box is yours also –

Edie[3] is here –

Your

Nell –

SMA, SCB6-A20

Envelope extant; postmarked 27 July 1886, Watford; addressed to Mrs Palmer, Kings Langley, Herts, marked 'immediate'.

1. Possibly Alice Comyns Carr; see n. 4 to letter 39, above.
2. Nannie Held.
3. Probably Edith Craig.

143. To Queen Palmer, 14 September [1886]

<u>14. Sep.</u>

Sweet Queen – May Edith & Ted[1] come down early on Saturday, instead of waiting for their Mammy & the midnight train? or – will they be a bother, for so long a time? I hope Tante[2] will come to my room at the Lyceum for the evening if she is going to be so sweet as

[p. 2]

to come for me tho' really it is only a <u>luxury</u>. not a "necessary." There's a train leaves Euston Station 12.30 Saturday morning, & I'd like the children to go by that, & will send them by it unless you write me, & say no.

I've got Olive[3] on my mind. & I can't rest – for I didn't see her, & I didn't write & I've a big debt of gratitude, & — We will have a talk about it all. I thought it wd

[p. 3]

be wrong to write to <u>Sara</u> not writing to Olive = I <u>am</u> glad to think I shall very soon be seeing you all. I wrote to our Alice, & heard from her yesterday = <u>Where</u> will be your <u>London</u> – <u>winter</u> home? Talking of winter Mrs Willie Winter[4] of New York arrives tomorrow & is going to stay with her little girl with me

[p. 4]

all winter I think – Poor thing – her boy – a lovely lad of 14 – was killed just outside her Staten Island home, & the place & it's [*sic*] associations was killing her, & so she is coming here – to try to <u>forget</u> a little – ? –

At least I pray the change may do her good = Particular love to Elsie from

Nell.

SMA, SCB6-A12

Envelope extant; postmarked '14 SP 86', Earls Court SW; addressed to 'Mrs Palmer, Langley Lodge, Kings Langley, <u>Herts</u>'.

1. Edith Craig and Edward Gordon Craig who, in 1886, were 17 and 14 years old respectively. ET makes arrangements for their safe travelling but had allowed her daughter to travel alone from London to Liverpool at the age of nearly ten years; see n. 2 to letter 39, above.
2. Nannie Held.
3. Possibly Olive Terry, daughter of Florence Terry.
4. See n. 1 to letter 128, above.

144. To [Queen Palmer], [11 October 1886]

Don't send round to me tomorrow at the playhouse if you go my dearest Queen I wd rather not see a very kind face. & I cant see you from the stage – I've been down here since Wednesday with my Edith – I sent for the children or I could not have endured I think.

~~You are sure to know that= to have~~

Edward (Godwin) went away – & shut the door behind him.[1] He is gone – & I'm wondering I don't die – one doesn't get

[p. 2]

much love – & he loved me most I do think of all who loved him.
Tell Fred I know he loved Edward. I came away into the country directly I heard from Louise Jopling & the going up to my work each night is good for me. Don't let Nannie[2] come round to me tomorrow & don't write to me, & don't let's speak. Only just love away at me not because I deserve but for Love's sake. & in pity.

[p. 3]

Ten days ago I wrote to Uxbridge, tell Fred, for rooms down there on the eleventh, – most 11ths I've just driven down & back again ~~but~~ –

Selfish Devil I am –

- –

Dear I hope you will be happy in London this winter & that I may see much of you. I have not yet written to Olive – I can't do much just now –

Your Nell=

My love to Nannie, & to the dear sweet buds–

SMA, SCB6-A10

Envelope extant; postmarked 'OC 11 86', Uxbridge; addressed to 'Mrs Palmer, 13 Phillimore Gardens, Kensington, London ='.

1. Edward Godwin (1833–86), ET's lover and father of her two children, had died on 6 October 1886 from post-operative complications. He was buried in a field in an unmarked grave in Northleigh, near Witney, Oxfordshire.
2. Nannie Held.

145. To Elizabeth Winter, 20 October 1886

Oct. 20 – 86=

You dear little Lizzie, you have had unfortunately bad weather – never mind – another time = meanwhile the best weather is not in London, but there is the best welcome "warm as warm" waiting for you at 33[1] – such as 33 is! Bless you my dear – I intended writing, but oh, Lizzie, it's an effort to do anything but just sit down & think – & think – & think =

[p. 2]

I am sorry you have dull news from your Willie Poet[2] – I wish, *wish* you could both just tide-over the winter & come together here in the spring

– You stop – & he come over I mean – I have "all-but", taken a cottage at Uxbridge[3] – such a *bit* of a cottage = You might live in it part of the time!! By George aren't we getting on with the sewing-machine[.] Tell Viola my mother has left her a box of chocolates & they are waiting for her – Waiting "for a good little girl" –

[p. 3]

The box is this shape[4]
a little bigger than this – straighter = & say to Willie his Bricks are here for him
– Yours my dearest Lizzie with much appreciation, sympathy & love
------ not Nellie
but
Nell=
Fog-soup for dinner to day!

FOLGER, Y.c.434 (21a)

1. ET was living at 33 Longridge Road.
2. William Winter, Elizabeth's husband.
3. The Audrey Arms, Uxbridge.
4. ET has drawn a sketch of a circle.

146. Mr and Mrs Henry Arthur Jones, 15 November 1886

My dear Mr & Mrs Jones[1]

I know this (tardy!) note will find you in the deepest, crapiest,[2] mourning for the loss of that lovely Tea-pot – to think that it is mine – &-no-mistake-about–it, is a delightful think, & I can't tell you how very kind I think you are to give it me – You know it

[p. 2]

is much too good for "The Audrey Arms – Uxbridge"[3] –, & so I shall keep it up here at my town mansion!! – & I'll promise you a really good cup o' tea from it if by chance you are in this neighbourhood & will come in about 4 –

I fear I shall not be

[p. 3]
down for the Meet on Tuesday, they are going to serve me up for supper to night at the Lyceum – hot – from the Witches Kitchen![4]

Thank you – Thank you for that
Tea = pot!!

Sincerely yours
Ellen Terry = 15.Nov-86-

BRO

1. Henry Arthur Jones (1851–1929), the dramatist who, at this time, had had several plays produced, the most recent being *Saints and Sinners* (1884). His most famous plays were to follow: *The Case of Rebellious Susan* (1894), *The Liars* (1897) and *Mrs Dane's Defence* (1900)
2. ET is probably referring to the wearing of black crepe fabric during mourning.
3. ET's second home.
4. Probably referring to rehearsals for *Macbeth* at the Lyceum Theatre.

147. To [Bertha Bramley], 19 November [1886]

19. Nov –

Bertha you dear darling I love to see your writing – That lovely rest time of Saturday – Sunday may not be yet – for a while – for the next month I'm ~~as good~~ as bad as buried – always inside the Theatre walls at least from 12 to 12 – It's really dreadful – but a month will end it for then we produce

[p. 2]
our play[1] – I cared so much to get your letter – it's so hard to smile when one's ghastly tired, but your handwriting made me all smile-y & soft for a wee while – Wait till the play is *out* & I'll laugh!
& I'll come to you then please, with much delight = & stop from the Saturday until the very last moment Monday evening – I know your work has ugliness in it, but it is Rainbow-lined, seen on the other side – the right side – of all dirty work it seems to me that Election work is the dirtyest – I've been told a good deal about it lately

[p. 3]
& I'd *sooner* be a stage player than the wife of a Candidate for Blackshire[2] – when you have another spare moment waste it upon me some time during the next month – the sight of an ~~cover~~ envelope addressed to me by some, does me *so* much good –

Your loving loving

Nell –

I so often think of you all at The Firs –

[p. 4]

Against that time – if ever that time comes
When I shall see thee frown on my defects
When as thy love hath cast his utmost sum,
Pall'd to that audit by advised respects –
Against that time, when thou shalt strangely pass,
And scarcely greet me with that sun, thine eye,
When love, converted from the thing it was,
Shall reasons find of settled gravity
Against that time do I ensconce me here
Within the knowledge of mine own desert,
And this my hand against myself uprear,
To guard the lawful reasons on thy part
To leave poor me thou hast the strength of laws
Since why to love, I can allege no cause"[3]

SMA, ET-Z2,021

1. *Macbeth.*
2. Bertha's husband apparently stood for election.
3. Shakespeare, sonnet 49.

148. To [Albert Fleming], 24 November 1886

Nov. 24 86 =

Thank you for telling of "Wonderful Walker"[1] – The reading of him has done me good – more more – give us more –
I hope you got the dresser-cloth safely – It did not fit my Buffet – it was not long enough nor wide

[p. 2]

enough & rather too grand – later on I'll send measurements, & ask for 2 cloths of your ladies – I've made my sheets!! & now I must lie on 'em.
I'm living at Uxbridge for I can't abide the city yet awhile – I've a <cottage> ~~cot~~ Really it is a little

[p. 3]

Pub <at Uxbridge>. – "a holy Tavern" – & the rent is only 5/ a week – taxes & all = It's a darling place with a long window 6 foot long – & the right way on.[2]

I hope your friend went to Mrs Stirling[3] – Do you really mean you want

[p. 4]

– a head of me by Louise Jopling?[4] – but don't bother to answer – you'll tell her if you want it =

I hope you are very well & very happy in the lovely country = I am – very happy because I've just received from my

[p. 5]

boy – Ted – a little pencil sketch of his school, & if my mother-eyes can see at all factly[5] it's a lovely little sketch – but I'll be artful – oh so artful, & ask a good man about it & not say it's Teds [*sic*]!! – oh that "good man" – will he break my heart & never

[p. 6]

know it!

Forgive me –
Yours faithfully
E.T.

SMA, ET-Z2,303

1. Rev. Robert Walker (1709–1802), known as Wonderful Walker, was portrayed by William Wordsworth in *The Excursion* (1814), Book VII.
2. ET includes here a sketch of a rectangle lying on its longest edge.
3. See n. 4 to letter 87, above.
4. See n. 2 to letter 84, above.
5. Objectively.

149. To Geraldine and Stephen Coleridge, [29 November 1886]

Monday =

AUDREY ARMS

Uxbridge

Darling Gill & Stephen

As I've not strength to act for at least a week, I can write to you! – At last that brutal fellow Adams will desist I suppose, & your sister will be obliged

[p. 2]

to do something to pay for the gentlemans [*sic*] vagaries – How about "going on the Stage"? The part of Goneril or Regan wd suit her to a T. & Henry may be doing Lear[1] shortly! –

[p. 3]

Won't you both come down here some morning early & go for a drive? Such a lovely Barn in the neighbourhood to be "flicked off!!".[2] I'm alone here with Mary to "do" for me, & am resting. I think I may have

[p. 4]

to go to Cheltenham on Thursday or Friday to settle about Edith going with Miss Malleson[3] to Dresden. I shall take her with me when I go to America.[4] I cannot be without one of the children. It wd be very nice if you cd come down on Wednesday morning. I want old Norman to come too. I cd put him up – or one any nice person.

There's nothing the matter

[p. 5]

with me, except that I'm tired – Life has been very hard of late – some months of disaster to me – I feel to be fighting for power just to use my life, not to enjoy it = I hope all goes well with you both & with the sweet boys[.]

[p. 6]

Didn't the fogs nearly finish you? They did me – No fogs here, & only the faithful "Fussie"[5] to enjoy the drives with me – tho' he don't much enjoy 'em, for I make him run –

[p. 7]

the old beer-barrel =
Do come & see my "Pub". – I think you'll like it – I want you to give me one of your photographs for it – & a wee book of some sort – please –
Oh, I'm tired –
Your loving
Nell =

GARRICK, Vol. III/10
Headed notepaper for the 'Audrey Arms'; envelope extant; postmarked 'NO 29 86', Uxbridge; addressed to 'The Honble Stephen Coleridge, 12 Ovinton Gardens, SW'; Coleridge's annotation: 'She took an old Inn and furnished it charmingly at Uxbridge. I was often there for the day, but I don't remember sleeping there. I used to come back with her to the theatre in the evening.'

1. *King Lear* was performed by Henry Irving at the Lyceum Theatre on 10 November 1892.
2. ET referred to sketching or painting as 'flicking'm which may have been a reference to the Impressionist style.
3. Mabel Malleson accompanied Edith Craig to Germany. Mabel's mother Elizabeth had taught Edith; see n. 6 to letter 109, above.
4. Edith Craig went to the United States on the Lyceum tour in 1895.
5. Fussie was ET's dog, later given to Henry Irving.

150. To Queen Palmer, [December 1886]

Monday =

Dearest Queen –

Don't "rebel" – against anything – I never tried it but once – it failed then – it always fails – I can't come dear just because I'm going away – to Paris – for a few days (to see Hamlet) when I come back I will – Tell Nannie[1] Paris is not

[p. 2]

"the seshaw" (sea-shore!) that I meant to write to her, but — couldn't – I often wonder how Alice is – yet I don't write to her I shall be [illeg.] better soon – just overworked & down a bit at present – When I come back from Paris I'll have an inspiration & – please you – come & dine

[p. 3]

with you & bring Edith[2] if I may – she will be home then – My Ted[3] sent me quite a lovely little drawing yesterday – my fond mother's eyes didn't make that there drawin? [*sic*] his fingers did the delicate work, with something behind them – When you write to Olive ask her to secure my loving thanks, thro' you, for a beautiful letter she wrote me some little time since = Love dear to you & yours & to Nannie

Nell =

SMA, SCB6-A13

1. Nannie Held.
2. Edith Craig.
3. Edward Gordon Craig.

151. To [Bertha Bramley], 23 December 1886

Home = 23 Dec. 86

Dear = I'm here – at home – "doing" nothing – (trying to rest). I'm not acting the last month because I've been ill for 3 months! but I'm better now, & commence work again on the 3rd –

I couldn't write in answer to your last letter – Edward Godwin[1] died just then & I have been *finished* by that – I shall seem well soon

[p. 2]

I think, but I didn't know how terribly it would alter me – I went on at my work for a time but broke down at last & sent for Edith[2] to be with me. Selfish & wrong but I couldn't help it – I think I shd have lost my wits from misery. =

I'm all right now – Edith did that. She & Ted are with me now, & I shd love to drive over to The Firs one day "on chance" if I may, of finding you & a welcome at home. Is your boy at home I wonder? Yes! Ted my boy has altered lately – looks rather shy now sometimes & is much quieter – Edith the same rum queer old Frump!

Are you the same-dear-darling Bertha – ? I'm coming to see [you] between Christmas Day & New Years' Day. Love to beautiful "Auntie" & all.

Yours very much
Nell.

SMA, ET-Z2,2023

1. Edward Godwin died on 6 October 1886.
2. Edith Craig.

152. To [Joe Evans], 31 December 1886

Margaret only comes to the children but you will be a child & receive her with love, since she brings love to you from E. T. & Edith & Ted =
Dec 31.
- 86 -7

NYPClub

Decorative New Year's card in two colours, with a triangle of blue comprising half of the design and with the image of a woman standing (presumably ET as Margaret in *Faust*) decorating the triangle of white colour; envelope extant; postmarked 'DE 31 86'; addressed to '[Joe Ev]ans, 36 East [...], New York, N.Y, U.S.A.' This printed card is similar in style to one used by Henry Irving, using red and white, and depicting him in red costume as Mephistopheles in *Faust*.

153. To Elizabeth Winter, [December 1886]

You darling Lizzie

Not a day passes but you are affectionately in my thoughts, & Boo[1] & I are constantly speaking of you with true love & sympathy & admiration, & yet I have not written!

How much I wish you & William S.[2] Winter & the little ones lived in England, I can never tell you – The dreadful anniversary[3] is near at hand, & I know how vivid will be your remembrance of the past – yours & his – but Lizzie dearest Lizzie is not Viola, are not the others depending upon your smile for sunshine – I know how you devote yr

[p. 2]

your [*sic*] time to them & your energies also, but Lizzie darling girl give them the happiness of being able to look back & remember their mother at her best – pretty & bright – for you are so pretty my dear when you are bright for a while – & so dear all ways you must be to those who know you even a little = I love you Lizzie so – I love you dearly – & I pray for you – but you can't care for that can you? I can & do & hope & hope I ever may – some day you'll see your Angel-boy again – who knows, perhaps in Viola or the others – but if you count him gone he'll never come – Lizzie sweet Lizzie be strong & be pretty for the sake of Willie & the children – – but oh, I feel for you & with you – Will you come & stay a bit in New York with me in end of the summer?

[p. 3]

Since you left I've been so ill – & have not acted all the while!! I'm going back on Monday – I knew I shd break down in the end, & yet how I did *try* not to "give in" – but "giving in" has given me strength of body at least, for I've been in the country & by the sad sea & am not nearly so tired nor looking so hag-ish – the dear Boo is far from well I grieve to say it but I depend upon the coming spring for her the dear old pet – The children are home & are very good & well & Ted[4] grown in 6 week wonderfully tall – I wish his brain developed! Edie[5] has

[p. 4]

tried her very best I'm sure at her "Exam", & I will try to be content even if she does not "pass" – Sweet Henry[6] was touched by your note to him – he knows how much I love you – He is a great dear – singularly flawless in his nature & admirable is his power = He was here last night at supper & we spoke of you & Willie & drank to you & to your well being. Please send the handkerchief to Mrs Edward Davis – c/o Mrs Gillespie[7]

250 South 21st St
Philadelphia
Pa –

I've not written to her yet, but will do so = a wretched putter-off – !! that's what *I* am! I'll surely send the parcel off from Mr Brereton[8] (when it comes) to Jones Esqre[9] = He is writing a new play for the Haymarket & my

[p. 5]

sister Marion acts in it – make me a name for your husband[10] – I cannot call him Mr Winter & "Willie" don't sound respekful![11]

My dear dear girl – take arms against your self & battle on the side of the children — (oh, lord what a humbug I am ! all the while I know you *do* May all the saints have you in their keeping – & from my heart I wish you Peace in the coming year –

Your loving loving

Nell=

[p. 6]

"Fine but endears through years & years"
My loving thanks to ~~W. W. – the gentle shepherd~~ your Willie for his card, & the sentiment is my sentiment.

FOLGER, Y.c.434 (63b)
Annotated 'Ellen Terry to Mrs Winter Dec. 1886'.

1. Elizabeth Rumball.
2. ET has written 'Shakespeare' vertically, leading from the S. of the name here.
3. Elizabeth Winter's son had died the year before and ET refers to the impending anniversary; see letter 143 above.
4. Edward Gordon Craig.
5. Edith Craig.
6. Henry Irving.
7. Mrs Gillespie, was ET's oldest friend in Philadelphia, the United States ; she was the great-grand-daughter of Benjamin Franklin; *Memoirs*, p. 221.
8. See n. 1 to letter 131, above.
9. H. A. Jones; see n. 1 to letter 146, above.
10. ET liked to invent names for her addressees.
11. Respectful.

154. To [Elizabeth Winter], [1886]

Wednesday =

Why of course – either Sat or Monday let me know which evening – I can but hope you have by this time heard from Will[1] that he is coming over for else he will miss an opportunity of better[ing]

[p. 2]

his health & spirits by having a real holiday with you as a real companion, & your visit to England unless he comes, will always be remembered by you as being just beastly! – I go to Uxbridge for Sunday (only dont tell the Jones's and I want to be quiet there, & do nothing[.] So unless you wd rather (?) be in London Sunday (!!) why don't you use Sunday evening for travelling here & go the next day to the Lyceum. Why of course The Crystal Palace. I forgot that! & I'll go too, if you

don't mind – perhaps drive there, & after dinner there, I can drive back alone, & you go with the chicks by rail to Longridge Road at your leisure
Love to the children & more to you –
Your devoted Nell=

[p. 3]

Kind remembrances to Mr & Mrs H. A. J.[2] =

FOLGER, Y.c.434 (60)
Annotated '1886'.

1. William Winter, Elizabeth's husband.
2. ET has sketched several different faces in profile.

155. To Elizabeth Winter, [1886]

Friday Night

Darling Lizzie –
I have told the Carrs[1] you may come or you may not on Sunday with us so now it's open to you to do as you

[p. 2]

like only let me know – somehow – by telegram?
Greatest haste
Nell=
Mrs Jones has sent me The Tea pot!![2]

[p. 3]

I will write to him on Sunday = It was very kind!

FOLGER, Y.c.434 (62b)
Envelope extant; postmarked '86'; addressed to 'Mrs Winter c/o Henry A. Jones Esqre, Chalfont St Peters, Bucks'.

1. Joe and Alice Comyns Carr; see n. 4 to letter 39, above.
2. See letter 146 above.

156. To Queen Palmer, [n.d.]

Tuesday =

Will you come with me my dear dear Queen to see Sonnenthal[1] as Kean next Saturday night – I have a box there – or perhaps you know, & wd rather *not* hear him, or – perhaps – many things will not let you come – but – I am ill – quite – with a horrid throat, &, rehearsing every day I simply fly

[p. 2]

from my work to bed – then to work again, & I haven't breathing time for a scrap of pleasure – Even seeing Sonnenthal is partly for work's sake – & I shall never see you, I do believe unless you come to me – You did come I know, & thank you – I have seen nobody –
Haste – Will you come Saturday? Yours faithfully
Eleanora =

[p. 3]

I wrote last night for over 3 hours & was too tired to write a note I wanted to, to her.

SMA, SCB6-A18

1. Adolf Ritter von Sonnenthal (1834–1909), Austrian actor born in Budapest.

6 HARD LESSONS (1887)

157. To Miss Morrison, 2 January 1887

11.I.87

Dear Miss Morrison

I'm very glad you wrote – I will send you seats for 4 on either Saturday or Monday – On second thoughts I enclose them, for Saturday, & may I ask you to return me the ticket at once, if you cannot use it for that night –

I have not forgotten the stockings & will send them to you in a few days –

[p. 2]

With all good wishes for the new year

Your truly

Ellen Terry =

33 Longridge Road
Earls Court.

PML, LHMS Misc Ray 188733 MA 4500

158. To Stephen Coleridge, [January 1887]

St Stephen's Church[1] at 12 Saint Stephen, not the other gentle – man!
I'm that bad – have been having supper at mother's, & rushing about all day – I can't have anybody at home

[p. 2]

Tomorrow since I'm packing & writing & what – not—so I've ~~had~~ ordered some luncheon at Bailey's Hotel close by the church at 1 o'clock – Henry & Gill George Stoker & Lady Gordon Mr Waldo (Parson) Boo, Ted, Edie, you, &

Nell =

"10 little nigger's"----

GARRICK, Vol. II/15

Coleridge's annotation: 'My dear wife put gentle pressure upon Nellie to have her natural children christened, which had some how never been done. Lady Gordon, Irving & my wife were the God parents.' This is bound out of sequence, in the section for 1883.

1. The christening was performed by the Bishop of Exeter on 11 January 1887 at Exeter Cathedral; see *Memoirs*, p. 195.

159. To Clement Scott,[1] [16 January 1887]

33 Longridge Road
Earls Court
Private

My dear friend –

What a funny man you are! You send me a pretty card & an affectionate wish, & that is sweet & dear & just like you – just like Clement Scott – now I take up the last number of The Theatre! – Well! I don't like Mrs Kendal[2] – off the stage – (perhaps because I don't know her well – she certainly doesn't know me!) but I do think that number of

[p. 2]

The Theatre is a disgrace to your name – Why did you let such a thing be done? You didn't do it yourself surely!

– Well at least I thank you for thinking of me & sending me your sweet wishes for the new year & from my heart I wish you – what I wish for most, myself, – peace, & a growing heart – (– as if it were a Bulb!!)

Bless you Clement Scott –

Yours always Ellen Terry =

HUNT

1. Clement Scott (1841–1904) was a drama critic for the *Daily Telegraph*, and for his own journal, the *Theatre*, founded in 1877; see N. Auerbach, *Ellen Terry: Player in Her Time* (London: Phoenix House, 1987), p. 296.
2. Mrs Margaret Kendal and her husband had joined John Hare in partnership as actor managers at the St James's Theatre, London, in 1879.

160. To [Clement Scott], 19 January 1887

Jan 19. 87 =

Well – yes! I quite agree with you in all you say about Mrs Kendall [*sic*], but I fail to understand why you should get less lofty, because she is so low –

I didn't notice the spelling![1] – I hope we shall meet again some day! You & I – (I don't want to meet Mrs K–!!

Yours always very much
Ellen Terry

HUNT

1. Scott appears to have corrected ET's spelling of Mrs Kendal's name.

161. To Stephen Coleridge, [2 February 1887]

LYCEUM THEATRE

No dear I can't come to luncheon with you tomorrow tho' I should have liked much to do so. I have arranged to take Boo & Alice Carr[1] to 'ampstead 'eath,[2] (The drive will do us all good) & have luncheon

[p. 2]

afterwards with some folk at the Carrs.

Idiot!! Why didn't you say Monday or Tuesday next.

Love to little Gill[3]

Nell =

GARRICK, Vol. III/11

Headed notepaper; envelope extant; postmarked 'FE 2 87', London WC; addressed to 'The Hon. Stephen Coleridge, 12 Ovington Gardens, S.W.'

1. Elizabeth Rumball and Alice Comyns Carr.
2. Hampstead Heath.
3. Geraldine Coleridge.

162. To Mabel Malleson, 5 February 1887

5.Feb-87

Dearest Mabel[1] – I think I apprehend the situation which is effective, but not "quite through", delectable – However as you have your private rooms it seems to me the less pleasant outside it's [*sic*] door the more you may, both, "seek the seclusion which the Cabin grants" – As to the giving a months [*sic*] notice of leaving from one particular date, you will see by Mrs M's letter,[2] which I enclose, there is not a word said – & it's

[p. 2]

all pickles !! (What's that now in your best German?!) & I shd say, wd not be insisted upon – however of course I know you will do your best to make the best of the situation – As to the Ball, why yes, Edith[3] may go (since you have asked for her, tell her this –) & I'll send off a frock of some simple kind on Monday from the Lyceum –// Let her wear out the brown (2) – red dress (1), & even then, 'twill be good enough for the boat, for this new one I have for her will be too warm & must be kept for

[p. 3]

next winter – thanks my dear little Mabel for your letters – I delight in getting them – for the manner in which you write is most satisfactory – & satisfying – Mrs George Lewis,[4] a very great friend of mine living here in London, has ~~two~~ *a* sister (at least) who lives in ~~Mauheim~~ Mannheim – Madame Hirsch – this lady will "make advances" shortly & I shd be glad for Edith to like her & to accept any kindnesses from her & invitations not interfering with her lessons–What kind of weather have you out there – the last three

[p. 4]

English days have been old-fashioned Spring Days – warm & moist & growing – soon-to-be-*greeney*! I have no news – Remember dear Mabel you are to judge & do the best out there, the best for Edith, & I shd ever be quite certain you wd do the right thing, for you wd not lightly break up arrangements made to [illeg] "Fly to others that you know not of"!!!

I'm in a hurry as usual

Farewell –

Yours always affectionately

Ellen Terry =

In case of the "19th" affair being insisted on, why in case of necessity a months [*sic*] money might be paid!

FOLGER, Y.c.1392 (96)

1. Mabel Malleson, daughter of Elizabeth Malleson (see n. 6 to letter 109, above), accompanied ET's daughter Edith Craig to Germany.
2. Elizabeth Malleson.
3. Edith Craig.
4. See n. 1 to letter 38, above.

163. To [Edward Gordon Craig], 25 March [1887]

25. March – Friday.

Sweet boy – Why have not you written to me this week? – I've a *great* treat in store for you when you come back – I am going to run over, in Holy Week to Edith[1] at Heidelberg & you if you're a good lad, shall go to the Sea for a week with Henry![2]

I think it is lovely of him, to say he'll take you – to Hastings or to Eastbourne – I suppose you heard of dear Mr Beecher's death[3] – the news made me quite ill for

[p. 2]

some days – that poor lonely lady! It wont [*sic*] kill her, for she is sorrow-soddened already I think – she has "so much endured – so much endures" – I send you an account of him from an American paper. Edie Lane[4] is here & so is Audrey[5] – they send their love with mine, & as I have not a scrap of news will end up – Send me a line or two at once – & tell me at the same time if you think Miss Bullen liked her work bag –

God bless you my dear –

Love to Grey & Finnes –

Your loving

Mummy

HRC

Annotated '1887'.

1. Edith Craig.
2. Henry Irving.
3. Mr Henry Beecher (1813–87), American preacher who led the Plymouth Church in New York from 1847. His sister, Harriet Beecher Stowe, wrote the novel *Uncle Tom's Cabin* (1852). He married Eunice Bullard White. He died on 8 March 1887, seventeen days before the date of this letter. See *American National Biography*.
4. Edie Lane was to be married in 1907 to H. A. Gwynne (1865–1950), journalist for Reuters and *The Times* and editor of the *Standard* 1904–11 and the *Morning Post* 1911–24. He was a unionist, imperialist and anti-Semite, prosecuted in 1918 for an attempted coup against the British government; see *ODNB*.
5. Audrey Campbell was a very close friend of ET. Their correspondence ran from 1887 to 1912, the year of Campbell's marriage. Campbell acted with ET on tour in 1903. see Auerbach, *Ellen Terry*, p. 408.

164. To Compton Reade, 3 April 1887

33 Longridge Road
Earls Court

April 3rd 87=

Dear Mr Compton Reade

The two precious volumes have arrived, & I beg you to take my best thanks (in anticipation) for a great treat =

Just starting for Heidelberg for two days [*sic*] sight of my little daughter[1] so pray excuse my hasty thanks.

Yours sincerely
Ellen Terry.

SMA, ET-Z2,229e

1. Edith Craig.

165. To unidentified man, 14 April 1887

33 Longridge Road – Earls Court
April 14 -87=

~~LYCEUM THEATRE~~

Dear Sir

I am exceedingly obliged to you for your letter – Sure enough my boy[1] is the culprit – Mr Irving[2] gave him permission to play in the holidays in The Grange Garden,[3] & to use his bow & arrows. I am very sorry, & such a thing, of course, shall not occur again – I am dear Sir

Your obliged
Ellen Terry=

FOLGER, Y.c.434 (130)
Headed notepaper for the Lyceum Theatre.

1. Edward Gordon Craig.
2. Henry Irving.
3. Henry Irving's property, The Grange at Brook Garden; see Holroyd, *A Strange Eventful History*, p. 182.

166. To Janet Achurch, 19 April 1887

April 19. 87

Dear Janet[1]

I spoke for Mr Charrington,[2] but was just too late – I spoke at once too ~~but~~ when I got your letter [.] Depend upon my remembering you both, if ever I think there is a good chance any-where – That you shd be in a good theatre[3] (& together if possible) for a longish period is the thing to endeavour for – Poor dear Janet – I'm so

[p. 2]

sorry you are troubled – I've often & often been coming round to see you, but oh, the work!! Everlastly some thing to do. If you can do so easily send me a nice (Cabinet) photograph of yourself & one of Mr Charrington – or, I'm scarcely ever in shops & so perhaps have not seen 'em, can I get them somewhere?

Yours affectionately
Ellen Terry =

FOLGER, Y.c.434 (4)

1. Janet Achurch (1864–1916) first appeared on stage in 1883. In 1889 she performed Nora in *A Doll's House* and subsequently became associated with the work of Henrik Ibsen. Other notable roles included those in George Bernard Shaw's *Candida* and *Captain Brassbound's Conversion*. In July 1887 she performed at the Strand Theatre. See *ODNB*.
2. Charles Charrington (d. 1926), an actor with the Benson company, married Janet Achurch; see *ODNB*.
3. ET was active in helping her colleagues secure work in the theatre.

167. To [Bertha Bramley], 2 June [1887]

Home Thursday. 2 June!

I've only secured these seats to day, so could not send before – So sorry Dear you have been ill –

I'm dead tired – To day a rehearsal of 5½ hours for The Amber Heart[1] (a pretty play we do on Tuesday morning next –) I wd send you tickets but it's for a little mans [*sic*] "benefit",[2] & I've

[p. 2]

given away to my people all the seats I bought –

If you are well enough & care to see The Merchant of Venice with the children I do think that's the perfectest play for chicks, & I'd send you a box for one of the next 2 Saturdays –

With very much love
to you all
Your Nell –
but no time![3]

SMA, ET-Z2,054

1. Alfred Calmour had privately printed a collection of his plays, *The Amber Heart and Other Plays*, dedicating it to ET: 'To Ellen Terry truest of friends, this book is dedicated by the author, as a mark of his regard and admiration for her many estimable qualities as a woman and her genius as an actress'.

2. This was first performed by ET on 7 June 1887. Alfred Calmour had had an accident and lost his hand, and funds were raised for him.
3. ET has drawn a line linking 'With very much love' and 'but no time'.

168. To Lady Monckton, 12 June 1887

33 Longridge Road
Earls Court –
June 12.87 =

Dear Lady Monckton[1]

It will suit me nicely – on Tuesday then July 19 = at 1.30 o'clock =

Many thanks for your congratulations upon the little play[2] – It's very odd, I never had ~~so many~~ more letters for any big part I've slaved at – much ado about nothing I think!

Sincerely Yours
Ellen Terry =

UCLA

Envelope extant; postmarked 'JU 13 87', London SW; addressed to 'Lady Monckton, Ettrick House, 159 Cromwell Road, SW'.

1. Possibly a relative of Sara Prinsep (see n. 8 to letter 1, above), who was named Monckton before marriage.
2. This may refer to ET's performance in Alfred Calmour's *The Amber Heart* on 7 June 1887.

169. To unidentified, 14 June [1887]

Thursday June 14–

Audrey Arms
Uxbridge

I don't know what to say! – but wd like to thank you for the lovely little picture you sent me by Mr Alexander – a picture of how I ought to look as Ellaline[1] – & try to ! but cannot = It is a picture of the spirit of Mr Calmours [*sic*] little play, & I love to have it, & I thank you very-very-much for giving it to me –

Sincerely Yours
Ellen Terry =

[p. 2]

P.S=

on the train

The two faint hearts puzzle me – Are there two Amber Hearts around & about Ellaline has one – I'd like the other – I *think* –
Perhaps you meant it for Ellaline's & Silvio's!!!
– Then Silvio's should have been very wee – scarcely to be seen it seems to me[2] –

HUNT
Headed notepaper for the Audrey Arms.

1. ET performed the role of Ellaline in Alfred Calmour's play *The Amber Heart* on 7 June 1887.
2. ET conveys her opinion of the character of Silvio in *The Amber Heart*. Ellaline suffers greatly from the callous behaviour of Silvio, the 'poet and troubadour', and is feared drowned towards the end of the play.

170. To Stephen Coleridge, 15 June 1887

June 15th, 87

Dear Stephen,

Here's the "Benefit" cheque – Please send me a hundred pounds of it, & do what you think best with the £306-12-6[1] – There were a few pounds more sent just as presents, but I've sent that to a Hospital & a few poor country friends.

You did look well yesterday!

Best love to the Jubilee Gill![2]

E.T.

GARRICK, Vol. III/12
Envelope extant; postmarked 'JU 15 87', Earls Court SW; addressed to 'The Hon. Stephen Coleridge, 12 Ovington Gardens, SW'.

1. There is an ink blot over the figure 6, which may possibly be a 5.
2. Geraldine Coleridge, Stephen's wife.

171. To Stephen Coleridge, 24 June [1887]

24 – June –

Dear – I have to be at rehearsal (Olivia[1] –) at 11.15 today, & there's no chance of my coming back until part 3 – !

I don't see how I can come at the time you mention! Couldn't I see you for 5 minutes on my way down again this evening about 7 o'clock I'll call in on the chance.[2]

Everybody is giving me books lately!! Delightful! 3 last evening,

[p. 2]

2 of 'em from strangers for Beatrice. (by the way I played rather nicely last night! –) Do you care to see Olivia any of the 4 nights it's done?

Thursday or Friday theres [*sic*] a box if you will have it – tell me tonight –

Best love to Gilly[3] – Hope you are all well –

I'm tired rather – such very hard work – but wonderfully well.

Nell

"Flick" away!

GARRICK, Vol. III/13

Envelope extant; unposted and presumably delivered by hand. Coleridge's annotation: 'The allusions occasionally to my "flicks" "flick away" etc., have reference to the rapidity of my painting'.

1. ET had first performed in *Olivia* on 27 May 1885 at the Lyceum Theatre. Its popularity meant that it was revived several times.
2. ET has marked in the margins the text referring to the time of the arrangements.
3. Geraldine Coleridge.

172. To Queen Palmer, 12 July 1887

Home

12 July 87

Sweet Queen –

That's all right is it? – all right & silly & ---- satisfactory – Instead of going into Gloucestershire as I intended for a few days between the 21st & the 25th I shall come to the dear mote & be as "as happy – as I 'ere can hope to be ~~where all is pain~~" – (that don't suit the mote!) – I am getting so

[p. 2]

Sick of all I have to do & the utter want of time & power to do it all –

Thank you for your letter & as you say "when you are well away from it" (!!) I will come to the Mote[1] & see Tante,[2] & [illeg.] May you have sunshine on your path all the way to Switzerland & back again & on to Heaven where I hope to ~~meet~~ "have the pleasure" of meeting you a few seasons hence perhaps there'll be a little more time there – fewer perplexities – & a few old friends!! Your loving Nell –

SMA, SCB6-A21

1. Ightham Mote, a manor house in south-east England; see following letter.
2. Nannie Held.

173. To unidentified, [20 July 1887]

Tuesday=

IGHTHAM MOTE
SEVENOAKS
KENT

Yes darling – on Thursday <tomorrow> then – that is the day that Nan[1] takes Edy up to London & sees her off to Dixton[2] = ~~You must come from the station at Charing X~~ A train leaves Charing X -10:15 for Sevenoaks – now a carriage (with perhaps somebody in it) will be at Sevenoaks to meet that train, as Edith will just have gone up to London) but

[p. 2]

if you still decide to come from Victoria by the train you named (11.35) you must take a Fly & drive "to the moat" – but come by the 10-15 from Charing Cross to Sevenoaks , as I say, if it be possible –don't take a return ticket for there's a nearer station I think to go back by – I was disappointed yesterday to see you twice "so near & yet so far" – no sleep last

[p. 3]

night , no penholder now so under these distressful circumstances fare thee well my lovey-Dovey –

your Nell =

UCLA

Headed notepaper for Ightham Mote, Sevenoaks, Kent; annotated 'Jy 20 87'.

1. Possibly Nannie Held.
2. Edith Craig was educated for a time at Elizabeth Malleson's house, Dixton Manor, Gloucestershire; see n. 6 to letter 109, above.

174. To [Elizabeth Malleson], 2 August [1887]

Inverness = Aug 2nd

My dear friend – I know you will be pleased to hear that I have had such a lovely, restful, enjoyable week that I have only written one letter (to Ted)[1] all the time, & will forgive me that I did not write to you – Your kind consent to take my boy for a little while, just delights me & I write you this line to ask that he may be met at the Cheltenham Station – (by Edy?)[2] the "usual train", which leaves London at 12 – I go on tomorrow to my sisters at Divach Cottage[3] – Glen Urquhart nr Inverness – I wonder will Mabel[4] be my friend as usual & send me a few lines giving me news of you all & of my young woman from whom I have had no line all this while, tho' I'm hoping a letter from her may await me at Divach = if it be possible I hope

[p. 2]

the children may go to Edinburgh [on the] 17 or 18 with Miss Herbert – please tell my Edith I have taken some beautiful rooms for all 5 of us (for Boo[5] stays on [illeg] little with us) at No 5 Melville St Edinburgh = Poor Mrs Rumball has been a rather feeble traveller, & at first I feared we should have to take her home again but each day now she improves & Mr Irving[6] is so perfect a person to travel with – so patient [illeg] gentle that he has made things easy but many a time I've longed for [illeg] for *his* sake as well as for mine.

We had great fun yesterday – [illeg] are full of our next production – Macbeth[7] – & being in Macbethshire we "go about" to the "different" spots. Well we came to the ~~damned~~ [illeg] blasted heath! – Lo, a fine potato field – & a sky line of waving barley. However we had secured a very warm invitation from the Thane (the Earl) of Cawdor to visit Cawdor Castle & to sleep there – & we went

[p. 3]

& stayed to luncheon (though not to sleep) & were most charmingly entertained by the old Laird & his daughter Lady ~~Margaret~~ Evelyn Campbell[8] – who took us for a wonderful drive ~~throght~~ through – first an oak forest then up higher amongst the furs then higher still where there was nothing but heather – except Grouse – oh, it was lovely – lovely – & we came to the conclusion we must build our own 11th Cent[ury] castles & blast our own Heath's, [*sic*] for there's nothing left to take pattern by ! – – but after all, "the play's the thing", & the people like us, & with that encouragement, we'll never say die!! – I'm writing all this twaddle in bed, & as it's nearly eleven o'clock (quite late, that, now for me!!) I must "end up", as Edward says – I can

[p. 4]

never tell you how kind I think it is of you to take Ted – it is such a comfort to me to think of both chicks being with you, now I cant have them – I meant to write & ask you a lot about Edith, but oh, dear, oh dear how tired I was a week ago, & I didn't[.] It was about her speaking neither french nor german! such a big girl – Can nothing be done? Time is going so quickly now, & the Damsel is nearly 18!!

Miss Herbert who will be with her now for 2 months or so has been the last three years in Paris – so I mean to see they speak & read french together every day – & the music will be all right – but music, drawing & those two languages[9]

I do wish she would work at it all for the next 2 years work in downright earnest – I really beg pardon for this long rigmarole & I send my dear love to you all at beautiful Dixton

Yours most faithfully & gratefully
E.T.

FOLGER, Y.c.1392 (2b)

1. Edward Gordon Craig.
2. Edith Craig.
3. Kate Terry's country house.
4. Mabel Malleson.
5. Elizabeth Rumball.
6. Henry Irving.
7. *Macbeth* was first performed by ET at the Lyceum Theatre on 29 December 1888.
8. Lady Evelyn Campbell (1855–1940), daughter of the Duke of Argyll, married James Baillie Hamilton at Westminster Abbey on 10 August 1886. See *New York Times*, 28 July 1886.
9. ET was concerned that her daughter should acquire the appropriate accomplishments for a woman of her age.

175. To Stephen Coleridge, 8 August [1887?]

Divach Cottage
Glen Urquhart –
Nr Inverness =

Monday 8 – Aug –

Oh, if you could but see this beautiful place! A storm is gathering over the hills & it looks portentous = I have intended writing to you every day, but somehow it wd not happen & in two whole weeks I've only written 4 letters – two to Edy – two to Ted = You see at first I was so very very tired & quite ill – but bit by bit I got better for I did nothing but rest & eat – & *now*, oh, triumph at last I sleep = I wonder where you are? You & Gill – I wish she were here with me in this perfect place, far away from everybody with only (after the family) The Curlews, & Hares, & Partridges, & Grouse to look at one & they are not so rude – don't even ask for one's autograph!
Next Thursday <week> we (Boo Henry & I) go on to Edinburgh – & we begin work the following Monday there. Boo is looking simply wonderful! Better than either of us – we have more to recover from. We all get on wonderfully well here, & to see "old Henry" stalking over the moors with ~~Fussy~~ "Fussy" at his heels in a high wind is too funny. I miss Edy now, always when she is away from me but Miss Herbert will bring both children to me in Edinburgh – she settled to come to me for about 6 weeks from the 18th but as she is rather in want of a resting

place I've allowed her to go to Longridge Rd & stay there for awhile – Boo will stay with us until we go to Glasgow = Please I want some money! I forgot to ask you for some when we went away, & Henry "treated" Boo

[p. 2]

& me during the week we took to travel to this place but I shall be wanting money before I leave here for, amongst other things, the servants = Miss Herbert too must have some to bring the children to Edinburgh – shall they travel 2nd, or 3rd class – ? I rather think, as the 3rd is as good carriages s the 2nd, they had best come 3rd as Dolly is with them. What think you? Ted joined Edy on Saturday last at Dixton, on a little visit to the Mallesons – Of course dear Stephen Edith is to be paid for there! Can you tell me anything about the enclosed papers? "Who is Viola"? Who is she? I have kept the £5-5-0- but I don't know anything about it! Is it Road Cars? I should be very glad to hear of you – Here is a wee silver holder for a flower, I send a bit of white heather in it ("Luck"=) which I picked Gill this morning "with a wish" – Give it her from me please with my dear love – What about Ted & Heidelberg – I expect you have been doing it all for me this time I've been away – Ted has I know to be there by the 15th Sep – I think Boo shall stay on & go up to London with him, & then you say the Masters will take charge of him to Heidelberg. Is this so? I shd like Ted to have the same pocket money in Germany as he has here = Have you a list of our tour – here & in America? If not Ill [*sic*] send one = We shall be in London for about a week before we sail from Southampton – & I'll come to dinner if youll [*sic*] ask me any day but the 18th Oct. (Kate's wedding day, & we all dine with her.) Do you know – have you heard that Flossy has twins? Well she hasn't but a fine boy is added to her already numerous family.

Give my dear dear love to Gill & the little boys & take a chaste salute upon your manly brow from

Livie=

GARRICK, Misc. 2

176. To unidentified, 24 August [1887]

5 Melville St. Edinburgh. 24 Aug–

Well I've not yet recovered from the fits your letter threw me into – but I'm better – You must know we didn't act on Monday at all[.] 'Twas impossible to produce a thing in two rehearsals that had taken all our Stage Carpenters & Scene Men 6 months to do – However all's well that ends well we did make 'em sit up on Tuesday & no mistake the audience thought it all lovely but we

[p. 2]

were not quite happy with roofless cottages – no lightening paltry thunder – & a few trifles of the kind – I send you a notice – but the best one was the Scotsman = What think you of these picters? [*sic*] I think the "Sunshine & Rain" is deftly placed. What do you think? It has been a true little friend & has got many a wetting at least – Oh, the lovely drives it and I have been together = all this week we do Faust – next week its Faust, Olivia & Louis XI – & the Merchant = Well, we have had our holiday & it stands us in good stead now – Directly Henry begins his work, he is to me the most wonderful creature under the sun – but when he is holidaying he's but a mortal man, & I don't think much of him! We have lovely lodgings here – Dolly is about the same – (not improved by having become a holy Roman!) Henry[1] is at a

[p. 3]

Hotel & he has only taken *5* rooms for himself & Walter[2] = Lou comes here I think for 2 days on the 1st Sep – Oh, how I wish --------
I've a mind to send her to one of Henry's 5 rooms! Oh, wouldn't Lou be shocked? But she'd go I bet, rather than not stay = Eden & Edy[3] are capital friends – at the present moment they are all (all but Boo who is here & sends her love) on the top of a tram going thrice round the city for 3d – a cheap, & interesting drive = Fancy your meeting Dr Bird! Don't you think Burnham Beeches lovely? I love the place – Did I tell you I was going to Oxford when this little tour is finished – on my way up to London – Just with Edy – Shall say goodbye to

[p. 4]

Ethel Arnold's poor mother who probably will not live till I come back from America & then I want to see a little churchyard in Oxfordshire[4] & put some white heather on it – but it will all be done in a day, & so I shall have only 3 days in London – Henry has to go & unveil a fountain in Stratford[5] on his way up to town – the gift of the rich, common, Mr Childs of Philadelphia – Dear I've no news – we are all pretty well & Boo is howling out I must go & lie down – (the usual thing you see!) so farewell my sweet old pretty = With a great deal of love & missing you dreadfully I am
Your old Nell=

UCLA

1. Henry Irving.
2. Walter Collinson, Henry Irving's servant.
3. Edith Craig and probably Robertson Ramsay; see n. 4 to letter 59, above.
4. Probably Edward Godwin's grave; see n. 1 to letter 144, above.

5. Henry Irving unveiled a fountain in Stratford upon Avon on 17 October 1887; see G. T. Noszlopy, *Public Sculpture of Warwickshire, Coventry and Solihull* (Liverpool: Liverpool University Press, 2003), pp. 62–3.

177. To Stephen Coleridge, 3 September 1887

Sep 3rd 87 = 5 Melville St = Edinburgh

Dearest Stephen – I thank you more than I can tell you for your long letter about Edward.[1] He shall be ready & packed & labelled ~~by~~ to start the time you mention – "8 p.m. Sep. 16, Victoria Station" – I think we have all his clothes quite ready. Boo[2] & I have been doing them all this week. ~~W a few books Mr~~ Mr Ted & I went out yesterday shopping together & bought a few books for the youth – & he has the following –

Two or three Dictionaries)		Latin Primer and Via [illeg.]
An Atlas)		
Lockes Arithmatic [*sic*]	)	Parry's Greek Grammar
Hall & Knights Algebra [*sic*]	)	
Todhunters Euclid [*sic*]	)	Cornwalls Geography [*sic*]

These Dr. Holzberg told

[p. 2]

me wd be wanted – As to Oxford dear Stephen you must direct me in the future – meanwhile I particularly wish Ted to be made to speak French & German well & to learn drawing & music. I mention these particularly for the rest I suppose will be settled out there in Heidelberg for him. I think it pretty certain he will be an actor & so that is what he had better be put straight for. He speaks naturally well, but stands terribly in want of grace of carriage – drill – "deportment" – This I shd wish attended to, at once. He is very lazy, & has no more reasoning power than a baby but I have no other fault to find with him. I should feel glad if he might be made to ~~speak in~~

[p, 3]

~~public~~ speak before the boys or masters or any audience at times – to recite – for he is nervous & shy & this wd help to overcome the terror of it (which I feel to ~~day~~ this day at every new audience –) I don't want Ted to be coming home eventually – if he could stick on there for 2 years, we might go & see him, if it might be contrived that he could be looked after during his vacations = Will you ask Mr. L. this for me? This is all I can think of –

Dear old Stephen I will be as "careful" as I can – & will save as much as possible – but I must ask you not to invest at ~~once~~ once, everything – as, getting Ted's things, & many bills coming in will not allow of it = Another thing too I want to do – a thing I never asked you about before & that is lend some money.

[p. 4]

Of course I have often loaned money to women & have always been repaid – but I cant lend £50 without coming to you for it because I haven't got it! Now this lady I want to lend it to, ~~woud~~ was my friend in my greatest time of need, & I very much wish to help her now – You will send me a cheque therefore for £50 my dear Stephen at once please – I can write all about it but she is sure to pay & most likely in November or December – Do this like a good boy at once for me. We are having a very happy time here all together Edy & Ted & I & Boo – always driving & walking, in the air when I'm not at rehearsal! The work already is very hard. Give my love to Johnston & Norman[3] & all the R's. Are not you lucky, & clever to have got rid of your house? I do think I ought to have

[p. 5]

let mine & put Boo with friends or in some pleasant country lodging = She is very well, but the least least self-made worry <or wine> & she is like a helpless baby – I fear she is growing terribly feeble – This is quite between ourselves but it is awful to me to see it = I must go now – I am so glad about the Dudley = Yes I've seen many good little "notices" about Demetrius – in the N.Y. papers amongst others – Bless you dear – Forgive me all the trouble I am to you – you're getting about enough to do!!! – & believe me your fond & appreciative Livie =

GARRICK, Vol. IV/1

Envelope extant; postmarked 'SP 3 87', Edinburgh; addressed to 'The Honble Stephen Coleridge, The Cottage, Addlestone, Surrey'; bound in the later volume out of sequence. Stephen Coleridge provides a full page of notes at the beginning of this volume of correspondence: 'This volume is full of Ellen Terry's anxiety about her son "Ted" afterwards known as "Gordon Craig". He had been finally expelled from the Heidelberg School, a fate which I succeeded in preventing on a former occasion by travelling out post haste myself to the school to beg them to keep him. He was "out at night" and was discovered – This was the beginning of his unprincipled career. His mother's pathetic efforts to put the blame on his masters, and my lack of response to this, make her rather angry and hurt! Poor dear, if she could have seen into the future – !!'

1. Edward Gordon Craig.
2. Elizabeth Rumball.
3. Forbes-Robertsons; see n. 4 to letter 61, above.

178. To Stephen Coleridge, 11 September 1887

Dearest Stephen, Henry[1] never thought "The Amber Heart"[2] a good play – & never said so – but he & I think it an excellent vehicle for the display of certain ~~[illeg.]~~ <qualities> in an actress & the public thought so too – "The Bells"![3] read the words of that! but I shd be sorry if the 3rd act of that play was never to be done again for Henry could not show in a Shakespere [*sic*] play all he shows in The Bells – Are you having a great deal of rain in London? I never saw anything in the least like it is here! It's a curtain of water all day long! Except to day – This is Sunday & we are going for a glorious drive presently – the last Sunday we shall [be] with dear old Ted for a long while = Dear, you know I can't see the lad[4] off by his train from Victoria ~~next Wednesday~~ , for I shall be in Glasgow – working = He leaves Glasgow Wednesday & Miss Harries[5] will meet him & look after him in London, & he has one or two things to do for me there = Miss Harries can see him off on Friday eve, but my dear friend your kind suggestion of going to Vic[toria] with him is so delighting to me that I beg you to do so if you can, & so give me great ease of mind & happy comfort = It's too absurd do you know the way that boy looks upon walking! Yesterday Bram Stoker[6] had a little spare time & kindly asked Ted to go for a walk with him – the walk was a good one, certainly – 10 miles – but Ted speaks of it as if it were a great feat to have accomplished – it did him a lot of good = He is very lazy – but I do believe far more capable than he is given credit for – at least by me! A few days ago he did some drawings for me – I never left his side for 4 hours & those drawings are just excellent – all I did of course was just to keep him at it, & point out

[p. 2]

a few things his lazy look didn't see, but the result was fine! But a few hours attention to Ted *and* my work thrown in every day, & I should be an elegant corpse by next year!! He has the sweetest temper & big loving heart, but he'll have to be made to work. We shall miss him here dreadfully when he goes, for we have had such a happy time all of us together. I shall keep Booie[7] on I think now to the end of the time for she likes it so & is wonderfully better – she is so strangely white tho' – I don't notice the fact, to her – she looks so bleached – face – hair – hands = but it's being with me the dear old thing likes so, & it will be dreadful when I have to leave her. I am going for a night & day into Oxfordshire on my way from Liverpool to London – to say good-bye to Mrs Arnold[8] – Ethel Arnold's mother, who wants to see me she says before she dies, & she can't, we think, live long – & I'm going to see Edwards [*sic*] little grave[9] & put some heather there. Edy[10] will be with me & that's all. Look at your calendar, dear. We act in L'pool 15 Oct[11] = I think I shall go by the night train if I can to Oxford = Tuesday the 18th I dine with Kate (her wedding day) & on the 19 I go to another wedding – so I'm counting upon going to you for either a few ~~days~~ hours on Monday, or Wednesday evening = Monday I think = & I want to see the Casellas too = I'm giving a few pounds to that dreadful Exeter affair, but not coming to you for it = The clearing up a bit of bill – clearing off of all is, I think ~~the~~ a capital notion of yours one of many you may claim credit for! – Yes the more I think of it, Monday night at the Cottage (or wherever you may be) then Tuesday morning to London – Wednesday I can see the Casellas, & Carrs, & Robertsons[12] – the evening with

[p. 3]

Boo, & the next day off to Southampton & N.Y.[13]

Now I must go dear little Stephen = I read all about Mary Andersons[14] [*sic*] dresses – how beautiful! It's so funny that I shd never have seen her act! I sent her a little tellywag[15] last night, & shall hear all about the evening from Laurence Tadema.[16] I wish I could have been there = Poor Johnston[17] = I hope he is fairly well – Leontes is rather an oldish part for him I think!

Dearest Gill.[18] Give my love to her, & when she has a moment to throw away ask her to send it to me –

Love from all of us to all of you =

Nell =

9 Mansfield Place,
Pitt St, Glasgow –
Sep 11 – 87=

GARRICK, Vol. IV/2

Envelope extant; postmarked 'SP 12 87', Glasgow; addressed to 'The Hon. Stephen Coleridge, The Cottage, Addleston, Surrey'; ET has written on the back of it 'Words – words –words!!!' It was bound in a later volume out of sequence. This letter was reproduced in *THET*, pp. 39–41. It was extensively cut by Coleridge to only three paragraphs, removing reference to Edward Gordon Craig and changing 'poor Johnston' to 'dear Johnston' (p. 39).

1. Henry Irving.
2. *The Amber Heart* by Alfred C. Calmour was first performed at the Lyceum Theatre on 7 June 1887 and repeated in May 1888.
3. *The Bells* was first performed by Irving at the Lyceum Theatre on 25 November 1871 under the Bateman management and again at the same venue under his own management, on 11 July 1879.
4. Edward Gordon Craig, referred to elsewhere here as Ted, ET's son, was at this point in his fifteenth year.
5. Miss Harries was an employee of ET, acting as her companion.
6. Bram Stoker; see n. 1 to letter 67, above. ET's correspondence in this period demonstrates that he, Henry Irving and Stephen Coleridge acted in a role of authority over Edward Gordon Craig.
7. Elizabeth Rumball; see n. 2 to letter 1, above.

8. Mrs Julia Arnold (1826–88), née Sorell, had been diagnosed with breast cancer. She, was married to Thomas Arnold (1823–1900), scholar and brother of the poet Matthew Arnold (1822–88), whose eight children included Ethel Arnold (*c.* 1864–1930), women's suffrage lecturer and author; the famous novelist and president of the Anti-Suffrage League, Mary Augusta (Mrs Humphrey) Ward (1851–1920); Julia, married to Leonard Huxley and the mother of the novelist Aldous Huxley.
9. Edward Godwin; see n. 1 to letter 144, above. This was probably the first time ET had visited his grave.
10. Edith Craig, ET's daughter, at this time in her eighteenth year, had been a great support during her mother's bereavement on the death of Godwin.
11. ET performed in Liverpool on the Lyceum provincial tour which included Glasgow, Edinburgh and Manchester.
12. The families of three close friends: Johnston Forbes-Robertson (see n. 4 to letter 61, above); Joseph William Comyns Carr (see n. 4 to letter 39); and Mrs Marie Casella (see n. 4 to letter 18, above).
13. The Lyceum tour started in the United States this year on 7 November.
14. Mary Anderson (1859–1940), American actor who had toured in the United States and first acted in London at the Lyceum in 1883 where in 1887 she performed the roles of Perdita and Hermione in Shakespeare's *The Winter's Tale*. She was the first to appear in both roles.
15. Telegraph.
16. Laurence Tadema (b. 1866), author and women's suffrage activist; daughter of Sir Lawrence Alma-Tadema (1836–1912), artist and designer of scenery and costumes for Henry Irving at the Lyceum Theatre.
17. Johnston Forbes-Robertson (1853–1937) performed as Leontes in *The Winter's Tale* at the Lyceum Theatre. He was also a painter and used his artistic talents to design the costumes for this production. In 1885 he had toured the United States with Mary Anderson in *As You Like It*, Anderson's performance as Rosalind having been praised by the critic William Winter; see Auerbach, *Ellen Terry*, p. 66. ET had known Forbes-Robertson for a long time, since they toured together in 1874 in Charles Reade's *The Wandering Heir*.
18. Geraldine Coleridge; see n. 1 to letter 58, above.

179. To Clement Scott, 26 September 1887

Theatre Royal – Manchester
26-Sep-87

My dear Clement Scott[1]

Mr Dutton Cooks [*sic*] statement[2] was in accurate – that's all – I didn't contradict it, altho' asked to do so by my Father at the time, for I thought it of little if of any interest – The very first time I ever appeared on any stage was ~~when~~ on the first night of The Winters [*sic*] Tale at the Princesses Theatre with dear Charles Kean[3] – as for the young

[p. 2]

young princes[4] – them unfortunate little men I never played not neither of them no ~~any~~ where = "What a cry about a little wool" = It's flattering to be fussed about but –

~~Facts~~ Fax is fax!! I hope you are very well – & your little girl also – I am very well & my big girl[5] is well – and I am yours ever

E.T.

[p. 3]

I was born at Coventry 1848[6] – & was, I think, about seven when I played in The Winters Tale.

HUNT

1. See n. 1 to letter 159, above.
2. Edward Dutton Cook (1831–83) was a drama critic for *Pall Mall Gazette* from 1867 to 1875 and then for the *World*. He was also a novelist. See *ODNB*.
3. ET's stage debut was her performance as Mamillius in *The Winter's Tale* for Charles Kean at the Princess's Theatre.
4. Probably in Shakespeare, *Richard III*.
5. Edith Craig, who was eighteen years of age at this point.
6. After ET's death it was revealed that she was indeed born in 1847.

180. To unidentified man, 4 October 1887

Liverpool = Oct 4- 87=

My dear Sir

I enclose cheque for the years [*sic*] rent of "The Audrey Arms"[1] – I suppose I ought to have sent it quarterly but I am terribly un-business like. I hope my mother will go & stay at the Cottage for a little while –

[p. 2]

We are doing splendid business all round the Provinces with Faust[2] & we sail for New York[3] on the 20th – How I shall long to get back to London – home – & to the Audrey Arms.!!

With very kind regards to your family

O (this is a circle!)[4]

Sincerely yours

Ellen Terry:

SMA, SCB3-A16

1. ET's second home in Uxbridge.
2. ET first performed in *Faust* at the Lyceum Theatre on 19 December 1885.

3. The third Lyceum tour of the United States began on 7 November 1887 and ended in March 1888.
4. ET draws a circle and then explains her meaning: 'family circle'.

181. To Clement Scott, 8 October [1887]

8th Oct – 1887
Liverpool=

Dear Clement Scott –

Yes! "bother these milestones"! say I too – your birthday – 6th October? – is my death-day[1] of the whole year – but it's past thank God, & since it borned you into the world, a dear sweet good fellow as ever was borned, it's [*sic*] offence shall henceforth be mitigated in my eyes –

Please don't publish my <other> letter – I never dreamt of it when I was writing to you – the facts can be used, but don't print the letter – No. I somehow missed the D-T[2] for Tuesday but have sent to get it – that wretched Ireland! you are sure to have said the right thing – the thing wanted to be said – about it.

Always yrs affectionately E-T-

Love to yr little girl, & Mrs Scott if she will have it

HUNT

Headed notepaper for Henry Irving, ET and Lyceum Company tour 1887–8.

1. Edward Godwin died on 6 October 1886.
2. *Daily Telegraph*.

182. To Amy, 10 October [1887]

Oct 10th Liverpool –

Dearest Amy – I loved to see your nice little fist! – & rejoice for your sake that you are by the lovely sea, instead of living in a filthy town such as ----- Liverpool for instance! oh, I get so ill here always, & you'll be sorry I know to hear that poor old Henry[1] is quite laid low (for the moment only, I hope) by a bilious attack. Men are such donkeys if they are left alone about eating!! They are very particular, but all the while are swallowing tinned soups, & canned vegetables & take them all to be fresh! Luckily yesterday was Sunday, & he had not to act, & I went down to his Hotel, & looked after the poor Dear's food & warmth a bit, & shall hope to find him better this morning – Isn't it odd, he doesn't know what pain is!! in all this attack of violent sickness, etc, not a bit of pain! not a little headache!!. & I can scarce see to write to my dear friend Amy for the neuralgia which seems to be gnawing at my head bones – Six months [*sic*] whole rest, is what I want – wouldn't it be nice to have it, & to go with you to Honibury = I shd just like that! & to take Edy[2] with me –

[p. 2]

We sail on the 20th, & so I fear there'll be no chance of even seeing you, let alone dining with you – we have only 3 days in London before starting for N.Y.[3] If you are in London however I'll run round for a moment & take my chance of finding you in – But in those four free days I have to run down to Oxford, & am asked to Stratford on Avon to see poor Henry unveil a Pump[4] – I beg pardon – a Fountain! The mace bearer will walk before him & these are to be regular jubilee juggins rejoicings – but I know I could not keep my gravity to see H.I. in such a situation, so will not disgrace him, but will keep away – "Faust" has been the greatest success everywhere[5] – I'm getting to loathe that Margaret – ! 600 hundred times uttering those idiotic words – the meekness of that woman is sickening – (as bad as E.T.= & she always was, & is, the veriest worm!) & I feel I shall throw her overboard, & not let her inflict herself upon the delightful Americans =

Edy is with me – (& three or 4 girls besides – relays <(?)> of friends meet us & stay with us at each new city – Ted[6] – my Edward has

[p. 3]

gone to Heidelberg – for 2 years! You have always been so dearly kind & sweet to him that I hope the enclosed photograph just done of the youth, will "find a place in your book" – How is the dear pretty Mr Skirrow? (shocking!!) – you positively don't mention him to me !!!!!!

You'll care I know to follow us <in imagination> from place to place when we are far away, & so I send you a little list of our tour – together with very much love, & hopes for your welfare, & blessings on your dear head – Your kind Dear farewell –

yr loving nell

HARV

Annotated '1887'.

1. Henry Irving.
2. Edith Craig.
3. The third Lyceum tour of the United States began on 7 November 1887 and ended in March 1888.
4. See n. 5 to letter 176, above.
5. ET first performed in Faust at the Lyceum Theatre on 19 December 1885.
6. Edward Gordon Craig.

183. To Stephen Coleridge, 18 October 1887

Oct 18 = 87 =

Dear Stephen –

Please write me a cheque for £100 –

There's a joke! but Henry has asked me to lend him a hundred pounds[1] – (I think he has made all his English money American – but of course I can't ask the why & the

[p. 2]

Wherefore –) Send it please to me *at once* ~~by Edy, who comes to say good bye & brings this~~

I'll run in tomorrow sometime for a moment –

Yrs devoted

Nell =

GARRICK, Vol. III/14

Envelope extant; marked 'By Cab='; addressed to 'The Hon. Stephen Coleridge, 7 Egerton Mansions, South Kensington ='. This letter is bound out of sequence in an earlier volume.

1. Henry Irving asked to borrow money from ET, presumably following their return from the United States.

184. To Elizabeth Rumball, 3 November 1887

Thursday Nov 3rd = 87 = Buckingham

"There's no place like home" – tho' New York is delightful! & our November is scarcely attractive! – I'm afraid I shall not be able to do much writing – I seem to be better, of course – after a month's resting I "ought to", & I think George[1] thinks it's all right – but oh, I am so far from well – I never seem peaceful if I rest ever so –

Edie[2] has music lessons 3 times a week – that I've managed & she practises very nicely every day – is doing so now as I write – I hope you'll go sometimes & see Mr McHenry – Edy & I lunched yesterday with friends of his, the

[p. 2]

Fowlers, & I met many friends there. Dear old George Stoker & so bright & good – I shall miss him dreadfully – he came in just now with a pretty brown hood he had bought for little Shula – so pleased – This Hotel is very nice – & very expensive. We (Edy & I) went to the Opera last night – Tristan[.] It was splendid, & every body was there – Mr Oram amongst others & Mr Sargent[3] the painter, the Duke of Marlborough[4] (who is in very bad odour here, in all the papers) came to speak to me – You shd just have seen all the glasses go up! –

Little Joe Evans[5] sends his regards

[p. 3]

to you – so does Mrs Anderson – we go to see her, & girlie, tomorrow – At present it's very little rehearsaling we can manage as the "Stuff" takes a tremendous time getting into its place. My greatest------- pleasure – is driving in the Park & a lady here lends me her carriage & pair – Carriage & 4!!!! 2 men & 2 hosses!![6] & that's nice =

We begin work now in a few days, & are going to do "immense" business – To all the Interviewers I say, "I have nothing to say but that I am glad to see my American friends again" & beg them to excuse me – I'll write more

[p. 4]

another day – Now I am tired. – We are just going to Brooklyn to see dear old Mrs Beecher.

Such stacks of letters to answer. Edie does some – Miss H – a few but it's awful – The brown dress of L & A I can't wear at all – the skirt looks as if it had been made up by Miss Harries – such a thing!! My black & my green are the two things, & the dark blue serge with Jersey from L & A's – Edy's black dress most useful, but it is horribly draped. We have just paid our 1st weeks [*sic*] Hotel bill. "Oh! My!!"

[p. 5]

I've written to Edward,[8] but had no letter as yet – Henry looks tired – he's out every day to dine with a lot of men. It is so queer in N.Y = All the men seem to go together & all the women together!! I like it myself a little more mixed I think. Joe Evans gives Edy a drawing lesson 3 times a week[.] She is pretty well engaged all day I can tell you one way & another – I wish I had continued to be well enough to have sat to Mr Grove[9] in The Amber Heart[10] before I left London – but it was impossible= You wd be so much

[p. 6]

amused if you could see Miss Harries in America – She is a good soul but she is real funny = Ask George Stoker about her being taken for me by the Custom House Officer!

I'm a little better – time too! & sleep better – The bags Nannie[11] sent me on board the Allen were just perfect – & I have 'em now hanging up all round my rooms. No 76. & 3 bedrooms besides!! Fourth floor – The Lovedays are in a lodging but have to go out, to get all their food! I want a picture of Kate & Polly & Floss[12] – there are none found here. Mrs Beecher sends you

[p. 7]

her love. She is looking very well – She told us all about his death, & I never saw Edy so much moved – it was a remarkable relation – & wonderfully told – Mr Sargent the painter is here – staying at the Clarendon where the Alexanders are. I may go there next time. Ask mother to send a message to Uncle Bill & Uncle John next time she writes. I have not seen 'em yet – but wrote when first I came = I enclose you a card of our daily fare which we choose from – Our weekly bill was pretty large I can tell you. For our 4 rooms we have to pay $84 –

[p. 8]

84 dollars & it's all on a piece with this. I shall send Stephen (let me know about Gill[13] from time to time) only half tell him of the hundred pounds Henry borrowed[.] He paid me the hundred today but there's no salary remember this last week – I've just heard from Ted – he seems all right now – I shall write to one of his masters & ask about him a little – Give my love to my friends & tell them I'm pretty well & Edy too, tho' she looks rather pasty! I'll keep this open no longer but will write again & tell you if the N.Y. public care for us as much as ever – God bless you sweet Boo –

Yr Nellie

SMA, ET-5,001

1. George Stoker, Bram Stoker's brother.
2. Edith Craig.
3. John Singer Sargent (1856–1925), artist and creator of the portrait of ET as Lady Macbeth.
4. The Duke of Marlborough was cited in the divorce case against Lady Colin Campbell; *New York Times*, 3 December 1886.
5. Joe Evans; see n. 1 to letter 126, above.
6. Horses.
7. See n. 3 to letter 163, above.
8. Edward Gordon Craig.
9. Window and Grove, a commercial photographer's company, operated from 63a Baker Street London from 1870s and *c.* 1890 opened another studio at Westbourne Grove.
10. *The Amber Heart*; see n. 1 to letter 167, above.
11. Nannie Held.
12. ET's sisters, Kate Terry, Florence Terry and Marion Terry.
13. Geraldine Coleridge.

185. To Joe Evans, [3 November 1887]

3 Nov 1887 Thursday 7.30

Sweet dear Joe

We jump at you ! – did n't dare ask if you "gave lessons"[1] – yet all the while were longing to ask you – How good you are – If you ever walk out in the evening it wd be good for ~~your~~ our health if you toddled up in this direction ! This evening it wd do us good, but perhaps you're not at home – or wd rather stay there – Yours affectionately E.T. & Edy.

NYPClub

Annotated '3 Nov 1887'.

1. Joe Evans gave Edith Craig art lessons.

186. To Edward Gordon Craig, 17 November 1887

Nov.17. New York = 1887

"Headache" & "in bed" – You! oh, I am so sorry my Ted. I wish I were near you to kiss your dear eyes, & soothe you a bit, & cool the poor beating head. You'd rest near me would not you dear? –

(Try hard) not to be kept in darling. You see that's their way of punishing, & we must all of us be punished to push on our intelligences a bit – Mrs Kean[1] used to punish me – but I'm better for it now I know. Goodness knows I'm not brilliant

[p. 2]

now, but I'm certain I shd have been much worse if she had not "given it me" when I was a kid! What <a> sweet little drawing of Bradfield[2] you sent me! I loved it – & the Sonnet cards too! Very pretty. More more drawings! I am feeling greedy!! Edy[3] is enjoying herself greatly I think – at the present moment she is having a drawing lesson from Joe Evans.[4] A large drawing of the head of the Milo Venus[5] – from a cast – Let me see now, many send you their love – Joe Evans the Lockwoods. Dr Bond. The Blashfields – Mrs Beecher – Mrs (Anderson) & Girlie – Johnnie Buck & Mr Buck (they are so

[p. 3]

very kind to Edy) Miss Klausen (who gives Edy music lessons 3 times a week at 9 in the morning). & many others send you their sincerest love –

Edy is such a good girl now she is always with me & Miss Harries has grown so fond of her. (You know she was not once – !!) Mrs Jinny Potter came this morning – Edy likes her very much – She – Mrs P – sends her love to "that dear boy" – She is not a success here, any more than in London – I think in time she'd act very well if only she wd do easier parts now – & she is so charming! Henry[6] is going to act 9 times next week!! & me – I – 7.

[p. 4]

A moving perf[7] of Faust for the Beecher memorial – A funny thing rather a play with The Devil in it, for a memorial to a Parson.[8] Will they notice it I wonder – Boo[9] writes she is pretty well – Awful Fogs in London! Glad I am out of 'em! Won't it be lovely when Edy & I come to see you in Heidelberg? Maybe when we go back from America we will go by Southampton to Bremen at once, before we go to London at all!! I'll see – & let you know. Mrs Winter & Viola, are coming to stay with me here a few days. Our business is enormous with Faust. Fancy there were 4,000 Dollars (£800-) in, last Saturday matinee!! Love to Pan, & tell her I am quite ashamed I never thanked her for the very pretty handkerchief she worked me – I have already had lots of presents here & we cant manage with so

[p. 5]

many flowers! Ask Dr Holzberg for me if you may have at least one bath a week – I hope you'll learn to skate or it will be foolish simply. Have you met any of Edy's Mannheim friends yet? Edy & I are to be photographed next week for your friend Moza! We'll send you some – here's one taken by a "snap photographer" on board the Tender. Look at Edy with her everlasting Handkerchief, & a half consumed apple! Now darling boy let me hear from you very often – & try to think that a little suffering is good for all of us – Anyhow good or not suffer we must – all of us –

[p. 6]

You'll know some day that your poor old Mum has had a great share, & when she was quite young too – only 17 years old![10] & lots afterwards too! So just work away darling – peg into your studies, & then you will have less to battle with later on –

God bless you my dearest heart – I am always thinking of you & always loving you –

With our love Edy's & mine

Your own old

Mum=

HRC

1. Ellen Kean (1806–80), née Tree, Charles Kean's wife.
2. Edward Gordon Craig attended school at Bradfield College in 1886–7; E. Craig, *Gordon Craig: The Story of His Life* (London: Victor Gollancz, 1968), p. 59.

3. Edith Craig.
4. See letter 185, above.
5. A large replica Venus de Milo stood in the hall of the house in Taviton Street which ET shared with Edward Godwin; *Memoirs*, p. 84.
6. Henry Irving.
7. Performance.
8. See n. 3 to letter 163, above.
9. Elizabeth Rumball.
10. ET refers here to her separation from her first husband, G. F. Watts.

187. To Stephen Coleridge, 23 November 1887

The Buckingham, New York
Nov – 23 – 87 –

Dearest Stephen – I am anxiously waiting to hear from you after your visit to Heidelberg. I can't tell you how good I think it is of you to go there & see how it happens that Ted[1] is such a bad lad – I wrote to him directly I read of his school report & told him how grieved & troubled & angry he had made me, & I also said it seemed to me we shd soon have to give up all idea of the stage for him, since he could not

[p. 2]

learn his lessons he'd not be able to learn his "parts", & told him that a training ship & the sea wd be more likely to be his future lot – I do feel that to stick at that school <for 2 years> (or at least a school in Germany) is his only chance – if he can be made to work, I think they'll do it there – I'll write more when I hear from you again. I'm almost blind from a terrible cold – though I have been ever so much better since I came to New York in general health – Edy[2] is very very good & sweet & industrious & in fact all she should be. She is now writing to Grandmama[3] – Miss Harries has grown very

[p. 3]

fond of her, & that's saying much for she did n't [*sic*] care for her before, all these years –

I am trying to be very economical – You ought to have recd[4] the full £200 the first (playing) week – for I told Bram[5] to send off the hundred & fifty, & to add fifty pounds of that one hundred which Henry[6] borrowed from me before we left London – I used the other fifty myself, for you see we were in New York more than a week before acting – I want you to be so very kind as to send Miss Kate Phillips the letter

[p. 4]

I send with this – first enclosing a cheque for £10. Do it for me at once, there's a dear, Stephen. I ought to have attended to it before – Take care the addressed cover (to Boo)[7] is enclosed.

What news of little Gill?[8] & the babes? How do you like your new dwelling place? Have you sold any more "flicks"!! I suppose I shall see the Yarnall[9] girls soon, for we go on to Philadelphia soon – Oh, this influenza! – can't see any more – I'll shut my eyes & think of you all at home – God bless you –

Nell =

GARRICK, Vol. IV/3a

1. Edward Gordon Craig was at school in Germany.
2. Edith Craig.
3. Sarah Terry; see n. 3 to letter 1, above.
4. Received.
5. Bram Stoker.
6. Henry Irving.
7. Elizabeth Rumball.
8. Geraldine Coleridge.
9. Mrs Yarnall of May Place, Haverford, Pennsylvania, refused to acknowledge ET on her second visit to the United States although she had sought ET's company on her first visit. Stephen Coleridge felt obliged to write to Mrs Yarnall to reprimand her for this behaviour. See Coleridge's annotation to his letter to Agnes Yarnall, 19 October 1884; Garrick Club Vol. III/2 letter.

188. To Joe Evans, 24 November 1887

Nov – 24 . 1887

You – or some you know – may care to go – He speaks very nicely I think – at least when you get used to the irish accent – ET[1] =

NYPClub

1. ET signs her initials in a distinctive way, with the T superimposed over the E.

189. To William Winter, 8 December [1887]

8th December=

Dear Dear Mr Winter

For fear it will be a long time before I find time to say more, Thank you for the dear picture –

I love to have it – & love that you gave it me – Thank you –

Yrs affectionately
Nell=

FOLGER, Y.c.434 (87)
Annotated '1887'.

190. To Florence Stoker, 19 December 1887

Philadelphia = Decr 19 – 87 =

Dearest Flo –

Don't think I fail to appreciate kindness because I have not sent you a word of thanks for your splendid bag – I'm not so dull – but, as no doubt you have charitably surmised, I'm pretty busy, &

[p. 2]

almost live at my little writing desk !

How very good of you & dear Bram to gift me – such a clever present – (tho' terribly extravagant ! Naughty Flo ! –) the very thing I wanted – to do for me from Saturdays to Monday visits in England –

Ever so many loving thanks to you both – Yours affect –
Nell =

I've seen yr photographs
not one nearly good
enough.

CLAREMONT
Envelope extant; addressed: 'To, The Lady, Florencia =, With love from E.T.='.

191. To unidentified, 23 December 1887

With much pleasure I sign my name for you – you speak of Charlotte Cushman![1] My dear mother[2] knew her well, & has often entertained me (& instructed me) with stories about her – in her art –

I sign my name with pleasure –

Sincerely yours
Ellen Terry =

Philadelphia =
Dec 23rd 87 =

FOLGER, Y.c.434 (121)

1. Charlotte Cushman (1816–76), American actor who performed alongside Macready and in the roles of Lady Macbeth, Rosalind, Beatrice and Portia as well as in the ordinarily male roles of Hamlet, Romeo, Oberon and Claude Melnotte in *The Lady of Lyons*. She also gave readings from Shakespeare. See Hartnoll (ed.), *The Concise Oxford Companion to the Theatre*.
2. Sarah Terry.

192. To Elizabeth Winter, December 1887

Dear Lizzie – from Nell

Dec'r 87=

Holland House[1] =
one of the "places of interest"
we did not visit!

FOLGER, Y.c.434 (64a)

1. Little Holland House was the home of G. F. Watts when ET married him.

193. To [W. T. Watts], [1887]

33 Longridge Road – Earls Court

You can always be thanked in words with Mr Swinburne by you but what I feel when I feel much I cant [*sic*] word –

But believe me very grateful to you for all your goodness in troubling for me – & grateful to Mr Swinburne also – -------as for the book!! if ever that reaches the destination intended for it I shall think the little American girl very fortunate, & have a good opinion of my own honesty – but oh, Lord we are all mortal ------ All miserable sinners------- Good Lord deliver us – I must not – covet my neighbours [*sic*] book!

Yours faithful & obliged Ellen Terry =

BL, Add. MS 70628, f. 54

Envelope extant; postmarked 'OC 18 87'; addressed to 'Theodore Watts, The Pines, Putney Hill', address crossed out, possibly redirected by the postal service.

Annotated '1887' and 'Look up Life of Terry at Brit Mus'.

7 'A USEFUL ACTRESS' (1888)

194. To [Elizabeth Rumball], 5 January 1888

Jan 5-88-Chicago-

Well my Booie dear I fear the letter you sent to "The Aldine Chicago" will never reach me! – so I can only hope there may be no deadly secrets in it!! Oh, such a lot of lovely cards & notes & gifts have come to me from England, & if only you could know the pleasure it gives me to get them from dear home – Chicago is not improved – We live in the heart of the town, for one thing, instead of on the Lake – & oh the dirt, &

[p. 2]

old Loveday[1] made us all rather chokey – However he is much better now – Mrs Loveday & Mrs Stoker are in New York – too rough here, for those who can stay in N.Y = We had a very pleasant fortnight in Philadelphia – chiefly due to the Mac Michaels –, the Platts – the Farnalls, & the Gillespies – & the crowds at Faust were enormous –

The sleighing in Chicago just delights Edy[2] – the Dexters are as kind as possible & the dear woman does everything for us – which considering the manner in which I treated

[p. 3]

her when she was in England, is generous to say the least of it! I have lovely letters from Ted[3] – he does put himself into his letters sometimes in quite a wonderful manner – Your news of Mrs Prinsep's death[4] shocked me greatly. Poor Mamie – she did treat me badly, beyond words once, but 'twas only through stupidity I do believe now – & I can't help feeling her death very much[.] She had excellent points of character – How strange that a vigorous woman like that should die before Mr W[5] – I think the vigorous people often

[p. 4]

<lose their> vigour in helping the weak ones to live! How some people never forget! I never do – I wish I were like the other sort – it makes it easier to get

along – & I think it's right too – Henry[6] is one of the "other sort" – After all you spill your milk, & it's no good crying then! – Ah! [illeg.][7] "If to do, were as easy", – etc, &c, &c, as Portia says = Lord help us we're all miserable sinners – but – "God above all", & his mercy is everlasting[8] = I think I shall write to Val –

[p. 5]

or to Alise Gurney. I have had a little silver box sent me from London with "E.T. from E.C" – upon it, & no letter, & I cannot think who it comes from!

Yes – Pay the bill at Edinburgh – one must leave a clearer understanding another time – & I must say the dresses have worn admirably & are most useful –

The Casella's sent us *lovely* cards drawn of course by themselves = I was <almost> beginning to think they wd not send & was feeling it very much – what a thing it is to

[p. 6]

be "spoilt"! Gill[9] sent me a ducky little paper knife Charles Fitzg[10] – a lovely blotter & paper knife – Audrey[11] a screamer of a letter!! (– I'm so glad she isn't getting engaged.) Kate[12] a beautiful lace pocket hankey – Nan some of her pocket handkerchiefs – oddly enough Florence Lockwood also sent me a dozen with Nell= on 'em – Hers are stouter – quite plain, & of fine linen – & her marking has a different N., to Nancy's – Nell= & Nell[13] = =

[p. 7]

When you see Mrs Casella tell her I was delighted [with] her chatty letter & think it most good of her to write me at such length – I hope London won't take away the good her travels did her! – I send you, in another cover, a white lace thing for your head, or your buzzim!![14] Accept it with your Nelly's love & best wishes for a happy New Year =

To night little Minny[15] acts & I shall anxiously look out for a good account of her – How sweet if she & Teddy act together some day –!! – Charlie will be nervous I know

[p. 8]

to night – I wish I could be there – I think I'll cable him a line – I can write no more dear now <to you> – for I've dozens of other letters to write & my American correspondence is pretty big I can tell you not counting any of you Dears in ~~London~~ Europe!

Fare thee well my little Booie – keep up the fires & don't send any more letters to the Aldine Hotel. Chicago for I am staying at the Grand Pacific in Chicago – Anyhow, when you get this, we shall perhaps be Boston ways – nearer civilization thank goodness! God bless you Boo –

Your Nelly.

SMA, ET-5,003

Envelope extant; postmarked 'JAN 5', Chicago; addressed to 'Mrs Rumball, 33 Longridge Road, Earls Court, London, England'.

1. H. J. Loveday, stage manager for the Lyceum Theatre.
2. Edith Craig.
3. Edward Gordon Craig.
4. Mrs Prinsep (see n. 8 to letter 1, above) died in 1887.
5. G. F. Watts.
6. Henry Irving.
7. Some characters are scored out several times.
8. *The Merchant of Venice*, I.ii.
9. Geraldine Coleridge.
10. Charles Fitzgerald.
11. Probably her friend Audrey Campbell; see n. 5 to letter 163, above.
12. Probably her sister, Kate Terry.
13. The character 'N' is drawn differently, with a longer tail on the top of the left or right vertical lines.
14. Bosom.
15. Minny Terry, daughter of Charles Terry and niece of ET; she performed at the Lyceum Theatre, including a role in *Olivia* on 14 September 1880.

195. To Joe Evans, 13 January 1888

Grand Pacific Hotel
Jan 13 – 88 =

You dear Joe –

You know how I felt getting that Rose – that lovely little picture – if you don't, I'm sure my words can never let you know –

Thank you Joe =

We are so well here in Chicago – isn't it funny? we are – "me most especially" – ! Chicago is a little – well a little rough, & very very dirty but there are some nice people here & they make all things nice for me –

[p. 2]

The cold weather suits me & – by Jove ! – it's cold enough for most people here[.] As I write it is 7 -° below Zero – & I feel chirpy, for an old 'un !! Sweet letters from Ted – Edy,[1] a little thoughtfuller, & ----- some others, a little kinder, & me, a little better in health for it all –

I want Mr Irving to do more of our plays when we return to N.Y. We begin with "Olivia". You'll all (36-E-31st) like that – (Kiss your mother for me this minute if you please – thank you. I consider it done you see ! –) Well, & then I want us to do "Werner" (I'm not in that but will see it

[p. 3]

with you – if you please –)

– & "The Lyons Mail", & "Much Ado" ----- & any other trifle we have with us –

I want to get back to New York & to be well when I'm there – Mr Blashfield has written me two letters & he must think me crazy, for they are difficult letters to answer & oh, Joe I have'nt [*sic*] answered them !!

I'm just off to work – & as 14 people's letters have been answered by me this blessed day

[p. 4]

& I'm writing to you who never wrote at all (oh!) I can't even look at a pen & ink tomorrow.

Bless you Dear – All good be round about you = With love to your Mother & Sister[.]

Ever yours faithfully faithfully Ellen Terry =

Tell me of a book ----- (*A* book!!) Well of a book to pass the time, & make one think of it at the time one is reading –

NYPClub

1. Edward Gordon Craig and Edith Craig.

196. To Edward Gordon Craig, 26 January 1888

Jan 26 1888

Boston – Vendome

January 26 – Snow deep – deep outside but my room is just filled with bowls, & vases, & jugs of Roses, of all manner & kind, all the spring flowers too Lilies, Daffys, Jonquills, [*sic*] unless you look out at the weather you'd think it the middle of Summer – Edy[1] & I are going for a sleigh drive this morning a splendid sleigh too it is. I've had crowds of people calling on me here but altho' I've been in Boston now nearly a week I've seen nobody for Chicago gave me such a cold

[p. 2]

& I've been terribly hoarse for the last fortnight not ill, but hoarse & not allowed to talk during the day time. It was quite killing about Henry.[2] Knowing this was a terrific big Theatre I begged & prayed that I might be "let off" the first night in Boston because of my voice & that Miss Emery[3] might play Margaret – no – he was like iron – like a rock about it, & I got mad & said "I do think that if your son, or your mother, your wife the idol of your heart were to die on the stage

<through> making the effort to do "the work you wd let it happen"! "Certainly I would," said he to

[p. 3]

my amazement! I expected he wd say "Oh, come now, you exaggerate" – so now I know what to expect[.] He certainly wd drop himself, before he'd give in, & there my Ted is the simple secret of his great success in everything he undertakes. He is most extraordinary of course now that I am better in health I can laugh, but at the time I was suffering so, I thought him brutal & said so – Poor Henry a man an inch less strong wd break down under such responsibility as he has – I was very glad to see by your letter to him that you had receíved [*sic*] his Shakespere – Very interesting isn't it? I don't like the binding – it's like a magazine

[p. 4]

cover – I guess you are having a good time during the holidays – 4 dances a week!! How do you like the German way of dancing? Tell me when next you write (such a time since I heard from you! You shd keep the excellent habit of writing to me every Friday or Sunday) Tell me if you asked Dr Holzberg, as I told you, to give you 20 Marks for me, for my Christmas box – Tell me – Mrs Skirrow I hear sent you a Sovereign – it was very kind – I hope you wrote to her & thanked her – oh, yes! surely – if not, by any accident, do so dear at once. Let me know of your holidays – When you get back to work put your great strong back into it, old boy, & don't forget it's the lost minutes that tell up against one the end of the Term. I was delighted the last report

[p. 5]

was so great an improvement upon the first – God prosper your efforts darling[.] Keep up the efforts, & soon it will be easy ~~ever so~~ easy – Edy is wonderfully improved in her music since she has been in America – she has never practised less than 2 hours every day – often more, & it's a treat now to hear ~~here~~ her play her scales!! "Susan" has just come in, & sends you a message that he "wishes you were here" – he says his rooms are miserable & ours are bright (we are staying in the same Hotel, The Vendome –) – So Edy & I tell him we "will decorate them for him when he goes out!! Let him beware Edy! eh? Look out for Squalls Mr Susan Austin!!! Did I tell you that when this <American> tour is over, & after a very short season (about 2 months) at the Lyceum, I am really going to take a 4 months rest at least. Previous to coming out (& being cut up!) as Lady Macbeth! How is the Drawing getting on? Edy has always said she "can't" draw free-hand – can only copy – however, now she is proving differently – & she went out skating with some people the other day in Chicago & has since been doing excellent sketches of the people on the ice from recollection

[p. 6]

but it is you who have the gift of sketching, & I do wish you wd encourage the gift – Dear old Boo seems to be very happy at the Groves – how kind they are! Do you know Lily Cox (Flossy's great friend) is going to be married? So many people have died lately that I know – the latest, are, Mr Chippendale, & Mrs Prinsep – When Henry said one night to Martha "Madam your husband's dead & sends his love", he wasn't so far out, was he? – Poor old Chippy! Now dearest I'm stumped for any news so I'll end up this *long* epistle with my blessing upon your dear old duck of a head – The Lord bless you & keep you – The Lord be merciful to me

A sinner
Who wants her dinner –
And doesn't get thinner –

(A born Poet you see my boy. A born ~~idiot~~ I mean Poet of course. Now you write to me Sir & give me news of yourself & tell me if you skate by now? I hear the cold is tremendous in Germany this year. God bless you darling Heart –

Your loving old Mother.

HRC

1. Edith Craig.
2. Henry Irving.
3. See n. 2 to letter 125, above.

197. To Bram Stoker, 3 February 1888

Please find 2 very nice seats= [Ellen Terry] for bearer ET=
~~Jan~~ Feb- 3rd 88=

[p. 2]

Ask for Mr Stoker =

HARV

ET's printed visiting card is used for this message to instruct Bram Stoker, as business manager at the Lyceum Theatre, to provide free tickets for the bearer.

198. To Major Pond, 10 February 1888

The Vendome – Boston=

Feb 10- 88=

Dear Mr Pond[1]

Thanks for your letter – my fear is, that I know too many "good people" & have so little time to do my duty by them, but I will with pleasure call upon Mrs Greely & her sister or write to them – since you tell me they are so amicable as to remember me & to desire to see me – many thanks for what you tell me of my dear Mrs Beecher – Poor dear lady she must have put out a little – Even she! – by the annoyances

[p. 2]

of being obliged to move so soon after fixing herself up in that pretty flat in Brooklyn – I am very sorry she is ailing –

Again thanks for your note & with kind regards believe me Yours truly

Ellen Terry =

CLAREMONT

Envelope extant; postmarked 'JY 23'; addressed to 'Major J. B. Pond, Savoy Hotel, Victoria Embankment'.

1. Major Pond is described by Stephen Coleridge as an 'American lecture' agent in the Garrick Club correspondence.

199. To Elizabeth Winter, 12 February [1888]

Monday 12 Feb =

Lizzy darling & how is it with you? I come across your Will's[1] brilliant trail in the Tribune from time to time & so seem to be with him & to hear him speak but of you I know nothing – Will you drop me a line saying you remember you are engaged to me for a week in New York – Can you come Monday or Tuesday? We hope to arrive in N.Y. on Sunday evening & will try to secure the room next to ours

[p. 2]

if you will let us know the day.

In greatest haste

With greatest love –

Your Nell=

FOLGER, Y.c.434 (65a)

Envelope extant; postmarked 'FEB 13' 1888, Boston; addressed to 'Mrs Winter, Box 18 Tompkinsville, Staten Island'; annotated '1888 Ellen Terry'.

1. William Winter, Elizabeth's husband.

200. To Miss Fisher, 14 February 1888

Mr Irving & Miss Terry regret exceedingly to know of Miss Fisher's sickness =
Feb – 14 – 88 =

HARV

201. To Mrs Aldrich, 19 February 1888

Hotel Vendome –
Feb 19 – 88

My dear Mrs Aldrich

I am very glad I have pleased you – You have given me much pleasure by your lovely little gift – "Our Lady of Kazan" shall have me in goodkeeping & I will wear her about me for the best part of my work – the little shrine you put her in, I will give to "Olivia Primrose",[1] it will perhaps teach her how to bear her body

[p. 2]

to bear her body [*sic*] more seemly. Will you accept my appreciation[.] Thanks & believe me

Sincerely yours
Ellen Terry =

Boston –
February 19th
1888=
In haste since I am just leaving Boston for New York –

HARV

1. ET played the role of Olivia Primrose in *Olivia*.

202. To Augustin Daly, 24 February 1888

The Buckingham =Friday = Feb 24 – 88 =
Dear Mr Daly[1]

I want a treat on Monday! – it's my day – & I don't act that evening. Can you spare me a box to see "The Midsummer Night's Dream"?

I long to see it – & Miss Rehan[2] – & Mr Drew – & Mr Lewis – & all –

Please give my love to Ada Rehan, & believe me Sincerely very yours

Ellen Terry =

FOLGER, Y.c.3076 (4)

1. See n. 1 to letter 110, above.
2. Ada Rehan (Crehan) (1860–1916), American actor who had acted for Daly in New York since 1879 and in 1884 at Toole's Theatre in London, and was particularly renowned for her role as Katharina in *The Taming of the Shrew* in New York in 1887; see Hartnoll (ed.), *The Concise Oxford Companion to the Theatre*. ET regarded her as her double; see Auerbach, *Ellen Terry*, p. 235.

203. To Stephen Coleridge, 3 March 1888

New York

3 – March – 88 –

My dear dear Stephen –

Are we not grateful that our little girl has passed safely through her time of trial? And so the dear mite has another mite – a boy again – a man child! Quite Lady Macbethian! –

I sent a cable to Boo asking about Gill,[1] & the next day Agnes Yarnall[2] telegraphed me of the event – Well I hope to see you all so soon now – Delightful – but it seems very true! – & very near & poyfeckly lovely.

[p. 2]

Dear Stephen I like America very much better, every time I come to it. I know so much better this visit what to do (& what not to do!) where to go, & all that – I know the first friends much better, & have 2 or 3 new ones. Then too they love me here in my work, better I think than in England – anything like good work is of course rarer here[.] Somehow too I do much better work here – am feeling so much better in health & spirits – "I guess it's the climate!" – Have I told you, or has dear Booie told you, that I am going straight on to Heidelberg (via Bremen) to see Ted[3] before coming to London? I can get 3 or 4 days there & I want to see Mr

[p. 3]

Lawrence, & see Ted in his school. I can't make out one or two things. No doubt, I think, that the boy is getting on better now, & is really trying to work – but when in my letters I ask about his lessons – his drawing for instance – he tells me he does not have any drawing lessons!! Now I want to see it all for myself, with my greenery – yellary[4] eyes! Miss Held will join me at Southampton & go with me – & I shall take Edy.[5] Please dear little Stephen will you write a line to Mr Lawrence (or Mr Holzberg?) & ask that Ted may have some free time whilst I am there (about 3 days I shd say I could

[p. 4]

be there altogether –).

I believe I sent you £50 – half of the hundred Henry borrowed our last week in London – & that since then the clear £150 has been sent to Child's Weekly. Is that not so? But I must tell you that has been done to keep accounts straight in London – for at times here we have closed the theatre for a night or two which, of course, made a difference in my salary, & a few subscriptions, for instance, <to> the Actors Benevolent Fund which was I think £25, all this was from my £50 a week – so I think you may find the last week

[p. 5]

of our New York visit will be short in payment by 50 or perhaps £100!! I tell you so you may not say "Oh, what surprise"!! – I'm glad you like your new quarters so much – My house hunting must begin almost directly I get home, for the melancholy of Longridge Road I can stand no longer – Either Campden Hill or Earls Court (near the Gilberts or the Casellas) I should prefer – & the rent must not be more than £150. I don't want to buy a house – I might not like it – Oh, how glad I am to think of coming home again.

[p. 6]

I dare say you know by this time that Polixina plays Margaret in the Provinces during the autumn, whilst I toddle off for a good long holiday. I think of going for a month to Broadway in the Cotswold Hills first of all, & then to Italy!! to *Venice* – to see the Merchant! — Oh, think of it – *Venice*, for the first time!! Too good to be true = Don't you think Boo might manage the move into a new house for me whilst I'm away?

I see Mrs. Jopling is married again! My stars – it will be me next ----- ? ----

[p. 7]

Will you come to the wedding? – Are you painting, dear old Stephen – more "flicks" – I'll come to the cottage during the summer this year if you can put me up – for we "change the bill" at the Lyceum & I shall have many a night off – I have had here, you know, & that's why I am so much better no doubt – Edy is practising – Mrs Lockwood & the Bayard girls are waiting in another room for me, I'm writing (in bed) to you & I'm due

[p. 8]

for an "Olivia" matinee in an hour – I must go dear sweetheart – but I send you, & my best Gill my best love, & I thank her for the ducky little paper-knife she sent me by Charlton –

Love also to the boys!! – that does sound funny! & wholesale!

Your devoted old

Nell =

GARRICK, Vol. IV/3b

Envelope extant, postmarked 'MAR 3 88', New York; addressed to 'The Honble Stephen Coleridge, 7 Egerton Mansions, South Kensington, London, England'. Coleridge's annotation: 'This letter alludes to the birth of my dear Paul at 7 Egerton Mansions'.

1. Geraldine Coleridge.
2. Agnes Yarnall appears to have been influenced by Stephen Coleridge's stern letter of 1884 and to have resumed socializing with ET in spite of Mrs Yarnall's concerns about her reputation; see n. 9 to letter 187, above.
3. Edward Gordon Craig.
4. 'greenery yallery' was coined by W. G. Gilbert in *Patience*, first performed on 23 April 1881. It was associated with the aesthetic movement and the Grosvenor Gallery and referred to a colour scheme popular with them. See E. Partridge, *A Dictionary of Slang and Unusual English*, 5th edn (London: Routledge & Kegan Paul, 1961).
5. Edith Craig.

204. To Mamie Metcalf, 9 March 1888

My dear Mamie

No doubt you have attributed my silence to the true cause – I have been very busy – & have had crowds of birthday[1] letters to answer from American – English – Scotch – Irish – Italian – Swedish – Canadian – German – French – & Russian friends & have not half got through with them yet –

It was very kind of you to send me such a pretty gift & I like it much better because you have made

[p. 2]

it yourself – it is very novel being made of leather too – I never saw one before – Thank you my dear child very much indeed –

If you see Miss Aldrich tell her I think of her every day, & wish she were in my life – I thank you for your affectionate little letter & am

always sincerely yours

Ellen Terry =

The Buckingham
New York – March 9. 88 =

HARV

1. ET's birthday was on 27 February.

205. To Mr Palmer, 10 March 1888

Saturday 10. III. 88 =

Dear Mr Palmer –

I accept with great pleasure the seat offered me between Mrs Palmer[1] & my friend Mrs Croly – on Thursday 16th

"I have a daughter"! I wonder what I shall do with her on that day – where I shall bestow her to see "the show"? Perhaps Mrs Croly's child will be there –

Sincerely yours

Ellen Terry=

HARV

1. Queen Palmer; see n. 1 to letter 108, above.

206. To Augustin Daly, 17 March [1888]

Victoria Hotel – March 17=

Dear Mr Daly

I have "a night off" next Saturday – & will be so delighted to come to your play, if you can spare me a box for that night – Yours sincerely

Ellen Terry =

FOLGER, Y.c.434 (8)
Annotated 'Ellen Terry March 17/88'.

207. To [B. I Dasent], [24 March 1888]

May I advise you to go early – the goslings have sold more tickets than there are places.

FOLGER, Y.c.434 (9a)
Envelope extant; postmarked 'MAR 88', New York; addressed to 'B. I. Dasent, 24 Irving Place, New York City'; annotated 'From Miss Terry March 24 1888'.

208. To B. I. Dasent, 24 March 1888

The Buckingham

Dear Mr Dasent

Mr Roche tells me you care to come to the little performance at West Fifty-Fourth St on Monday evening – & so I enclose 2 seats – Do I in knowing Mr I. R. Dasent know your brother? If it be so I'm <sorry>, you have not cared to call upon me since I should have greatly cared

[p. 2]

to make yr acquaintance – You must not expect a ripe performance from the young people on Monday – my daughter takes part in it & I'm greatly excited over the event –

Sincerely Yours
Ellen Terry =

March 24 – 88=

FOLGER, Y.c.434 (9c)

209. To Joe Evans, 29 March 1888

29 March 1888
Wednesday 12 o'clock

My little brother

Darling Joe – We are stuck here in the mist, & it seems as if we are never to start – Mr St Gaudens[1] & his wonderful gift! – I will think you both gave it me , & live [illeg.] to deserve such good fortune – How good you have been to us – I cant [*sic*] speak words to tell you of our gratitude to you for your just being you – To Mother & Sister Anne our love & devoted thanks

[p. 2]

What a miss not to have begun to know each other when we might some years ago –

I'm like a bit of leather now – an hour ago I was one smart – but, "but theres [*sic*] nothing like leather" –

When I am able to I'll write – I love you dear dear brother with all my heart –

Leather Ellen –

NYPClub

1. ET was introduced to Saint Gaudens by Joe Evans; see *Memoirs*, p. 204.

210. To [Geraldine Coleridge], [3 April 1888]

For Tuesday, darling –
Oh, if I could but make a little time!! When the Amber Heart is out, may I come & stay a few days with you?
Nell

GARRICK, Vol. III/unnumbered
Envelope extant, postmarked 'APR 3 88', Chelsea; addressed to 'The Honble Mrs S. Coleridge, 7 Egerton Mansions, South Kensington'. This letter is bound out of sequence in the Garrick Club volume just after a letter dated 18 October 1887.

211. To Stephen Coleridge, 8 May 1888

Tuesday = May 8 =

No dear Stephen I think you will never get that house for £150 – if you can, I'll jump at it!! However, if you can get if for 170, or even £180, I shall still take it = All right I think dear, about the expense – remember, in a few weeks you'll have an extra £10 a week – then too I can't stay here any longer – I hate[1] the dull street so, with it's [*sic*] line of silly peering faces all along opposite, watching me when I come in & out when I get up in the morning & go to bed at night.

[p. 2]

They are welcome enough to see everything I do the Lord knows, *only*, without asking, it's so rude! & I hate it –

I'm not well – too queer to go to the New Gallery to day – & I did so want to! – I'm tired – think I was born tired – it's just overwork I know, & my holiday thank God is near at hand, but I must take care of myself, or I shall be breaking down before the work is over =
Does little Gill expect me to dinner next Sunday? At the mansion I suppose, not the country cottage.
Best love to her & to you

From Nell=

GARRICK, Vol. IV/4
Envelope extant; postmark illegible; addressed to 'The Honble Stephen Coleridge, 7 Egerton Mansions, South Kensington'; ET writes on the back 'I wd take it for 7 years – E.T.'

1. The horizontal stroke of the 't' in 'hate' appears to have been drawn several times.

212. To Edward Gordon Craig, 10 May 1888

May.10. 88 =

Darling Ted –

I have written for your summer clothes to be got for you, I have written for a fishing-rod for you (if you are a good lad). Now what have you got for me – I'm a woman – you're a man – you should try to give me more than I give you (?) – Have you given me more hard work? or a victory over your little temper – 'eh? If all the Masters are exceedingly kind to you & lenient (which I am certain they are) it's nothing particular that you shd field them back all in your power of trying-to-do, & obedience, & sweetness, for it's mere duty on your part to do it

[p. 2]

<but> supposing if any of them are exacting or impatient (which I very much doubt, considering how you boys must try them) then it becomes a slight virtue in you, & a little sort of gift to me, if you still with all your might, try to please better & to work better –

Remember dear <it's> your duty to please them, not the Master's duty to please you –!! It is perhaps rather more their duty to displease you boys, for I fear it seldom pleases us, (especially when we are young) to be told when we are not doing right. And when you think a thing out you are generally a sensible boy so "think" a little now & again, all by yourself, & argue against yourself, & you will do more

[p. 3]

good, than by discussing your fancied ills with other lads – Remember my darling boy I look for more in your nature, of fineness, & nobility than in other boys, for you have many advantages of life, which should not leave you a common-place, ordinary lad, & you should rather lead, towards good, than be led towards bad – The Tug of War!! – & you must win – but by Jove! You must never leave off pulling the rope, or the others have you over the line, & it's a sight harder work to get back again =

Here endeth my Sermon!

(Tho' I hope you will read it until you know it, for I write from my heart, to your little heart dear Teddy – open it love – & let in my words – quick! quick!! –

[p. 4]

About the Army House – For Xmas I have left that entirely to the judgement of the Masters – I wrote & told you so – And whether they decide to place you there, or decide you are to stay where you are, that decision is absolutely right, which ever it may be – Why of course! "it goes without the saying" – & I guess it will depend entirely on your own conduct, & obedience, as to whether you go there next term – prove that they can trust you, & then they will – + (You know darling you have lately proved to yourself (& to me) that you cannot trust yourself!!!) I saw Mr Lane last night at the Lyceum – he seems a very very nice man – at his

[p. 5]

asking, I am consenting that you shd have the boating – under certain strict conditions which he will write to the masters about. Ain't I a kind old Mummy? I shall be rather nervous for some time, so call your common sense into play, & don't be careless. I played my last act nicely last night all through Mr Lane! for he & I were talking of you just before it came on, in No 2 Box – & he spoke of you so sweetly, that it made me feel soft – & gooder – & happier, & then of course one does ones [*sic*] work better – I rather think dear that now with the boating in view, the Tricycle need not hurry itself – for we (Edy & I.)

p. 6]

are going down near Dixton, for the first two weeks of my holiday & it wd be very kind if you were to lend it to us for then, & we then might bring it on to you when we come later on to Germany – What do you think? Do you pay for your own posting stamps? Mind you answer this question for anyhow you are too extravagant with the Queen's Head – not when you send me a real letter, but when you send a line, or a circular in another cover when you cd enclose it in your letter! No particular news here. We are slaving at rehearsals[.] Henry is at rehearsal every day at ten oclock – & generally sticks there for 5 hours – He is the wonderfullest man – & his is *the* way to succeed. With all his great powers & popularity & he says, Work – Work – Work –

[p. 7]

& he Does "work, work work"! Says, & does it too – Edy recites next Wednesday[1] but I dare say she has told you ----

We are all pretty well – Poor Nanny Held has left the Palmers – I don't think they treated her kindly – at present she is staying with me – Little Minnie[2] has made a great success in "Bootles (Baby)" – Poor Polly is ill – & there's no more news –

God bless my boy ---------

I am his very loving

Mum –

HRC

1. Edith Craig gave a recital on 18 May 1888 in London; see note to letter 214, below.
2. Minnie Terry, daughter of Charles Terry and niece of ET.

213. To Stephen Coleridge, 15 May [1888]

Tuesday 15 – May

Dearest Stephen

Please send me down this evening without fail, a cheque for £50 – it is to make up the £200 for my New Gallery[1] shares – I haven't quite enough to do it by myself.

Send it by Cab to the Lyceum, only be sure & let me have it tonight –

Love to Gilly flower & the buds

Nell =

GARRICK, Vol. IV/5

1. Joe Comyns Carr and Charles Halevy opened the New Gallery in Regent Street at this time.

214. To Joe Evans, 30 May 1888

33 Longridge
Road – Earls
Court . May
30 – 88 =

Isn't America a long way off? You dearest Joe but you did send me a lovely letter all the way from there.

22 – Barkston Gardens . Earls Court

"Better something than nothing" the German folk say . this is the *17 Nov !! =* & I can only send my love (some of the best I have) to you, & the dear little Mother & Anna & tell you there's not a day but I think of you with gratitude & tenderness – I just can't write a letter that's all – We are all very happy & well-er, & in a nice new house

[p. 2]

Altho' I can scarcely be said to be "in it" yet, for I only returned from my travels yesterday & tomorrow I'm off to Birmingham, to begin rehearsals of a new play – "The Thane of Glamis & his attractive spouse" – (rather a clumsy title) ----- dear me! now I feel as if I could write along for some time ! but I must go & try on the robes of Gudrun & go to see a little Kid at the Hospital ----or else write to my dear little brother Joe------- I shall go to the Kid & the frocks!!!

Nell =

NYPClub
A press cutting attached to this letter describes Edith Craig making her first public appearance in England at the Horns Assembly Rooms, Kennington Park, where she recited Saxe's 'Song of Saratoga' and Loring's 'The Crimson and the Blue' while Miss Campbell recited Tennyson's 'The First Quarrell'. The event was in aid of funds for the South London Homes for the Aged Deserving Poor; annotated by ET '18 May 1888'.

215. To Edward Gordon Craig, 27 June [1888]

Wednesday 27 June

It's too too bad of me my Ted not to write more but these are bustling times I tell you – the holiday coming there's so much to be done – Then too I have taken a new house (we enter it in August)

No. 22. Barkston Gardens
Earls Court.

it's close by here – just the other side of the Earls Ct Rd & it's nice, I tell you!

Dear Edie acted at ~~St James's~~ Georges Hall last night – I send you the Programme & some notices – The Daily Telegraph is splendid! Just think! The first English Critic Clement Scott = she had two wretched parts to play but

[p. 2]

at least they were different. She was not as good as she was in "Barbara" in New York – & I long to see you & Edy do that little play together = just suits you both = Mr A. Longridge, the noble Author of "Woolgathering" is Freddy Kalisch, but there's no reason why you & Edy shd not get to know some funny German plays (wee ones) & translate 'em, & then we cd all three you & she & I adapt them to the English stage. Has Henry[1] written you anything about the Holidays & Lucerne? Do you know he is going to take us all there? To Lucerne! I know it well – the perfectest place. *Such* a drive from Lucerne to Interlaken = I'll write my plans to you shortly – soon= We may not be able to get to you quite so soon as your holidays

[p. 3]

begin, & if this is the case, I've arranged you go to Karlsruhe for a week (or perhaps two –) until you join us somewhere[.] If so you will stay with ~~the~~ lady who has had Charlie Fitzgerald living there the last 2 years[.] She is very kind & nice,

& you must make her like & respect you (not a very difficult task I guess –!!). I think of staying with Edy in Germany, close by you, even when your holidays are over! Won't that be fine? I am very much pleased your writing is much neater now – & you spell more carefully upon the whole – try darling boy from now though to do without a paper underneath – I used to do it I know, but it gives you strength of character to depend

[p. 4]

upon yourself, even in the small matter of writing, & not upon a line[2] – Don't forget – it will seem quite easy in a month's time = Oh, how I long for the holidays!! I must enquire & arrange all about your drawing lessons – but more of that anon! & also about your music – I met Mr Walter Lawrence's Father yesterday. – I like the Son the best = My Benefit comes off on the 7th = the last night of season. We don't change the bill = Very sorry about Pan – she must be having lots of botherations. I think you'll miss her when she leaves Heidelberg – Thanks for the photographs – What a funny

[p. 5]

boy ~~Phllips~~ "Phillips" seems to be!! Who is the little lady near you? I mean ".-----."= You do seem to be the man among 'em all. I like the other picture too – you & the welsh boy together: Did you get the Academy & New Gallery illustrated Catalogue. I sent 'em off to you some time since – Why yes by the way, "Dawn" was in one of 'em[.] You were doing it very well 'till you came to the drapery & then you cd not get along. Edy also is doing a book of Costume! She is copying all my framed costume things, into a book & they look very nice = I seem somehow my darling to have no news

[p. 6]

for you! Except, that, thank God, we are all fairly well – I go to Uxbridge for a few nights tomorrow[.] Edy & Tante go too, & Edie Lane & Audrey will visit us! Booie is pretty well, but she feels the heat – Write & tell her mother said she thought she wd like to hear from you – Henry sent you the Shakspere [*sic*] then? A very good Vol: I think don't you? Donelly be blowed he's a vulgar impudent fellow. Think of his daring to kneel on Shakspere's grave at S. on Avon!! – Unless perhaps it was to pray God to forgive him for trying to blast a fair & beautiful memory.

God bless you my dearest love

With truest affection I am every your devoted

Mother =

HRC
Annotated '1888'. The year is inferred as 1888, since she refers to moving house to 22 Barkston Gardens in the coming month of August.

1. Henry Irving took ET and family on holiday.
2. ET gave advice to her son on letter-writing, revealing the extent to which she took seriously the presentation on the page. Some of the early letters in this volume appear to have made use of a guide line as described here.

216. To [Edward Gordon Craig], 15 July [1888]

Sunday = 15 July

Here are some "Amber Heart" Photographs for my old sweetheart – The Honble. Stephen[1] has written to the Doctor about your going to Karlsruhe – you will be there a fortnight, & then pray god we meet, well & happy – I intended writing to the Doctor about a few shillings for you but my letters decrease, as my time diminishes = However I enclose for you as a little present one pound, & now dear Ted if it goes at once, remember you will then be at Karlsruhe without any money & I really cannot help it – you must learn to keep money, & not let it slip unheeded through buttery fingers – Money is very

[p. 2]

valuable= "with out it there is neither life nor love" = I've been told so, & I believe it, though these are scarcely the sentiments you wd expect your Mother to utter I guess! But I tell you, so you may begin at once to take care – "too late" are such awful words.

Now my darling I must tell you a friend of mine from New York, Mr William Purrington may come & see you – Give him hearty & courteous welcome & give time & manners to him – he is to be at Karlsbad, & I think will go & see you at Heidelberg, – or he may send for you to go & see him & his mother & sister = & then you may go for a day – On second thoughts I will send you 5/- only & when you get to Karlsruhe I

[p. 3]

will tell Mrs Pastor to give you the other 15/- I think this will help you – you weak little boy – You darling, don't think I cannot appreciate the difficulties= I do = but all you have to do is to learn to be strong – strong for honour & for the right – & you will!

The Theatre is shut, & now a few dinner & luncheon engagements & then I hope my holiday will really begin – Edy goes to Uxbridge tomorrow with Edie Lane & Louis Winter, & they are going to take a paint pot & disfigure the place. I know they'll spoil it, but after giving 'em permission to paint the Dresser green, I've

said they must go up to the attic, & there they may spoil, "make or mar", as much as they darned pleased!!
Make a good end-up my darling sweetheart at your school & please the Masters & then ((beigh money))! for our holiday. I shall bring or send the Tricycle for sure = I hope you & Charlie Fitzgerald will do duets together for Piano & Violin – I should love that – Encyclopedia my dear boy. Not "a Cyclopedia", as you write it – Yes I know the Longfellow bit, where it is most lovely.
God guard you my darling son I long to see you & feel your dear face against my own. Best love from all of us.

Your Mother.

HRC

1. Stephen Coleridge.

217. To Miss Mills, 20 July 1888

My dear Miss Mills

I'm not good at this sort of thing. Will the enclosed be of any service? If not, send me a line & I'll alter it – Remember, it will do for any Manager. When all is said, you'll find, that should he be in want of someone for his Theatre he'll have you, & if he isn't he won't! – Anyhow of course one can't sit down & fold ones hands – & I wish you "Luck"

[p. 2]

& Good Fortune where ever you may be. Edy & I are down here enjoying ourselves greatly – driving about the whole of the day & eating – drinking – sleeping, & laughing a great deal from morning until night, & in August we go to Lucerne, then on to Germany & Italy,[1] & perhaps we may meet in December.

I hope you are well

[p. 3]

& as jolly as usual

With very best wishes

Yours always sincerely

Ellen Terry =

The Audrey Arms
Uxbridge – July 20 = 88

SMA, ET-Z2,219a

1. ET was to go on holiday with her children and Henry Irving.

218. To Audrey Campbell, 20 July 1888

33. L. R'd Sunday

How I wished for you yesterday my darling little Audrey – I had quite an – old-time-day, at the "Pub"[1] & although little Edie Lane & my Edy felt it & liked it, still it wanted you more than any I know, to just enjoy yesterday along with me – for Nan (the old original-none-like-her-Nan) – came down with Mrs Maudsely & stayed the whole day there, & it was all lovely & only you wd have known *how* lovely it all was, &

[p. 2]

she was – We all came up to town together last train, last night – It was all lovely. The Drive all of us seated anywhere in the carriage except upon the cushions designed to be sat upon = The Brook – through which we all waded –(round a corner) so the coach man couldn't see our ankles – *etc *— !!!) – The Dinner at 7 (a great success –) & above all The music afterwards!!! – That was perfect joy – oh, how she plays & sings= & how she looks while she's a doin' it = she & Kay M– played

[p. 3]

lovely duets & the soft black & grey of Kay, & the red of Nan's head, was a sight! with the jet of gas in that rummy [?] little room shining down upon them. I called them Hoary & Gorey – Lord how we all enjoyed ourselves – & laughed — & it was all too much for the other dear old Nan "Lo – the poor Indian" had to retire into the next room & have it out = How I wished for you, all the time you'll never know – but Nan F-H does – we wrote "Audrey Arms" = very big in white paint on our best big tea tray &

[p. 4]

with the help of the Lord & Edy, & a new broom handle we shoved it out of [the] window where it hung to the admiration of all beholders = ~~Tomorrow~~ To day I'm up in town to luncheon with Kate,[2] to dine with the Casella's, & tomorrow I trot off to Winchelsea to Alice[3] – coming back next Thursday – Friday or Saturday = Don't yet know which – & then I suppose we all start for Lucerne on Sunday or Monday – Thanks for your letter my Audrey –

Do you mean to tell me you won't be in town until I am gone?

[p. 5]

nonsense – you, also, will be up in town, "Friday or Saturday – don't know yet which" = Will you be pleased to hear I have settled very definitely *not* to go to America – this time! – I had a bad time rather – because – you may be surprised to hear me say so – common sense, cried aloud to me it wd be better for me to go , & better for everybody concerned – but I couldn't – simply = & that's over = & now for Lady Macbeth – in which I feel certain I shall fail – but I mean try to win

[p. 6]

I wish I could be with you = where you are now – for a few days – Ask 'em to ask me! – they'll be delighted! I'll come on Thursday – my dear I can't sleep yet. – which you confess is provoking –!

Have you read Rudder Grange the Book of books for you to read out loud where you are now = Every line is a shout of jolly laughter, & you'll thank me for telling you of it when you come to Pomona = Bless your sweet face my cherub – You will write me one little line to The Cottage Winchelsea, & make glad the heart of

Your Nell =

UCLA

1. The Audrey Arms, Uxbridge.
2. Probably her sister, Kate Terry.
3. Alice Comyns Carr, who lived at Winchelsea.

219. To [William Winter], [July 1888]

Longridge Road
Tuesday

Sweet William –

& Louis – Goodbye I start tomorrow for the Continent, & you are away from The Grange, or I intended running round to see you, & kiss goodbye to Louis =

I can't thank you enough for writing those lovely lines in my Edy's book – nobody but you could put so much in so little – Thank you & thank you – I'm delighted to have had the chance of making better acquaintance with Louis – to KNOW him

[p. 2]

is to love him – he is great darling = Ask him not to forget me nor those young Demons of Uxbridge = By the way in a letter from Lizzie this morning she seems to know about Louis being at Uxbridge & yet does not appear to have recd a letter a long letter I wrote her some weeks since, nor a photograph which shd by this time have reached her! I addressed her Mrs W. Winter (Box 18) Tompkins-

ville P.O Staten Island N.Y. – is that right? Godbless you my Dear – my friend I shall hope to see you again not very far off –
Great haste you will "excuse" & believe me yr ever affectionate

Nell=

FOLGER
Annotated 'Ellen Terry Recd July 30 1888'.

220. To Edward Gordon Craig, 2 August 1888

HOTELS SCHWEIZERHOF & LUZERNERHOF
LUCERNE

Hotel Schweizerhof =
Lucerne =
August 2. 1888 =

Here we are my pippen – Henry Edy – Tante & Nutter[.] All letters to be directed here for the next month, since these are our headquarters, we making our excursions from this place. Be quick & send me a letter quick – quick – quick – I think you have recd a letter from Mr Purrington – my American friend – & I hope you have answered

[p. 2]

it – if not, sit right down & do so at once – About next Saturday week we shall send for you!! This is a beautiful place, but oh, the rain – Is it the same with you? We were all weighed this morning before our holiday begins, & then at the end of it we shall be weighed again. You see I must lay on some fat for Lady Macbeth! Did you get a very clever Pamphlet upon Donnelly's idiotic ideas Shaksperian? Henry sent it you – the best

[p. 3]

thing that has been said I think – I'm tired after being in the Train all night so will end up – Mind you write me here*at once* – & tell me how you *think* you will like being at Fran Pastors – Love to Charlie – I fear he is only staying at Karlsruhe just for you – it's very kind = God bless you my darling boy. We all send our best love –

Your old
Mummy:

Has the Tricycle yet arrived?

HRC
Headed notepaper for the hotel.

221. To Marie Casella, 9 August [1888]

Thursday – Aug. 9. Schweizerhof = Lucerne

Dearest Marie – I write as soon as I definitely know – quite for certain, that instead of my lines lying in October in Venice I shall now most probably be in Berlin!! for I think I have to be there to look after some fresh schooling for Ted, & Henry will take me to Venice during this holiday of his, instead, unless it is too piping hot – any way in a few days that will be settled & I'll write then further = It is perfectly lovely here, but for my part I like a much quieter place – but Henry asked

[p. 2]

"is it a lively place", & being told it was, he settled upon it for our headquarters from which to make excursions. Yesterday & to day have been splendid & very warm, but it seems to me that if it continues warm Venice will be the last place in the world to go to! However if I get the chance off I go of course – my dear old Ted arrived last night & is looking splendid & seems rather nice I think & improved – he & Edy are glued together = I wish one of "the Casella gals" wd drop me a line & tell me when you all start on your holiday & where you go – Mr Toole[1] & his daughter

[p. 3]

have just arrived here for 2 days on their way back home.

You know my little friend Audrey Campbell don't you my darling? Well she is engaged to be married – I've no news except that Henry is getting fat!! & I'm getting fatter – when our holiday is ended we shall only be fit for Barnum's Show![2] – or as an advertisement for Thorley's food for cattle – That imp Miss Edy has been using my pen I find – please therefore to "excuse" my wretched writing.

[p. 4]

Here we are![3]
Meph = & Margaret,[4] after their holiday!

We are all going for a drive now – – will write further when it's settled about Venice.

SMA, ET-Z2,064

The date has been inferred from the address. During this period in 1888 ET was on holiday in Lucerne.

1. See n. 5 to letter 118, above.

2. Phineas T. Barnum (1810–91), American showman. See *American National Biography*.
3. ET has a sketch here of herself and Henry Irving in costume considerably overweight, reproduced in K. Cockin, 'Ellen Terry and Henry Irving: A Working Partnership', in R. Foulkes (ed.), *Henry Irving: A Re-Evaluation of the Pre-Eminent Victorian Actor-Manager* (London: Ashgate, 2008), pp. 37–48.
4. ET played the role of Margaret and Irving of Mephistopheles in *Faust*.

222. To [Audrey Campbell], 22 August [1888]

Lucerne – 22 – Aug –

Darling – We leave here tomorrow for Basle & on,[1] the next day to Cologne (Hotel Du Nord), & on Saturday morning we start for Berlin to stay there some time – So if you send a word at once to Cologne (telling me how you are) or after that to Hotel de Rome – Berlin – Remember as I write a letter may be coming here to me from you if so I'll get it tomorrow before I start –

I pray you are better & happier
With tenderest love your Nell=
Henry & Joe go to London Saturday =

HRC
Envelope extant; postmarked '22 VIII 88', Luzern; addressed to 'Miss Audrey Campbell, Hotel de l'Europe, Aix le[s] Bains, Savoie, France'; annotated '1888'.

1. ET was on holiday with her children and Henry Irving.

223. To [Audrey Campbell], [August 1888]

Hotel du Nord = = Cologne =
Don't we wish you were here! & I know you'd love it. I wonder would Pa have let you come with us? Never thought of it 'til now & have just asked for E.D.L.[1] = She "can't guess" she says – I guess *I*can guess! I feel quite wonderfully different already, altho' this morning we all felt very queer – but we have been for a 2 hours drive in the cool of the evening, & now we have polished off a rather good supper – sitting in the gardens writing this with the old moon above us, I tell you it's just poyfect. – we go on tomorrow by the early train to Dresden – Edy[2] meets us there on Saturday – we stay there Sunday, & most like the whole of Monday – & on Tuesday start for Krummunhubel – our address in Dresden is Hotel Bellevue, Dresden – & afterwards – Krummunhubel –

Riesen gebirge
Schlesien – Germany

[p. 2]

That poor little Victoria! I wonder how she is? You great ugly big Cowards to let the little thing go all alone = go out to her at once or else come to us!! I cut all Nannie's hair off this afternoon, & now send you a lock of it! She is very handsome now = I've met with lots of folk I know – but not, not Pur[3] = poor Pur – dear Pur = I wrote Boo this morning – also Henry – also Ted – also Edy – also not Pur! poor Pur!! = Edie L. is going to read out loud every day and Nannie and I hope Edy! – but I don't "reckon without my" – Edy! – We wish you were here – Why did I not ask Pa? Bestest love to you my pet – This is just to let you know we are flourishing & to send you the H.A.I.R = Write to me often like a real Audrey, & don't get into mischief this time in my absence – Your own old

Nell –

UCLA

1. Edie Lane; see n. 4 to letter 163, above.
2. Edith Craig.
3. Possibly one of the Purringtons, an American family with whom ET was friends.

224. To [Elizabeth Rumball], 29 August 1888

Hotel de Rome. Berlin
Aug-29-88

Darling Boo – Your letters have come all right – from Lucerne as well. All right about Ted's shirts = Berlin is a lovely city – so clean & such nice shops – splendid – A beautiful Park – & beautiful Soldiers (!) & beautiful Music everywhere –

[p. 2]

if only the "darned" *Bands* would give over playing day & night – Just fancy "Olivia" going to be done here for the first time by Possart – Of course we shall go & see it – I hope you will not go to Brancaster – really I think it is unsafe. Mrs Gibson *I* say, for a fortnight at least, & then if you like it, for longer = Yes by all means the inner door to the Hall & the Bells ringing up stairs – (the next is for Mr Roberts –)

[p. 3]

Both children are very well – They were both *frightfully* naughty 2 days ago but I told them that the slightest repitition [*sic*] of such conduct & I'd pack Ted back to Heidelberg, & put Edy in a Convent for 2 years, & then finish my holiday peacefully & quietly alone(!) for I'd bear not one thing further from them

– They were just devils – & there's no doubt about it, that at Karlsruhe, Ted was as bad as ~~bad~~ as a naughty boy could be.

[p. 4]

– There – "so much for Buckingham"!! – I dare say you have seen Henry by this time – Give my love to the darling boy & tell him we are having a Capital time, & that when the 16 Sep is past & we have seen Barmay in his new Demetrius we shall be nearly ready to leave Ted in Heidelberg, & settle down to a different sort of life – quite quiet – of course it's much better fun for Ted to be in a town & see all

[p. 5]

the plays & hear some splendid music – besides he & Edy are having the best of music lessons now & I like this place immensely = & the Barmays are – oh, so kind=

I want you to go to the Groves & ask them to send me 4 or 5 photographs of "Olivia" & "The Vicar" – for the sake of the dresses – at once please – not big pictures – just Cabinets= I shall stay on here at The Hotel de Rome.

[p. 5]

It made me quite ill at first, but of course we must not suppose we are not to have any trouble with them – suppose or not suppose, we shall. At present all goes well – Wonder how long it will last = !! I think now I'll finish up for we are going to an Oculist about Ted's eyes –

God bless you dear – Love to all my friends & love to my best friend Booie from her Nelly=

SMA, ET-Z5,004

225. To Bram Stoker, 10 September 1888

Hotel de Rome =
Berlin – Sep 10 . 88-

My dear Bram

I wish "it" divided into equal parts – please – one half to be "lodged," the other half sent to me (here or wherever I may be .) =

//How did Florence[1] like Captain Tree ? I must tell her some day what H. said of it – she wd appreciate what is too good fun to be lost = I hope you didn't let her overdo her strength whilst she was in Switzerland, you great big dear old darling stupid Bram! I've heard about Parsifal from 5 different ~~peop~~ persons who saw it this year – Now I must gather from you & Florence when I see you, & I guess I shall be puzzled finally –

[p. 2]

Madame Nordica[2] gave me a wonderfully *vivid* impression how it all looked – how it all – listened ! I think she is a very bright woman = I am very well thank you Bram, & the 2 pickles are exceedingly conductious [*sic*] = Ted sends you back the "sympathetic kick", but nothing will induce Edy to part with that "Kiss"! – The Barmays are such nice folk – I'm sure you'd like them – so gentle & generous & simple – their's [*sic*] is a delightful home – & being there a good deal, as we all are, helps to make my holiday delightful. I rather think of returning to England towards the end of October – but I shall go to some sea side place for a while before coming back to rehearsals –

[p. 3]

We are all getting on well with our German, & get great fun out of the Theatres – going to some place of amusement nearly every night = Berlin is a very joyous place it seems to me = German Art of all kinds is a little "too German", else there is much to divine, & a performance of Romeo & Juliet we saw tonight, – (it's now only a few minutes past 10, & we walked home after the play –), – was really good = Dont [*sic*] mention that I've written to you – (I don't mean Henry of course –) Hoping Noel is quite well again now, & with most affectionate regards to you & F

Yrs ever & hers
Eleanora –

CLAREMONT

Envelope extant; postmarked '10 9 88', Berlin; addressed to 'Bram Stoker Esq, Theatre Royal, Glasgow, Scotland'.

1. Florence Stoker, Bram's wife.
2. Lillian Norton (1857–1914), American opera singer known as Madame Nordica, who had by this time performed in New York and Milan. Her husband, Frederick Gower, had died in 1885. See *American National Biography*.

226. To [Stephen Coleridge and others], 15 September [1888]

Berlin – 15 – Sep

Dearest young people –

I was glad to hear you are in ~~Heaven~~ – Venice = I shall expect a sketch – a "flick" – for my new house!! When do you return to England? Now 2 or 3 lines & that's all, for I have neuralgia =

1st – Thank you for the cheque dear Stephen = Bram Stoker sent me the first weeks [*sic*] money entire (the Season began at Glasgow on the 10th) ~~After that~~ & now for the future will send me 30 & lodge 30 at the Bank = When I begin work again at the Lyceum it will be more =
2 – Ted returns to Heidelberg ~~next~~ Saturday = I want you please to give them notice at the College (if notice now be necessary) that Ted in all probability will leave Heidelberg the end of the term – He must now go to a school where

[p. 2]
nothing but German is spoken & I think the school should be here in Berlin = I am exceedingly obliged to all the masters for the trouble they have taken with the youth = – & regret he has not been wiser ~~than~~ & taken more advantage of the opportunity they have given him = I wrote to Mr Lawrence & asked all about the Karlsruhe affair – he answered my letter politely enough, & ---- it made me ill = for I had to tell Ted he had behaved like a snob, & had broken his promise to me & – well, no good talking of it all now. –
For the last 5 weeks both children have been exemplary in their conduct – doing German & music every day & getting on excellently with German speaking =
I think of leaving Berlin for England about the 2nd of October. I am going to take my mother to the sea somewhere for a fortnight =

[p. 3]
Herr Hollander (who is the Herr Director here of most of the best musical affairs) is teaching Edy splendidly & if he & his wife – a very nice lady – will consent to take her, I shall leave Edy with them for a year probably – she wd have a lesson every ~~day~~ other day from him, & her practising wd be superintended by one of his pupils – a lady – she wd have German, French, & drawing lessons also – Edy is very much interested in her music & is always practising!! I have been asked to act here – & have declined of course – Think of the Beatrice & Portia speaking one lingo, & the rest another language altogether!! We are all well (except the last 2 days I've had this severe neuralgia) & very happy = Where are your children?

[p. 4]
Send me a line or two quickly here, & tell me your movements. Mind, whilst on the spot, that you visit Verona – Padua – Mantua – Best love to you both, & darling Gill don't over-exert yourself by rushing about.

Lady Macbeth interests me beyond expression how much – I fear she will be beyond my expression !

Your loving Nell =
Hotel de Rome – Berlin =
Sep 15 =

GARRICK, Vol. IV/6

227. To Stephen Coleridge, [11 October 1888]

'Ammersmith

Please dear Stephen do not send in deed – or lease – or what you call it – just yet – as I find ongoing [*sic*] to [the] mansion this morning that the paint is all wet & varnishing not done[.][1] I have been obliged to put a stop to any

[p. 2]

moving in – on this account – as it is quite out of the question = And now – as I am unable to take possession – I am — ! if I am going to pay rent from Sep 29. Do you see? I daresay it may be a fortnight more before I can let my household removal by road – take place!

Nell=

GARRICK, Vol. IV/7

Envelope extant; postmarked 'OC 11 88', Weybridge; addressed to 'The Hon Stephen Coleridge, The Cottage, Addlestone, Surrey'.

1. ET refers to her taking up residence at 22 Barkston Gardens, a four-storey house off Earls Court Road, with a residents' garden.

228. To Stephen Coleridge, [21 October 1888]

26 Ethelbert Crescent –
Margate =

Dearest Stephen – I have been ill here & obliged to get Dr Hutchinson down from London – I'm weak, & the news about Ted has not strengthened me! When I hear from Lawrence (I telegraphed him for particulars –) I will write to you dear – at present I'm just obliged to keep still & quiet, Dr Hutchinson says I must stay on here until Friday week at least – I telegraphed my Father[1] to meet the youth at the station & take care of him for a few days.[2] Directly

[p. 2]

I hear from Heidelberg I'll ~~let~~ write to you, & I hope when you hear you'll write to me – I won't see the boy – for many reasons – one, that I shall be unable to do my work if I go – do anything but rest for a week.

I can't write – I'm much better to day than I was yesterday – have been poisoned in some manner or another & have become completely prostrated –

Best love to little station-left-Gill.

Yr loving
Nell=

GARRICK, Vol. IV/8
Envelope extant; postmarked 'OC 21 88', Margate; addressed to 'The Hon Stephen Coleridge, 7 Egerton Mansions, South Kensington, London'.

1. Ben Terry; see n. 3 to letter 1, above.
2. Edward Gordon Craig had been expelled from his college in Heidelberg.

229. To Stephen Coleridge, 23 October [1888]

36 Ethelbert Crescent
Margate – 23 – Oct –

I do not misunderstand you my dear Stephen but I do think you are sometimes the silliest gentleman I ever met with, and – sometimes appear to be the most uncharitable –

I am unlikely to "minimise the boys' [*sic*] present danger", on the contrary I think this is one of the most dangerous moments of his life –

Dear friend I know how earnest you are, & how with all your heart you serve me but you are so very unreasonable ~~at times~~ & – – at least in

[p. 2]

manner & expression, – so hard, that you often thwart the good you intend= In this case for instance as to the lad being "unfit to enter any other school" because of this foolish freak it is simply ridiculous to say such a thing, whatever we may pretend to Ted, for his narrow wisdom = The boy is not a bad boy but he is unlimitedly foolish & undisciplined, and — he is 16! It seems to me that many at 35 might be in proportion better diciplined. [*sic*] ---- (You and I, are, of course, exceptional! – Ah this is stupid of me, for naturally

[p. 3]

we wish our children to be better than ourselves =) ~~It seem~~

I must take time to consider this affair, & for a week can do nothing but consider – for I've had a sharp attack of illness which has left me very weak. Meanwhile my Father is looking well after the boy & making him do lessons regularly & I shall certainly not see him myself. That was <my> instant idea, & yours too I find – I shall feel very grateful for ~~[illeg.]~~ advice in this matter from 3 or 4 of my friends – Henry Irving has given me his – (or rather is giving it! – since he in his turn is seeking counsel upon the subject from authorities —)

[p. 4]

— & others also are: helping me = If you will give me your advice I shall value it exceedingly as coming from the love of one of my best friends =

Best love to my dear little Gill.

Nell =

GARRICK, Vol. IV/9
Envelope extant; postmarked 'OCT 23 88', Margate; addressed to 'The Hon Stephen Coleridge, 7 Egerton Mans, South Kensington'.

230. To Rev. E. Wilkinson, [21 October 1888]

dilemma dilemma dilemma dilemma

Dear Mr Wilkinson
<I am in a sudden dilemma>[1] & ~~I~~ am going to ask you to do me a great kindness = & to help me by helping my boy = & in this manner – His first schooling was with you & <it> was an uninterruptedly happy time <for him> – then he went to Bradfield for 2 years, & then <as I wished> ~~wishing~~ him to ~~know~~ speak German ~~thoroughly~~ well ~~I sent~~ & to be made to work ~~harder~~ I sent him to Heidelberg. He has been there just a year – the masters were exceedingly kind to him, but complainded of his laziness, & sometimes of foolish impertinence ~~but~~ they all ~~seemed to~~ said they liked the boy.

[p. 2]

~~Yesterday~~ I am not well & am staying with my Mother at Margate gathering strength for a great deal of hard work which lies before me in December – Yesterday I was startled & distressed to receive the following telegram from Heidelberg – " Wardell ---------
Wondering & pondering upon the best course to pursue I have come to this conclusion = That it is best the young gentleman shall not find it an easy thing to rush from his duty at school, to "Clover" in a Mothers [*sic*] arms – therefore it is best I do not see him (at least ~~for~~ for a little while) & his Grandfather ~~therefore~~ meets him tomorrow at Charing X & will take care of him for a few days until I decide <what further> = Meanwhile I don't know his offence – but if (& I feel I could

[p. 3]

pledge my life that it is so)* if* I find by tomorrows letters from Germany that there has been *no* ~~vice shown~~ vicious fault shown by the lad, but probably some fault of ~~ignorance, omm~~ omission – ignorance, or grave foolishness, then I beg you will help me in my perplexity by ~~consenting to~~ allowing him to come to you & join in lessons for 2 ~~week~~ 3 or perhaps even 4 weeks, whilst Mr Coleridge & I find another school for him in Germany = I have <only> lately parted from Ted ~~(only about~~ having gone to Germany to ~~spend~~ be with him in his holidays – He is just the same lad he was when he was with you

[p. 4]

& you were kind to him, only older & stupider because he thinks he's wiser = If you will consider my request I will of course forward you the Masters [*sic*] letter if you desire it – I fear I can't hear before Tuesday, & the boy arrives tomorrow, however my Father will take care of him only the quicker he gets to work again the better I feel it wd be for him = It wd be such a friendly kind thing of you to do = of such inestimable ~~of~~ advantage to the boy to go to no new school for so short a time, that I beg you to help me ~~but~~ by doing this thing, which I quite understand whilst I'm asking it, to be no common kindness – As haste is of the greatest importance ~~may~~ will you let me hear from you as soon as you possibly can –

SMA, ET-Z2,286

The date is inferred from the reference to the telegram ET received from her son's school in Germany.

1. There are numerous alterations to this letter, suggesting that it may have been a draft from which ET made a fair copy to be posted. It seems unlikely that she would have sent a letter which revealed so much uncertainty about spelling and expression.

231. To Stephen Coleridge, [27 October 1888]

Saturday =

Dear Stephen – Will you please send me the letter Mr Lawrence wrote to you. The instant I heard about Ted I telegraphed to L. for full particulars. I will send you his letter directly I get it back from Henry.//I expect you have guessed it – In thinking of helping hands in this time of necessity Mr Wilkinson came in proscession [*sic*] to my minds [*sic*] eye

[p. 2]

& I wrote to him even before I heard from Lawrence, and asked him to take Ted if it were only for 2–3 ~~or even~~ or 4 weeks – & telling him I expected a letter from Lawrence & ~~wd bring it him~~ at once wd let him have it before he sd decide to take the boy. There's a great deal of the Angel in W. & his letter to me was so kind, that I determined to go & see him, & get something settled to ease my great distress of mind – for want of sleep & your jumping to the worst conclusions had

[p. 3]

nearly sent me out of my wits – Of course it wd be absurd to trouble the W's with a great boy <like Ted> for any length of time, but his beautiful kindness just when one wanted help is another proof of what I've always felt, that almost every other person you meet in this strange & difficult world is an angel, & I thank God I don't meet them "unawares" – Please send me quickly Lawrence letter.

Yrs. Affec'ly
Nell

All who know Gill must be convinced of her "goodness" – as to "sound judgement" – ~~that will be bettered I should think by years , & experience~~.

[p. 4]

that will be bettered I should think by years , & experience =

GARRICK, Vol. IV/10

Envelope extant; postmarked 'OC 27 88', Margate; addressed to 'The Hon Stephen Coleridge, 7 Egerton Mansions, South Kensington, London'.

232. To Stephen Coleridge, 2 November [1888]

Nov – 2 –

My dear Stephen – I hope by this time, that Johnnie is hims [*sic*] dear little self again & your great anxiety past – Have you heard from Mr Lawrence yet? If not I shall write to him (of course I wd rather you did once more, instead.)

~~Making every allowance for the temptation that (it was entirely Mr L as I am convinced) Mr Lawrence~~ I know (no one better) what an exceedingly thoughtless, careless & lazy boy, Ted is, but it = seems to me that if every schoolmaster expelled every boy who was thoughtless, careless & lazy, it wd be peculiar – as for obedience I thought that was *taught* in schools – the boy has always been obedient to me during his holidays, & expelling a boy & so handicapping his future career is a course which were I a man & [in] your place (of friend to me & to the boy) shd not go unrebuked = Remember all that has been said against Ted has been by Lawrence who disliked him & was disliked by him.

[p. 2]

This morning brought me a beautiful letter from Mr Wilkinson who speaks well of Ted & advises for him in the immediate future one of 3 courses – I'll forward you his letter the day after tomorrow. He will keep him until Christmas so to gain time = ~~Next~~ Tomorrow week I come to town, & on the 18th start for Birmingham for my regular rehearsals, & then on for 5 weeks of incessant work – every day & every evening =

I'm better than I was, but even a miles [*sic*] walk or 2 hours "go in at" my part tires me considerably. The best reports about Edy from the people she is with

– & she is practising her music 5 hours a day & sings in the Choir, which is very good for her.

Tired to death – can't write another line. Nell=

GARRICK, Vol. IV/11

233. To Stephen Coleridge, 4 November 1888

Dear Stephen – Mr Lawrence has a right to make his own rules for his own school, & I do not say he has been unjust , but he has been jolly unmerciful & <(to the boy, & inconsiderate to me.)> I can not but hope that his "vulgar night work", will be treated <with> more consideration (!) "in the sweet bye & bye," & that a softer punishment than expulsion may be found to fit his case – But I'm sick of the theme & cannot but

[p. 2]

be glad for the boys [*sic*] sake that I'm not quite as stern as you & Mr Lawrence = As to my spoiling the boy he has been away from me for 5 years, & I have in writing & ~~[illeg.]~~ <personally> begged his masters to treat him with the greatest severity if severity were necessary. – I want no "excuses" made for Ted – he has none for his foolery – but I won't have a stain of viciousness imputed

[p. 3]

to as white a nature as ever was God made[1] – You did impute this, but like a dear fine fellow as of course you are, you confess you were in error, & <you> cannot find fault with me for defending my own cub! Ted is <my kitten> – only half made up, – like Richard – & never will be a scholar – but tho' I'm sorry <for that> I'm never going to believe him

[p. 4]

black before he's black. It seems to me it's *very* difficult for any of us to do the thing we wish but ~~as~~ the song says – "It's no matter what you do if your heart be ever true" – & I pray Ted's heart will ever be "true to Poll" – "Poll", standing for – Well, you know ~~as well~~ we all know what Poll does stand for —

Let's talk of something

[p. 5]

else please.

Poor little ~~Johnnie~~ Jack – Poor little Gill! – hope they are both better now & will get quite right very very soon –

Please send me a cheque for Edy's people by return – Every first of the month I am to receive a "report" of the damsel together with her "bills" from Mr Holländer for her music, French, German & Drawing lessons, & her Pension expenses. The report was excellent – they say she is a most contented good girl & very industrious (!) ~~practicing~~ doing daily lessons of 7 hours, & is very obedient – ~~I don't~~ & 8 hours
Mr Holländer in Berlin stands better than Mr Dannreuther does in London she cd not get better musical instruction, & altogether I don't think £20 a month at all expensive – They have no other ~~lady~~ person staying with them, & only took Edy because their sister in England is an old friend of mine, & because Edy showed great promise as a Piano pupil. Mr H wrote his report on the first & sent me his receipt so I want him to ~~get~~ hear from

[p. 6]

me as soon as possible, so please send me the cheque (£20-12-6-) as quickly as you inconveniently can! –

I'm by no means well – sleeping scarcely at all – it's terrible= – & we come up to town Saturday or Sunday next. Then a week in London slaving at my dresses with Mrs Carr, & Henry comes up on the 18th to take me down to Birmingham

[p. 7]

for rehearsals – & no – mistake – about – it!!

Love to Gill & the babies – "Excuse" this rigmarole

From your loving

Nell =

Margate – Nov – 4 – 88 =

GARRICK, Vol. IV/13

Envelope extant; annotated by ET: 'Cheque to be made payable to Alexis Hollaender $20-12-6'.

1. Stephen Coleridge has written against this in the margin of the bound volume of letters '!!! poor dear blind Nellie!'

234. To unidentified, 5 November 1888

Miss Ellen Terry
26 Ethelbert Crescent
Cliftonville
Margate

Just had serious telegram from Toole from Edinburgh Flossie[1] critical state 3 doctors – Toole given up engagement this week in Carlisle – best love

SHAK

Telegram from ET; in unidentified hand; headed notepaper for Mr Henry Irving and the Lyceum Company tour (listing seven different dates from 10 September in Glasgow to 19 November in Birmingham).

1. Florence Toole, daughter of J. L. Toole; see n. 5 to letter 118, above.

235. To Stephen Coleridge, [5 November 1888]

Monday

Well dear Stephen I will send more weekly in a very little while but not just yet – not 'till I get settled at 22 – When I was in Berlin I bought linen which was sadly wanted at home, & the bill for that, and for 2 or three other things was paid for at the time by Miss Held who was with me – Altogether I had from her just £50, & so that's what I've been doing lately with my money – each week paying her 10 pounds – but soon now I shall send each week to the bank £60: – but not just yet. ~~Such things as~~ Thank you for sending Mr Hol–

[p. 2]

länder's cheque so promptly – Dear Stephen I don't think it is at all expensive to pay for what Edy gets – & the people with whom she lives are so exceptional. I cannot but think myself very lucky, if all goes on as well as it has begun with her.

I do trouble you dreadfully. I am so sorry, but I can't help it!

I think I'll catch this post – (?)

Nell=

GARRICK, Vol. IV/14

Envelope extant; postmarked 'NO 5 88', Earls Court; addressed to 'The Hon Stephen Coleridge, 7 Egerton Mansions, S. Kensington, London'.

236. To Edward Gordon Craig, 8 November 1888

Margate= Nov 8 – 88=

Dearest boy – Yes the one drawing is most careful, but I can say nothing whatever good for the rest – I don't call it at all a good show for a week! Next week let it be better. "Nothing to copy"!! What do you mean? You have 2 Shakspere's with you, surely – & isn't one a new one?

There's a man, Mr Herbert Railton, who draws most beautifully in the English Magazine, I shall ask Mr Wilkinson to give you pocket money (while he

[p. 2]

very kindly keeps you with him) the same as the other boys*less*sixpence a month –

Then I'll tell you what I'll do – I'll give you this year for your Christmas-box all the numbers, bound, of the "English Illustrated Magazine", from the beginning – I think it's been going on for 2 years – Now ask Mr Wilkinson if there could be a nicer present? – Just think what a lovely little Library you are getting together – & they are such lovely friends – good books –

[p. 3]

Then I will see that you get the fresh number every month ~~week~~ <you paying first> – I think it is the best illustrated magazine we have – there is nowhere, such a six-pennies worth!! I wd go in for a bit now for drawing landscape – & nothing that isn't beautiful (your tree in yr last sketch was good) & "drop", Gordon Browne for a while = You want more breadth & Herbert Railton combines that with the greatest delicacy of drawing & carefulness –

[p. 4]

How odd the sister of the boy you "fagged" for, being at (Tunbridge)! – Did I tell you I had splendid report of your sister? – You will be very sorry I know to hear, that poor Florrie Toole is dead – So young & pretty – it's too terrible – & it has nearly finished poor dear Mr Toole & the Mother their boy died, just about the same age, & now they have no more children – I sent 2 white hearts to-day in flowers for the poor girls [*sic*] grave – (she is to be buried to day –) from

[p. 5]

Edy & Teddy Wardell & wrote on the card ---- "Death lies on her like an untimely frost

Upon the fairest flower of all the field"[1] –

Poor old Justin too, is terribly cut up – & Henry grieves sorely for his old friend Toole = I go down on Sunday week to Birmingham to rehearse Lady M – I've too much to do, & I can't sleep, so it's wonderful that I'm as

[p. 6]

well as I am – Now during the very busy time that is approaching, I may not be able to write regularly, but on no consideration must you miss yr Sundays letter to me, or I must complain at once = We go back to London today & I have a weeks [*sic*] very hard work before me – My grateful greeting & kindest regards to Mr & Mrs Wilkinson – & my tenderest love to you my darling = Grandmama sends love, & Tante, & Drummie also! Yesterday I went a-sailing oh, it was cold!!

God bless you & guard you – Mummy

HRC

1. Shakespeare, *Romeo and Juliet*, IV.v.28–9.

237. To Stephen Coleridge, [17 November 1888]

Friday night

22 Barkston Gardens,
Earls Court, S.W.

Dear Stephen

First, thank you for the wee bookie. It's just lovely – best of all I like the four lines to Geraldine = You said them, or wrote them, to me once but I'd no idea they were yours! –

Your letter to Lawrence was very nice I thought – & temperate (for you!) just as I shd wish – Of course I wd rather not have any bother about the money if it came to that, although I can't say I see much

[p. 2]

for the £31-15-4= still that does not so much matter – & it's nothing ~~since~~ since we have received his assurances that he does not think my boy a vicious scamp – not that I ever imagined he did – the fact is my dear Stephen they are very weak to be obliged to expel a lad for insubordination =

About that precious Tricycle. Do advise me – It cost me a good bit to send it out in a packing case & locked up to be free from damage – It was in perfect condition then, just 2 months ago, Ted could not have used it more than half a dozen times, & it must

[p. 3]

have been in proper condition ~~to have taken~~ <when he took> that most unfortunate ride of 20 miles – Then am I, I wonder, to understand the masters have paid £5-7-6- since Ted has left? It seems so – The other boys constantly went out on their tricycles – Are their parents charged in that absurd fashion for such a preposterous item! I've just been writing Master Edward a long letter, & have now added a P.S. asking him all about the tricycle – I go down to Birmingham tomorrow, or the next day, but although I feel much better, I am scarcely as strong

[p. 4]

as I ought to be for the months [*sic*] terrific work which lies before me – we hope to produce Macbeth on the 22 – if not, immediately after Christmas, & I'm as nervous as a Cat about it. I've been staying with Lord & Lady Macbeth at their place in Scotland (Glamis Castle) & I find she is not in the least like that clever portrait of her by Siddons – & between you & me, I think the portrait far finer, as a great standing-out figure – 'tho' she should not have been made masculine – she's *quite* feminine[1] = When I come back I want to ask you a few things about her – Love to Gill & the children –

Yrs. Affec'ly

Nell –

GARRICK, Vol. IV/14

Envelope extant; postmarked 'NO 17 88', Earls Court; addressed to 'The Hon Stephen Coleridge, 7 Egerton Mansions, South Kensington, London'. Headed notepaper for 22 Barkston Gardens, Earls Court SW.

1. ET draws a long upward-sloping line here.

238. To Mrs Jeune, 19 November [1888]

Birmingham!

Queens Hotel – 19 Nov.

My dear Mrs Jeune – Please "excuse" this paper, & take my thanks upon it for your kind invitation to drive – I shd be much delighted, only, I'm a little too far off for you to fetch me I fear!!! For I'm at Birmingham – came here yesterday & tomorrow we begin rehearsals for Macbeth.

You will be glad I think to hear our dear Henry Irving is very well, but looks tired – & no wonder! –

It was naughty of you to trouble to write, but it was very nice to hear from you. The Alexanders are looking exceedingly well, & seem very jolly & I dine with them tomorrow – I have moved into a new home & I enclose the ~~new~~ address.

In haste, Affectionately Yours

Ellen Terry

SMA, ET-Z2,202

Headed notepaper, Mr Henry Irving and the Lyceum Company tour 1888 (listing seven different dates from 10 September in Glasgow to 19 November in Birmingham).

239. To Audrey Campbell, [November 1888]

Queens Hotel

And did you get home tired & cold, & *do* you think me just having to have let you go alone?

Oh, how I asked before THE hour came – & the train was an hour late!! – That poor dear thing from 11. to 6.30 – & oh, how green he was from fatigue & so ill – no voice – glad enough was I to be there, tho' my fatigue was awful too – need I tell you any rest whatever – for even one [illeg.] minute was impossible = never mind – Sunday night slept like ten tops & I'm all right now & happy enough & so is he I think – or rather we are both settled down again to work as if I'd never had a holiday. I'm nearly due at rehearsal my poppet & I want you to do something for me at once (not another Bonnet! – not 'till the spring & then it shall be grey please!! –)

[p. 2]

I want the book of German Soup I bought in Berlin – you remember it? It's on the Piano I think = Do send it me at once – theres [*sic*] a dear little chubkins – I'm rather Down about Lady M. I fear Henry doesn't like it – & I dont either – well it has to be done –

Bless you my pet – give my love at 22 – I've no time to write – Polly does Margaret[1] quite beautifully – she's grace itself – it's not simple enough quite, but it's beautiful – she looks like a Princess.

Goodbye my Audrey
Nell=

UCLA

Headed notepaper; Mr Henry Irving and the Lyceum Company tour 1888 (listing seven different dates from 10 September in Glasgow to 19 November in Birmingham).

1. Winifred Emery, ET's understudy, played Margaret in *Faust*.

240. To Stephen Coleridge, 21 November [1888]

Queens Hotel
Birmingham, 21 Nov.

~~22 Barkston Gardens~~
~~Earls Court, S.W.~~

Dear Stephen,

The poor Tricycle in itself is not harmful – in fact Mr Wilkinson was saying it kept many a lad healthily employed & kept 'em from mischief, – & do you know it was a ~~beaty beaty~~ "beauty" – & cost £25. Of course I didn't buy it! It seems a great pity to sell it – Ted writes "When I arrived from Berlin I found Dr Holzberg had given leave to the boys to ride it, & the result was it had got broken – then Dr H

[p. 2]

said he wd give me an order to get it mended, & I sent it to Frankfurt" ==

I'm very hard at work down here, rehearsing all day, but I get to bed every night at 10!!

Lady Mac will be the death of me – I know I shant do her well, & I'm miserable about it – for it has to be done – Gill & the boys at Broadstairs! I've just come from there! I hope Baby will House-keep well!!

Love from
Nell =

GARRICK, Vol. IV/15

Envelope extant; postmarked 'NO 21 88', Birmingham; addressed to 'The Hon Stephen Coleridge, 7 Egerton Mansions, South Ken'.

241. To Edward Gordon Craig, 22 November 1888

Queens Hotel =
Birmingham.
Nov 22.

Yes, your writing was much better my dear Ted – bolder – clearer & not so affected as it has been of late = I hope you told Mr Wilkinson[1] exactly what I said about why I did not write to him! I mean to do so however this evening or tomorrow. Tell me what you are going to recite, or act, the end of the term!

Yes the Germans are very odd at times in their estimate of character. I think it is the man you quote from ~~who~~ (Garvinus)[2] who libelled poor Ophelia – but

I wd not listen to him for a moment = My head is better thank you dear & I'm hard at work down here at Macbeth rehearsals =

[p. 2]

Henry[3] is pretty well, but looks sadly tired – he works so very hard, & has worked all his life – that's the meaning of such a brilliant record of successes.

Nothing great is done without it, Ted, & oh, believe me, if you were not blind & foolish you'd understand (& will some day & <regret>) how wicked it is of you not to take the golden opportunities you have & profit by them. Work is a blessed saviour = If now, you had improved your time & had got something into your big head you might have been with us playing "Malcolm" – it's a small, but very important, very difficult part – anyhow you'll have to play Malcolm before Macbeth – or Macduff = I'm off to rehearsal – Edy was singing in a chorus at a Concert given in Berlin on Monday – Singing!!! think of it! – God bless you – Best regards to Mr & Mrs Wilkinson – Your loving Mother –

HRC

1. Edward Gordon Craig was being educated by Mr Wilkinson, having left college in Heidelberg.
2. Georg Gottfried Gervinus (1805–71), German author and historian, who wrote numerous studies of Shakespeare, including *Shakespeare Commentaries* (1863).
3. Henry Irving.

242. To Henry J. Jennings, 22 November 1888

~~22 Barkston Gardens~~
~~Earls Court S.W.~~

Room 19=
Queens Hotel – Birmingham =
Dear Mr Jennings –

No – no – for a hundred reasons – I'll give you a few of them, if you will call & see me some day either at 3.30 – or after 6.30 = I shd be very glad to see you again if you have an unbusy moment to come = My mother is here – or rather she is with Marion at "The Plough & Harrow" – & Kate is coming down to day![1]

[p. 2]

a nice little family party! –

With very kind regards (& hoping to goodness I thanked you for your portrait! – but I am careless!!)

Believe me

Yours sincerely
Ellen Terry =

Nov 22 – 88=

PML, LHMS Misc Ray 188740 MA 4500

1. ET refers to her sisters Marion and Kate.

243. To Stephen Coleridge, 26 November 1888

Birmingham ~~28~~ Nov – 26 =

22 Barkston Gardens
Earls Court S.W.

Dear Stephen = Let me know quickly, by ½ a line, where you have told those blessed people to send the Tricycle = I'm sorry you put that P.S., but you always mean to do the best, I know – I know – <& of course "It hit the nail on the head"!> I feel sure it is better now to fight right out & deny the liability of the whole sum, or to pay the whole sum, tricycle bill & all, with a polite remark = The last is the best. A dear old man I know, & a great school master advises

[p. 2]

me never to mention the word expulsion to Ted, or to anyone <in speaking> about Ted = for he says it doesn't mean the same thing in England & on the Continent – & it is unfair to the lad, for he considers the whole affair has been a storm in a tea cup & that Lawrence & Co have behaved <in a> childish manner = I'm sure fighting Mr Cad Lawrence wd be very expensive, & I can't afford it – if it were an English master one would have to – but no English school wd have done

[p. 3]

it of course – they wd only have let Ted go on, idle or not idle, & not bothered about him, & then he wd not have been rude, & <so> none of this could have happened. The way our ends are shaped is strange – & I think all will come well in the end =

I return to town next week & shall have to ask you several things. – I'm ever so sorry you have all these things to botheration about. I 'm off to rehearsal =

Polly[1] plays Margaret beautifully – but she is a Princess of the Middle Ages & not a peasant child =

With love –
Nell =

GARRICK, Vol. IV/16
Envelope extant; postmarked 'NOV 26 88', Birmingham; addressed to 'The Hon Stephen Coleridge, 7 Egerton Mansions, South Kensington, London'; headed notepaper for 22 Barkston Gardens, Earls Court SW.

1. See n. 1 to letter 239, above.

244. To [Stephen Coleridge], [27 November 1888]

Later on =

On second thoughts it seems to me quite abominable that a whole quarters payment shd go, for one months [*sic*] tuition recd, when they have sent the boy away unjustly. What do you think of sending them a months [sic] payment for, as it were, "goods recd", & telling 'em to sue me for the rest – What I so fear is, that you have already paid the full term money (I forget) & that this is something extra!
Let me know please – Poor Stephen, what a lot of writing! –

N.

GARRICK, Vol. IV/17
Envelope extant; postmarked 'NO 27 88', Birmingham; addressed to 'The Hon Stephen Coleridge, 7 Egerton Mansions, South Kensington, London'; marked 'Immediate'.

245. To Edward Gordon Craig, 3 December 1888

Monday. Dec 3. 88=

22, BARKSTON GARDENS,
EARLS COURT. S.W.

My darling boy – I am very busy & can only send you a line to thank you for your little drawings & letter & tell you all's well with us = Tell me in your next, when the boys begin their holidays at Mr Wilkinsons = I enclose a letter which came for you a few days ago, & which was sent down to me at Birmingham & then followed me up here again = Who is it from? do I know the writing? Tim Fantz [?] will be here soon – he is going to bring with him from Heidelberg several things you've left behind. Your Shakspere amongs [*sic*] other things = Tim comes to England just before Xmas: Edy writes to me now long letters in German. I should love to have you home here for the holidays but I fear I cannot – must not – for it will be just in the thick of my work & I want helpers, instead of children who need help. The quicker you mature my dearest lad the better, I pray God you may mature in the right way & I believe in you for your (our) bitter little experience of the last two months I hope

[p. 2]

will have had the effect of making you a little wiser at least = You shd have learned one lesson, that rebellion against orders, is only childish – That the manly thing to do, is to endeavour to obey them = If you have not learned that lesson, then I fear, much suffering is before you, & before me too! But you must care for me at least, & try to avert trouble from my poor head, instead of bringing it on me = I like this sort of weather don't you? it makes me feel up in the sky for my work = Have you settled about the farce yet? If I were you, I should recite something not play a farce (one of the most difficult things to do – requiring no end of careful rehearsals, & a fellow actor to "play up" to one = Why don't you recite[?] I'll send you a list of things to choose from if you'll let me know = Just off to rehearsal = I enclose you a little coin it's modern! but I don't think you'll mind that = God bless you my Dear Son=

Your old loving Mother=

Stamps are best

HRC

Headed notepaper for 22 Barkston Gardens, Earls Court SW.

246. To Stephen Coleridge, 4 December 1888

4 Dec – 88 =
22 Barkston Gardens,
Earls Court, S.W.

£23-7-6=

Please my dear Stephen will you send me a cheque for Alexis Hollaender[1] for £23-7-6= Yesterday I was at rehearsal from 11 to 6, & we only did one act. H.I.[2] was "at it" again, all the evening, but I was quite tired out, & could not go. I have written a very long letter to Edy this morning & as my rehearsaling is due in an hour from now "Excuse" this scrap of a note & believe me yr. Loving

Nell =

GARRICK, Vol. IV/18

Headed notepaper for 22 Barkston Gardens, Earls Court SW. Bound out of sequence in the Garrick volume after a letter dated 22 December.

1. In payment for his music lessons given to Edith Craig.
2. Henry Irving.

247. To Joe Evans, [13 December 1888]

22 Barkston Gardens
Earls Court SW

It is perfect – although for stage purposes it wd have to be made double the size, or at least half as big again – still – all in proportions so it wd remain lovely. What a dearest Joe it is! all who know him must love him –

I'm coming to "call" upon him to day – or rather upon "hims" mother & sister, & shall leave this for him shd it chance he shd be out –

Nell=

Do be careful, & not go out in these cruel fogs.

NYPClub
Headed notepaper for 22 Barkston Gardens, Earls Court SW. Annotated '13 Dec 1888'.

248. To Joe Evans, 14 December 1888

22 Barkston Gardens
Earls Court SW

Is this the way you keep out of the fog ? you bad boy ! –

I'm up high to day – in my blue room amongst the Iris blooms – laid low – with chest & throat = Yes of course I'd sooner you did the letter than anybody in the world but we must discourse about it *first* = I was going to send & ask you, mother, & Anna if you'd be so sweet & kind as to come here to supper at 7.30 on Sunday – Then I shall be quite free from all business for a few blessed hours & we can

[p. 2]

have a quiet little time together[.]

Sweet Joe do make 'em come , & come your dear self – & then the letter can be settled –

Nell =

NYPClub
Headed notepaper for 22 Barkston Gardens, Earls Court SW. Annotated '14 Dec 1888'.

249. To Edward Gordon Craig, 17 December 1888

22, BARKSTON GARDENS,
EARLS COURT. S.W.

My dear I am sending you shirt – tie – stud & all, together so to be quite sure – now dont [*sic*] forget you have 2 of your best evening shirts with you now. I hope you'll like the Stud – it is a beautiful pearl, & there are 10 wee diamond sparks, so learn to put it in the card in the box directly you have done with it, or you'll lose it, by having it sent to the wash, or some such thing & then I shd be *very* sorry & you wd have to put up with any common thing instead, & that wd be a pity = Have you written to Mrs George Stoker to thank her for

[p. 2]

having you? To think you'll see Macbeth after all!!! Now don't leave that school like a little blind oaf as if you were leaving for an ordinary term – You must understand the W's have been truly your friends[1] in great need, & have helped us at a time when everybody wd not have done so – & you must not be just only a silly good little boy, but give them when you leave a fine young fellow's manly acknowledgement of your understanding how much you are in their debt – & never forget it!

Dear I can't give you tips about your recitation for I haven't got the book – but one thing I remember in the chorus [?] you must be rapid, & convincing – & look pleased all

[p. 3]

the time – the other, "The Confession" take in slower time & *never* *once* (until quite the end) let them think it is acted pathos – Take your time – not a loud voice don't look all the time at the audience in this – but sometimes at yr fingers as you pause, abstractedly – when you come to –" it's that confounded cucumber (or whatever the words are) speak the line sharp – look at the audience, & speak the line in a slightly higher key= oh, I could tell you if you were here lots of things – but take your time in The Confession – & think it out – I'm laid up with cold in my bedroom, or shd not find time to write this to you – I can scarcely see –

[p. 4]

Edy got your letter & she seems to have had a "lovely birthday" – She is very happy where she is & thank God all goes well = I'm dreading Macbeth, & am frightfully nervous. However Sunday week must come & then it will be all over =

I hope the 19th will pass off grandly – my best of good wishes, for it to be a fine success – Bless you my Ted –

This is from your old
Mother=
17. Dec. 88=

HRC

1. Mr Wilkinson had taken Edward Gordon Craig in to complete his education after the boy had been expelled from college in Heidelberg.

250. To Stephen Coleridge, 22 December 1888

22-Dec – 88 =

22 Barkston Gardens,
Earls Court, SW

Dear Stephen –

Will you please send Wilkinson <or me> £25 for Ted's 8 weeks. I told him to send to me, & not to you, at the same time assuring him we had not "quarrelled" – much !! It's a comfort to me to hear the Wilkinson's speak as they do of the youth after the late complaints of him – Poor Ted, as long as he's not tempted to be naughty he is ever striving & wishing to be good – but he is weak. I tell him of the saying ----
"Pray away devoutly
And hammer on stoutly" – he came

[p. 2]

back yesterday, & directly I've time to turn – (that means, when the 29th is past & gone ! –) I shall send him off again = Meanwhile I think I know of a place for him – Wilkinson is making enquiries about it =----- but I can do nothing, think of nothing but my work, until the 29th is past. Whether I shall play the part well in a months [*sic*] time, I can't yet conjecture, but I know I shall play it precious ill the first night – & I'm terribly nervous – & cannot rest at all = All right about the seats for you & Gill =

Best love – from Nell.

GARRICK, Vol. IV/19

Envelope extant; postmarked 'DEC 22 88', Earls Court; addressed to 'The Hon Stephen Coleridge, 7 Egerton Mansions, South Kensington'; headed notepaper for 22 Barkston Gardens, Earls Court SW.

251. To Joe Evans, 25 December 1888

22 Barkston Gardens
Earls Court SW

It has come "To Nell" – & I don't know why, but I always cry when any thing from you comes into the house – Darling Joe. The last thing in the world I can do is to "speak" – but that signifies nothing to you, for you always know –

Its [*sic*] Christmas Day –

God bless you my brother – my good friend – I'll change that name with you – & now I'll go to my work

[p. 2]

to the Lyceum – Did I tell you you had done your work for me to perfection ? I hope so – but perhaps not – I am confused, & all nothing plainly but

29 =
Dearest boy –
Speak to the Little Mother for me & to Anna –
Your Nell =

NYPClub
Headed notepaper for 22 Barkston Gardens, Earls Court SW; annotated '25 Dec 1888'.

252. To [Elizabeth Rumball], 25 December 1888

The Only Boo!

With her Nelly's dear love!

On Christmas Day –
1888

SMA, 5,006
Envelope extant; addressed to 'Mrs Rumball, Brancaster, Nr Lynn, Norfolk'.

253. To Joe Evans, 29 December 1888

Thanks & thanks it will 'do nicely' –[1]
Now comes the tug o 'war – & the
"Production"
will have it –
Love – Love –

NYPClub
Annotated 'To JE in London 29 Dec 1888'.
1. This line may be written in another's hand.

254. To Clement Scott, 31 December [1888]

Private 31 Dec

Dear Clement Scott

After feeling miserable a bit, about what you were going to say (for of course I guessed it – having just about enough wit to keep myself warm) I must confess I laughed, when I read what you did say[.][1] You have hit the blot! "an empty & a barren cry" – indeed it was, when I called on the spirits to unsex me – I acted [illeg.] that bit just

[p. 2]

just [*sic*] as badly as anybody could act anything =
It was most kind of you to suppose that I could act Lady M – you write from that point of view, which in itself is a very great compliment = For my own part I am quite surprised to find I am really a useful actress – for I really am!! to be able to get through with such different parts as----- Ophelia – Olivia – Beatrice – Margaret – & Lady M.
& my aim is usefulness – to my lovely art, & to H.I.

[p. 3]

This is not a very high ambition – is it? but long ago I gave up dreaming & I think I see things as they are (especially see myself as I am, alas) & off & on the stage only aspire to help a little=
– Mind you though Mr Clement, although certainly I know I cannot do what I want to do in this part, I don't even want to be "a fiend" & won't believe for a

[p. 4]

~~moment~~ Cant [*sic*] believe for a moment that she did "conceive" that murder = that one murder of which she is accused = most women break the law during their lives, ~~but~~ few women realise the consequences of ~~wh~~ that they do to day = In my memory I have facts, & I use them for (not for my "methods" in my work <thats [*sic*] where I fail, so dismally in this> but for) reading women who have lived, & can't speak & tell me = I am quite top full of – ~~dr~~ (not direct cruelty I hope but) – womens [sic] secrets = (& I have my own !!!) & my women – my friends–

[p. 5]

were not wicked — & you say *I'm* not = !!

I do believe that at the end of that banquet, that poor wretched creature was brought, through agony & sin to repentance & was just forgiven –

Surely did she not call on the spirits to be <made> bad, because she knew she was not so very bad? I'm always calling on the spirits to be made good, because I know I'm *not* good – not strong in good, although all the while desiring it above all else – No – she was not good, but not – much worse

[p. 6]

than many women you know – me for instanse [*sic*]– my hankerings are not for blood, but I think might, kill for my child, or my love, ~~&~~ blindly – & see & regret & repent in deepest sincerity after – You would have laughed the other night though – the man at the side put the paint – the "blood" – on my hands, & in the hurry & excitement I didn't look, but when I saw it I just burst out crying = I don't believe you think I'm very bad – I am – Perhaps when I tell you I loved, you won't believe it, when at the same time

[p. 7]

tell you I broke the law & forged for my love[2] – I tell you I did love & forged – said money was owed by him to me when it wasn't – in order to get it again for him of course[3] – Do you think I thought that wicked then? I thought it was right – I couldn't have done it with my baby at my breast if I had seen it as I see it now – You say I can't be Lady M whilst all the time you see I am quite as bad – – Don't have me hanged drawn & quartered after this – You are quite right I cant [*sic*] play Lady M – but it's because my methods are

[p. 8]

not right & oh, nothing is right about it yet – To be consistent to a conviction is what I'm going to try for =

If you don't put this in the fire this moment may my eternal Cuss fall on you! "Go into the fire Jew – Go into the fire" – Now I've my work before me haven't I? I've not slept for a month, properly, & these fogs frighten me – I wish I didn't act, or you didn't write, then perhaps I might see something of you = Forgive this horrid scrawl which is written to assure you I am a real bad person, & yet somehow in the person of Lady M. [illeg.]

[p. 9]

have contrived with evident subtlety, to make you think I can't assume bad 'cos I'm good! Don't you think it's all rather humourous [*sic*] ? –

It's good of you to have "let me down ~~so~~ easy", but I care more for what you think, than because you say it to others in print =

Was it not nice of an actress she sent me Mrs Siddons[4] [*sic*] shoes – (not to wear, but to keep with me –) I wish I could have "stood in 'em ="! *She*played Lady M. (her Lady M – not Shakesperes [*sic*] – & if I could, I wd have done hers, for Shakspere's Lady M, was a fool to it – but at the same time I don't think I'd even care to

[p. 10]

*try*to imitate her imitators. I wish I could have seen Helen Faucit[5] in the part – I do believe she was the rightest = although not to be looked at by the side of the portrait by Siddons, as a simple effective figure –
Can you ever forgive me, or can I ever forgive myself this long horrible scrawl?

Ah, but I *do * wish you & yours a happy
New Year –

Yours always E.T.

Fire-Fire-Fire!

HUNT

1. Clement Scott reviewed *Macbeth* in the Daily Telegraph on 31 December 1888.
2. Approximately four words are scored out here.
3. Possibly Edward Godwin, whose financial situation was difficult while ET was living with him.
4. Mrs Siddons played Lady Macbeth in 1779 and later in 1785 in London.
5. Helen Faucit played Lady Macbeth in the 1840s onwards.

255. To Julia Arnold, 1888

1888

Mrs Arnold[1]
C/o Mrs I. J. Fields
14 = Charles St=

I regret I cannot be two people & come to you & go to my friends –

Ellen Terry=

HARV

Telegraph; headed notepaper, Western Union Telegraphic Company

1. See n. 10 to ET's letter of 11 September 1887.

256. To Elizabeth Malleson, [1888]

22 Barkston Gardens
Earls Court SW

You Dear –

(I believe I never answered yr last letter whch [*sic*] was full I recollect of all manner of kind things.) I'm very glad you are coming to London – You will surely come to see our play = I'll try to keep my box free (or get it back from someone!) for one day in the week & I'll come up either Thursday or Friday from Uxbridge[1] where I am staying for fresh

[p. 2]

air with Teddy) & if you will come now to[2] – this place to eat your luncheon I shd like it very much or, I will come to you – What you will ! – Edy was nicely when I saw her in Berlin & I think of going to Germany in July to join her again – She is very happy & greatly beloved – – but more when we meet –

How lovely Dixton[3] must be looking now !! Now I must be off to my work. Our 1st Matinée – such a hot day for my[4] hot clothes as Lady Mac.[5] Affectionate greeting to you all –

E.T.

HARV

Headed notepaper; annotated '1886'. The year of this letter has been inferred as 1888 (in spite of the annotation) since this was the year in which ET moved into 22 Barkston Gardens.

1. Probably the Audrey Arms, Uxbridge.
2. ET has drawn a line indicating the address of the headed notepaper.
3. Elizabeth Malleson lived at Dixton Manor Hall, Gloucestershire.
4. This could be 'my' or an embellishment above the word 'Mac' on the lower line.
5. *Macbeth* was first performed at the Lyceum Theatre on 29 December 1888.

257. To [Bertha Bramley], [1888]

Private (or they'll say I'm lunatic)
Saturday

Who was the "one member of the family" who thinked such a thought!! Edgar? No – he doesn't think at all! (Goodness gracious!! I mean of me!)

Dorothy! Dorothy!!! That is the party – naughty little girlie –

Dear old Bertha – did you ever feel so crushed (that's exactly the expression)

[p. 2]

– I'm not fooling – so crushed out of all individuality that people & all things, seemed unreal, & that it was just impossible to reason or to do reasonable things

– oh! how dreadful a time I've passed through – In truth I've been brave in the long-while-ago –, through heavy sorrow & trial, & now <that> theres [*sic*] nothing to bear

[p. 3]

with, now that the Sun does shine for me, I am in the tight merciless grip of Melancholy for the first time in a very long life – Ah! But the terrible time has past, only now you will understand me when I tell you I couldn't write letters – couldn't see people could not do ~~any~~ "those things which I ought to have done" – The time began when I was at The Firs!![1] What do you think of that?!!

[p. 4]

Let me come to The Firs again, & bury the corpse of "my Melancholy" under one of your Fathers [*sic*] trees! 'twill hurt no one, as my melancholy is a dead 'un!

The Shakespeare calendar says the 17th is a Sunday – You says you are coming to Faust[2] that day!! oh! you naughty little Bertha! would you mind telling me the day you really are coming! Saturday or Monday I 'specks[3] – Saturdays the play goes best =

[p. 5]

Now this "Faust" is out – launched – floating – the part of Margaret is not particularly exacting, & should you chance to be in town late, it's so warm & comfy in my room at the Theatre! (for a Theatre-room) & I shd so love to see your dear sweet face & beautiful eyes looking, as they always do at me, as if they cared for me a little. Will you give my love to The Firs in general & to your kind Auntie in particular & forgive me taking up your time with all this rubbish about myself for I am

your truly devoted Nell = (33 L. Road.)[4]

SMA, ET-Z2,014

1. The home of the addressee.
2. *Faust* was first performed on 29 December 1888 at the Lyceum Theatre.
3. Expect.
4. ET lived at 33 Longridge Road until her move to 22 Barkston Gardens in autumn 1888.

258. To Bertha Bramley, [1888]

33 – Longridge Road
Earls Court = Saturday =

Dearest Bertha – Thanks for your warm welcome, and for the Lozenges! (the wee black ones are splendid –) In the midst of a whirl of work (directly – I come back home) I can only find time now to tell you how glad I am <about> [it], & how I long to see, the new specimen!! – but no boy will ever beat that last girl – that elf Gogo – the sweet thing – my love to her – & to Auntie & to – oh, ------- the whole lovely "bag of tricks" – (Oh! how dreadful!) I hope your Father

[p. 2]

The King is well – & dear Mr Bramley – If Edy & I drive down some Sunday I do believe you will give us luncheon or tea, as the case may be! = Won't you?
Talk of the American climate being "trying" – an English springtime takes the cake – a Blizzard in New York is a trifle, compared with a gentle breeze from the East in old London –

It is past midnight – Friday & Saturday & I must get me to my little bed – good night –
"Goodnight, I have to say goodnight To such a host of charming things"[1] – Do you know the lines beginning so? – Aldrich –
God rest you – God rest you – Nell –

SMA, ET-Z2,017
Annotated '1888'

1. 'Palabras Cariñosas', ll. 1–2, by Thomas Bailey Aldrich (1836–1907).

259. To unidentified, [summer 1888]

HOTEL DE L'EUROPE
MARSEILLE FRERES

Venise – Monday 13 – 18
We have been racing about ever since & now we are in Venice!! It is sweltering hot but we don't mind that, for it is all just wonderland to us – We arrived last night only Henry & I & the [illeg.] – for H. thought it a little too much of a joke for us all to come – so Miss Held is taking care of the children until we go back to

[p. 2]

Lucerne on Thursday – The colour of the place delights & amazes us & it seems to me a dream – it's perfectly mad being here I know in such weather, but Henry never heeds the heat, & I don't mind it under the circumstances –

This is only just to let you know we are here, & therefore that I shall not be here when you are here in October – I want to know where you will all be before October = goodbye my dear Dear –

We are just off to stand in St Marks □ & be roasted in our attempts to get to the Ducal Palace.

I do pray you are better – Please give my love to the children & with a fond hug believe me ever your very loving

Nelly

SMA, ET-Z2,2067

The date of this letter is probably summer 1888, when ET was on holiday with her children and Henry Irving.

8 UNDATED LETTERS (TO 1888)

260. To Mabel T. Batley, [n.d.]

Tuesday
33. Longridge Road
Earls Court

Dear Mabel
I send you the box for Thursday anyhow, in spite of your mother being away, perhaps you will like to take your cousin if you cannot use it, will you kindly send it back at once

Yours affecly

E-T-

BL, Add. MS 62702, f. 117
The letter has been dictated and is written in another's hand, but signed by ET.

261. To Bertha Bramley, [n.d.]

In bed. Tuesday.

Bertha dear ever since I saw you upon that lawn I have been what is called "stretched upon a bed of sickness" – only a "chill" – but such a choice chill! no ordinary affair I assure you –
You were coming tomorrow, weren't you? but you must not now please, & at this rate never no more shall we meet on this distracted globe! – forgive but don't forget.

"Livie" =

Mrs Prinsep[1] was here yesterday.

[p. 2]

Tho' I'm fooling I'm in such pain.

SMA, ET-Z2,050

1. See n. 8 to letter 1, above. Mrs Prinsep died in 1887.

262. To Bertha Bramley, 14 January [no year]

<u>33. L. Rd</u> <u>Thursday 14. Jan.</u>

Dearest Bertha

I thank you, more than I can say, for yr letter – next Sunday with you all at the Firs wd be the delightfullest [*sic*] thing, but the children have a birthday on <on, Saturday, & we "keep it," on Sunday> ~~that they~~ & if I were away, they say it wd not be a birthday = The next 3 Sundays I'm engaged, but after that

[p. 2]

I'd be very much obliged if you'd engage me!

I'm just off with the children & my sisters to see the Indians at Battersea Park[1] – a charming day & <u>spirits is up</u>!!

I wish Dorothy were with us –

With a great deal of love

Yours ever

<u>Nell –</u>

I wish you'd send me round the <u>numbers</u> of your seats at the Lyceum.

SMA, ET-Z2,015

1. Arthur Liberty organized an exhibition of Indian craftsmen in an 'Indian Village' in Battersea in 1885; see J. H. Mackenzie, *Orientalism: History, Theory and the Arts* (Manchester: Manchester University Press, 1995), p. 128.

263. To Bertha Bramley, [n.d.]

<u>Friday</u>

Dearest Bertha

Many thanks for your pleasant proposition, but I am off on Sunday evening to Heidelberg to get a 2 days glimpse of my Edith[1] – send the boy to me & I'll get him a stall <u>if I can</u>, or

[p. 2]

at least a seat <u>somewhere</u> – 'twill be pretty crowded I guess the last night for a whole week – I'll <u>gallop</u> through with Margaret[2] so he may catch his train you may depend upon it

Best love my dear old Bertha – from <u>Nell =</u>

Isn't Auntie going with you?

SMA, ET-Z2,040

1. Edith Craig.
2. ET played the role of Margaret in *Faust* for the first time in December 1885.

264. To Bertha Bramley, [n.d.]

Sunday Just starting for New York[1]

Farewell for awhile [*sic*] sweet Bertha. This has been a very difficult year for me – always breaking down in my work – next month I hope to be back & to see something of you. Love to the dear sweet Auntie & to all of them – your tired devoted Nell =

Edgar sent me some of his exquisite Carnations. It was good of you to tell him to! They were just right for Margaret[2] =

SMA, ET-Z2,051

1. ET went on tour to the United States for the first time in 1883.
2. ET first performed Margaret in *Faust* in December 1885.

265. To Bertha Bramley, [n.d.]

Sunday

STAR AND GARTER
RICHMOND

My dearest Bertha

I seem in the way of losing <sight of> my friends in this world for the rest of the short chapter – & all along o' my cussed health!! Last Tuesday & Wednesday I was so weak & worn out that Mr Irving let me off ~~for~~ 4 nights work ~~tomorrow~~ & I slipped away down here alone with my maid to take care of me & have simply lain on bed & sofa

[p. 2]

since Thursday – just think Bertha dear I could not go down last Sat – & Sunday to Oxford to hear Henry Irving speak,[1] & see him honoured, nor to dine with him at the kind old Vice-Chancellors, & oh, I did want to – so = Tomorrow I go back to work (tho' not fit).

How long are you staying in Richmond Terrace? Any evening but tomorrow if you can come to the Lyceum do – do – do – for tho' it's warm weather my room there is cool & I never else shall see you –Your loving old

Nell –

SMA, ET-Z2,052
Headed notepaper for Star and Garter, Richmond, with the motto 'Honi Soi qui mal y pense' ('shame on him who thinks evil of it', French; the motto of Order of the Garter).

1. Henry Irving spoke at Oxford University on 'Four Great Actors' on 26 June 1886.

266. To [Marie Casella], 12 August [no year]

Wiesbaden =

~~22 Barkston Gardens~~
~~Earls Court S.W.~~

12 Aug –
Dear – whoever it was answered my <telegram>!

Don't you think I did quite a clever thing in sending to ask you about the Hotel in Paris? Who should know the way about there, if not the Casella's's's! = What are you doing at Folkstone & why not Ramsgate since Henry has been there so long? Thanks many [*sic*] for replying to my telegram = I'm only going to be in Paris a week or perhaps ten days – I want to see the exhibition, & get a dress if I can from Miss Sara's[1] dress ~~dress~~ maker – Felix I think it is = Where is poor Mummy? & is she much better = Henry[2] is rested – & as for our party we have had a good time in the teeth of opposition!! for of all primitive places in Germany, I think we were at the primitivest [*sic*] – Such beds!

[p. 2]

Such food!! Such roughness!!! – but on the other hand such air!!! Such sunshine, & such fun!!!! –
Edy[3] went on to Berlin yesterday with her people = & Nannie Held, Edie Lane & I, came on here to see Audrey's[4] aunt, for a day, & tomorrow we start for Paris – & I hope for the Hotel Les Deux Moules = We telegraphed just now for beds = Henry will join us, & give us treats!! *One* treat he'll give us will be Loveday!![5] He never travels without his Loveday! Oh Lor'!! If you are at Folkestone when I return I shd like to stop there a few days – are you at an Hotel or Lodgings? Do drop me a line one of you two children. If it was Mama or Papa who [illeg.] answered my telegram, please

[p. 3]

give them my dear love & thank them for me =
I heard from Boo[6] that your poor old Doggie was very ill & had The Dances!! – Whatever that may mean! – Ted has been staying with Henry & he says he's a perfect love of a boy – & gives him the best of characters – I've always suspected Ted of goodness, & now my suspicions are confirmed!! Well I hope to see you all soon – either in Folkestone or London, & shall hope to find you as well as this

leaves me at present! – I haven't learned my new part, & feel as lazy as can be =! – With much love

Yours ever affectionately

Nellen T =

SMA, ET-Z2,066

1. Sarah Bernhardt (1844–1923), French actress.
2. Henry Irving.
3. Edith Craig.
4. Audrey Campbell.
5. See n. 1 to letter 194, above.
6. Elizabeth Rumball.

267. To [Stephen Coleridge], [n.d.]

It's very sweet & dear of you Stefano to want to help me – (again –) but arrangement have been made & I shall not be detained 2 moments – Thank you Thank you. – So sorry your head is bad.

GARRICK, Vol. III/1

268. To Stephen Coleridge, [n.d.]

Sunday =

Here is the Buenos Ayres &c paper signed, my dear Stephen (thank you – –) & I also send another paper – I still stick in the country for it is most lovely there – Directly I come back for good, I'll come to you, & we will talk of the play, & you'll read me the rest of the romance – ?
Much love from Nell.

GARRICK, Vol. III/15
Coleridge's annotation: 'I think this "romance" was Demetrius'. This undated letter is bound in the volume at the end of the letters for 1887 and before those for 1890.

269. To Stephen Coleridge, [1887?]

Ted returns on the 5th August – I shd like him to be with me from 3 weeks to a month & then go to Heidelberg –

[p. 2]

Here is another circular Stephen dear – Now don't 'ee lose 'em.

GARRICK, Vol. IX/11
Unsigned note in ET's hand, inserted in bound volume of letters from 1899 but probably dated 1887, inferred from the reference to Heidelberg, where her son was at school.

270. To [Edith Craig or Edward Gordon Craig], [n.d.]

VINE COTTAGE
KINGSTON VALE

Wednesday Evening = Putney
Here are the ~~stalls~~ Dress Circle seats my dear – 4 seats – (only had 2 stalls.)
Bobbie is here with me for the night – He is a gem = Such a fine chap –
I've not forgotten about the 20-box.

[Page 2]

Why didn't you answer my letter? – I shan't write if you don't =
I've Charles I[1] now on my mind – after that some peace from studying for awhile!
– Sans Gene is a slaving part =
Love from

Mother

HRC
Headed notecard, Vine Cottage, Kingston Vale.

1. ET performed the role of Henrietta Maria in *Charles I* for the first time at the Lyceum Theatre on 27 June 1879.

271. To Edward Gordon Craig, [n.d.]

Friday =

22 Barkston Gardens
Earls Court S.W.

No, we haven't much news for one another, only the news that you are better, is the best news in the world for me = I send some newspaper cuttings, & that "Faust" is to be done in February is certainly "news" = The Poor "Sick Monkey" is just the same & sends his love & a shake of the paw to old H = I can't think of anything to give Henry — Fact is, I can't think just now of anything but rehearsals – I go to bed

[p. 2]

tired as a slave! = Henry looks frightfully tired too – but we are both pretty jolly = Hope you'll not get cold at "Called Back" –

Would you like to come back to rehearsals alone first? & go & see some plays in the evening with Edy? – or, wd you like to act at once as well? I advise the first – (rehearsals alone) Tell me at once & I'll arrange it with Henry = Henry loves to get yr sketches of H.H. – They make him laugh – Best love from us all –

Yr loving
Mother =

HRC
Headed notepaper for 22 Barkston Gardens, Earls Court SW, where ET moved in autumn 1888.

272. To Edward Gordon Craig, 9 April [no year]

Home = 9. April =

Ted my darling I never know whether you receive things or not that I send you. So theres [*sic*] not much encouragement to send 'em"! Now that your time at Southfield Park is coming to an end, I'll send you one jolly good Hamper – I'll send (if you'd like them A cake (2 cakes) 3 Boxes Sardines – Some Biscuits. Bon-Bons (to pull) Some Jam – Toffy = (or some kind of sweets) & some Oranges. Now I think that will be a splendid

[p. 2]

Hamper!! Don't you. Why did you not answer Violet's nice letter? Very rude – Now sit down & write to me – Are you getting on better with your work now? Keep your record for "good conduct" clean at least, to the very end of your stay with Mr Wilkinson. Aren't you sorry to be leaving them all? I think you'll remember your first school–days for ever with much pleasure – (& I fear with regret also, at the thought you might have worked much harder.) Do write to me & tell me what you think. Shakspere! Why surely you have a Shakspere with you. You shall have the Walter Scott when you come home. Have you written Edie lately? Have you heard from her?

[p. 3]

Olive Seward is here (from Rome) & sends her "best love to Ted" – I'm expecting Mrs Lockwood & Francis & Florence soon after Easter – Dear Hamlet is very well – as usual – & –, as usual, is ever at work morning noon & night – Do you know that Edie is at work to pass for Girton? It's "a coiker" to pass & I shd say her spelling – like yours – wd have to improve first – however Mrs Malleson says "she can pass easily" – & <as> all Mrs Mallesons [*sic*] girls are Girton Girls, she ought to know. Now let me have a nice letter from you. Nicely written too for you've plenty of time tomorrow & Sunday. Give my love to Louis, & best regards to Mr & Mrs Wilkinson.

[p. 4]

Boo[1] is well – so is Fussy & Puffy & the bird, but I have one of my severe colds, & cannot sleep.

God bless you my darling boy.

Yr Mum =

HRC

Annotated '1888[?]'. The date of this letter is slightly uncertain as Edward Gordon Craig was educated by Mr Wilkinson in two separate periods, one *c.* 1883 and one at the end of 1888 after he had been expelled from school in Heidelberg.

1. A sketch of a face has been drawn next to the text on p. 4.

273. To Edward Gordon Craig, 24 July [no year]

July 24 = Krummhubel =

I liked the drawing you made me, "from the life", very much for I know it's much more difficult than to copy= I enclose autograph= as I find you asked for it in the letter before the last, which I have already answered: Don't take your tall hat down to Ramsgate nor yr frock-coat – it's a case of, "flannels, generally, & one nice get up in case of need": I am much better today, & we have heavenly weather= I write to you in a Hammock, & it's rather wobbley!! Be extra polite & good in your conduct with the Gortons do leave a fine character behind you = & don't leave your clothes – your things behind!! Farewell my laddie –

Mother =

HRC

274. To Edward Gordon Craig, 20 August [no year]

20 Aug

Winchelsea = 20 Aug.

Sweet drawings all of them! specially the Lavender & the Saxon Arch: thank you my very dear boy: I love your drawings.

It depends upon how folk see "pathos" – The most pathetic I think, is, to see the afflicted bearing with cheerfulness & resignation what is then fate – Of course some folk are different – they are "not built that way"! A blind man boisterously cheerful wd of course seem discordant, but I don't fear that in you for it wd be an error of taste & – well I hope – believe it wd be impossible. Give my love to Paul, & to his Mother my thanks for inviting you: I do hope we may meet. I fear it is impossible for me to come to Northampton – Audrey is here now – Goes up tomorrow – Henry returns to town on Sunday. We are all well. Best love from

Your Mum

HRC

275. To Augustin Daly, 27 July [no year]

27 July=

Dear Mr Daly –

So many thanks, but after all I dare not come, for I'm as ill, as can be ill = & so I return the box & wd be grateful if you cd spare me instead 2 seats for Wednesday or Thursday evening for my young daughter who is dying to see our Ada Rehan![1] (the nice bright creature –) Edith (my girl) wd like to go

[p. 2]

round 'tween the acts or after the play to see Miss Rehan, & the other ladies, if she wd not be in their way for a few moments! –

Mr Irving fears it wd be impossible to run in to see "Nancy",[2] as we both have crowds of work that day – We are so sorry – so sorry –

Very sincerely yours
Ellen Terry =

FOLGER

1. See n. 2 to letter 202, above.
2. Possibly *Nancy and Company* at the Strand Theatre.

276. To Charles Dodgson, 15 March [no year]

March 15
33 Longridge Road,
South Kensington

My dear Mr Dodgson[1]

Will you be kind enough to give this to Ethel Arnold for me.

Look out for new business with Hero in The Church scene.[2] I'm sure it's much

[p. 2]

better now – Also am I quite sure you are in the right about some other things you said one day at Kate's about this same church scene – it's too long to write about for I'm a poor worried woman[3] & have too much work to do. Tell the little

[p. 3]

girl Lucy that, so she may envy me & with affection
believe me yours yours [*sic*]
Ellen Terry =

FALES, 5:453 XV-232
Headed notepaper for '33 Longridge Road, Kensington'

1. Probably Rev. Charles Dodgson (Lewis Carroll); see n. 1 to letter 103, above.
2. ET had performed as Hero in *Much Ado About Nothing* at the Haymarket Theatre in the 1860s.
3. 'woman' is written diagonally down the page.

277. To Joe Evans, 23 September [no year]

22 Barkston Gardens
Earls Court SW
Monday 23 . Sep

Dearest Joe – Thanks for pretty sketch = but a misunderstanding somewhere. I do want to wear powder for 2nd part of play – I do want to wear a high head – but I want a pretty example to give Mr Fox the wig maker – who is rather stupid like me – we can find nothing but huge exaggerated articles, & it don't "go" with the pathetic situation = Behold your stall!!
Nell

NYPClub
Headed notepaper for 22 Barkston Gardens, Earls Court SW, where ET moved in autumn 1888.

278. To Joe Evans, 27 January [no year]

22 Barkston Gardens
Earls Court SW

I found this <letter enclosed> a few days ago in my bag – stowed away – when it was written I don't know – but a long while ago I'm sure = – it had been put away waiting for an enclosure, which I did not attend to – Don't think me silly because after all I do send the letter –

Sweet Joe. I had such a lovely letter from you 2 days ago – & I must tell you of a terrible Tragedy ! You sent me a photograph of yr picture [of] the outside of Audrey Arms – I saw it as I was

[p. 2]

just starting in my usual haste for the Lyceum – & since that moment no human eye seems to have beheld it!!! Search has been made, & I am sorry to say I suspect that either Rose burned it in horrible mistake – or that Miss Campbell Stole it – but I barely had time to say "take that up to my bedroom" before leaving, & ----- I've never seen it again!! Do send me another one my very dear Joe= – Thank you for yr message about Mr Purrington = – Indeed he is not in my debt – it was my neglect in answering letters caused a mistake – but that has been put right = We have all been ill. Ted first, & then I – broke down & cd not play act – but now we are all well again – & I am ever yr loving Nell =

NYPClub

Headed notepaper for 22 Barkston Gardens, Earls Court SW, where ET moved in autumn 1888.

279. To Joe Evans, [n.d.]

We're kind o' shut up like whooping-cough people, but hope to be let loose tomorrow or next day at latest –

Will you come down to the Theatre this evening about 8 o'clock & I'll find you a draughtless corner if such a thing is about anywhere –

We send you our love – don't send it, but put it inside your inner coat pocket & keep it hot !

Yours ever E.T. =

NYPClub

Headed notepaper for 1887–8 Lyceum Company tour.

280. To Joe Evans, [n.d.]

Monday . 2 o'clock

Half blind from pain & totally stupid, I send this line to tell you I could not see you ~~this~~ this morning or – surely it goes without the saying – I wd have been so glad – Drenched with a cold I must obey the Doctor's orders & "remain in bed & see nobody" –

Oh! if I have to "give in" this last week, just from weakness of the flesh how I shall despise myself – but the Doctor fears

[p. 2]

it must be so ---- (*I* don't!)
Suppose time goes by, & I am not well enough to see you all before I go!!
Will you understand !
"My love is strengthened though
more weak in seeming
I love not less though less the
show appears –"[1]
Teddy will take this to you & I hope he'll have the luck to find you in –

Remember you'll come to me when you come to England – if you please – & Remember – oh! but I'm sure to see you again soon –

God be with you
ET –

NYPClub

1. Shakespeare's sonnet 102.

281. To Joe Evans, [n.d.]

22 Barkston Gardens
Earls Court SW

Darling little Joe

'ere be the ticket. Audrey Campbell sees me so very seldom (!) she wants me "all to herself that day in the coming & going" – so her orders to us are that you are to "make yourself very scarce", & not venture to address us, except when we arrive at Bushey" – then please let us "give you a lift" (mercy! What a lot of slang!!) – from the station to the Theatrekin – for it is a goodish long way.

[p. 2]

We <Audrey & I> shall get in (going) at Willesden at 1.50. so pop yr head out & look for us –

I know Anna had a dull time last night at the workhouse – tell her to try again ~~ag~~ & it will be better next time =

I pray for a fine day on Monday – it wd be almost better if they put off their visit 'till Tuesday *if* it's a threatening looking Monday morning – Your loving old sister

Nell =

NYPClub
Headed notepaper for 22 Barkston Gardens, Earls Court SW, where ET moved in autumn 1888.

282. To Joe Evans, [n.d.]

Tuesday =

God be with you – Very soon shall I see you again I hope – me there – or you here – The talk of to day wd not have been but you told me of [...][1] & out from my soul there went a prayer[,] a

[p. 2]

great wish for her happiness & that she might never desire more than – she is likely to get ! Oh, I cannot word it – I just wish her well[.] I wish you well my beautiful dear young friend & I love you very much & <so> does Edie – & Ted – "Nell"!

NYPClub

1. A piece of paper has been excised from p. 1, rendering the text obscure and indicated by the ellipsis.

283. To Joe Evans, [n.d.]

Midnight = Sunday =

Victoria Hotel

My dear Mr "Joe Evans"

Here's the box for Hamlet – (for next Thursday :) I send it to you , & <"the others"> with my love – which is the only thing I can give you – You said something about coming to England ! How much I hope you will come, I cannot tell you – When you (or "the others" come, I want you to promise me you'll make 33 Longridge Road –

[p. 2]

Earls Court – S.W. London ~~your~~ (that's where we live – my children & I –) your Inn for [illeg.] as long as you can endure it = If you are ever passing this Hotel about <12> I hope you will look in upon me – I go to rehearsal about 12.30 = or 1 o clock = & I wd be the better for a glimpse of your kind face = & I want my boy to know you – Thank God he is not <so> dull but he can know & understand what you & "the others" did for me, in giving my little treasured book –

Always yours Ellen Terry:

NYPClub
Headed notepaper for Victoria Hotel.

284. To [Albert Fleming], [n.d.]

33 Longridge Road. Wed.

Have you guessed I have been ill, or cut to bits, for I did not write to thank you for the lovely stuff? How good of you to send it & I do thank you now. Please accept my thanks as I thought, my "level-headed" little daughter

[p. 2]

was able to spin ~~before~~ 3 days after trying to – she went back to school yesterday (leaving me wretched for the loss of her) taking her wheel with her, & some good flax – she will send me a specimen of her thread soon, & I will ask you to find fault with it, or to praise it a little –

[p. 3]

I will read your letter (again of course) & answer it a little later on .] Excuse me now, as I am in bed really ill unable to read, write or to understand the meaning of the simplest sentence. Idiotic I suppose!! "Oh! for rest – rest" –

[p. 4]

My beautiful big dog is dead – my bullfinch I fear is dying, my children are away

Isn't it ~~it~~ all grey? I hope it is all better with you in the lovely country –

ET =

Please don't write & say you are sorry I'm ill –

SMA, ET-Z2,299

285. To [Mary-Anne Hall], 25 [n.d.]

My dearest little pale Mary

I am very anxious to hear of your health.

You may have been led by my silence to think I didn't care, but indeed darling I have very often thought & even dreamed, of your poor little thin pale face, & of your sweet kind manner to me when last

[p. 2]

we met – & have often intended to write but oh! Marion I am so busy, & am very far from being well myself. My old face is the looks like a tallow candle, only theres [*sic*] not so much colour in it – & I am in such bad spirits & can't account for it –

[p. 3]

At some private theatricals given by Lady Collier I met Mr V. Vernon Harcourt – (If you remember, I have spoken to you about him.) He was so kind, & so nice altogether to me & has asked Tom Taylor to invite him next Sunday to Lavender Sweep to meet us – & we are going – Please excuse this blotchy writing for I have a "quill" which has seen its best days, & ink which

[p. 3]

is greasy – & I have also a very bad cold & can write no more to day but must go to bed.

No news darling chick whatever have I got for you I hope you will send me a little bit of news which will be most pleasant to me – That you are well but don't write if it worries you.

God bless my sweet tiny handed Marion –

Every your loving
Nell.

My best compliment to yr sister Emily –

V&A

286. To Mrs Hill, 1 July [no year]

33 Longridge Road – Earls Court=

Sunday . July 1.

My dear Mrs Hill

That I hold my life scared to my work must be my excuse for terrible neglect of my good friends at some times – We are bewilderingly busy at the theatre now – so forgive me – will you? here is my esteemed

[p. 2]

my revered, autograph!!

With much affectionate thought of you, I am ever yours

Nelly (not Ellen please.)

FOLGER

287. To Elizabeth Malleson, 13 September [no year]

Sunday .13. Sep.
Home

My dearest Mrs Malleson

I send you my girl[1] again – It seems to me that slothfulness is her difficulty – or rather *our* "difficulty", in regard to her, for she seems unconscious of the –"difficulty" !! I do regret regret *regret* being unable to see you & talk with you about her – & of course I regret the <lost> treat of being with you a few days in your own beautiful home for my own sake – however, you will I'm quite sure be glad

[p. 2]

to know I had a "perfectly lovely time", – never before such a real happy holiday & <that I> am much stronger & better in health for it – Edie will tell you (perhaps!!!) how she enjoyed herself, Mr & Mrs Carr seemed to enjoy it, & as for the dear Vicar,[2] he was a picture of perfect content, all the while – even when [illeg.] one of us lost £60 for him! Does a good digestion come of a good temper, – or one's l-v-r[3] being – "all right", does complacency set in! ? – (I rather think ones [*sic*] digestion may

[p. 3]

be kept in order!)

If you please I wd like Edie ~~go to to go~~ (a crowd of people talking in the next room) to go on with her drawing under Mr Goodwin's direction for the present at all events –

Many Thanks for sending me his letter – a delightful one – most interesting & clever – Still I don't think Mr Goodwin has seen what she seems to me to do so ~~well~~ much best – She, one moment, scribbles so vilely, & the next, draws so well!! (slothfulness) – One thing I shd much like. To get (myself) some drawing

[p. 4]

from her once a week. I will offer her a prize for every half dozen careful drawings she sends me – May I suggest that when any of you are "to be had" – your heads – one your hands – she may make use of the Malleson family !?!!! I hear that "reading aloud", goes on, at the Manor House, & that some of the ladies ~~work~~ at their needlework at the same time – this delightful picture suggests that, some of them might work with their pencil at the same time –

I must go – for the holidays are nearly over now & I am

[p. 5]

told by Edie & Ted, that I am "always writing" ! – (how very contradictious [*sic*] to my friends who maintain that I "never write"! Edie is sorry to leave us – but longs to see you all again – "Joy Poole" is a great delight to her – & we joke her about "*Trouty* Pool-e" – the dear thing she is so very serious over a joke – I hope you'll not think we have spoiled her during the time she has been with us – I try not to – & I hope she will not trouble you too much. Poor Miss Mabel I fear gets the worst part of her – for which I am very regretful.

Will you give my love to her, & tell Mr Malleson not to forget me.

Your grateful & affectionate

E.T.

FOLGER, Y.c.1392 (1–29)

1. Edith Craig, who was taught by Malleson; see n. 6 to letter 109, above.
2. Henry Irving.
3. Presumably, liver.

288. To Mortimer Menpes,[1] 23 February [no year]

Feb 23. 33

Longridge R^D^

Goodbye my dear big Genius – When I got back home just now after calling at Osborn Lodge to see you, I found Mr Irving, so he just sat down & wrote you a hasty line – "better late than never" I told him!! –

I can never thank you enough for the dear little head, you have given me.

It's absurdly like what the

[p. 2]

child was then – (she is now a very fine young woman !) Dear Mr Menpes I wish I could do something for your wife whilst you are away – I liked her at once, & this morning she was so sweet I loved her – I hoped to see you to day – believe me I am Yours most gratefully

Ellen Terry =

(greatest haste)

Goodbye – which means "God be with you", doesn't it?

CLAREMONT

1. Mortimer Luddington Menpes (1855–1938), Australian artist, studied at the Slade School of Fine Art in London with Walter Sickert, both of whom became assistants in the studio of James McNeill Whistler. Menpes married Rosa Grosse in 1875 and their daughter, Dorothy Whistler Menpes, was born in 1887. Menpes

visited Japan in 1888 and it may be this trip to which ET refers here. In 1888 his artistic decorations for his home at 25 Cadogan Gardens, Kensington, were featured in an article in the *Pall Mall Gazette*.

289. To Mortimer Menpes, 29 July [no year]

July 29 :

Dear Mr Menpes –

I pray you to remember your promise & send me the wee sketch of my girl, if only to "look at" & <send> it back to you. I was very glad to see you the other night.

Yours sincerely

Ellen Terry =

Did your red friends like the play? –

[p. 2]

33 Longridge Road
Earls Court – S .W.

CLAREMONT

290. To Mrs Nixon, [n.d.]

Lyceum Theatre

London =

Dear Mrs Nixon

Here is Miss Portia

Will she do?

I wish now I had dressed the lady in her scarlet robes as Doctor of law – as it is she certainly looks better by candle-light –

With warmest wishes for your splendid schemes Sincerely yours

Ellen Terry =

FOLGER, Y.c.434 (1–140)

291. To Queen Palmer, [n.d.]

<u>Sunday =</u>

Oh you darling Queen How sweet you, & a lot of other people are. You don't mind my mixing you up! Because the others are good to be mixed with – I couldn't write to thank you for your letter – but I couldn't even write to Fred – kind lovely Fred – I think I've been a little bit mad since a few days = Nothing but rage & despair could find room in me, & I've been away still down at Uxbridge unfit to be seen by any who didn't love me – Away = "lest the wise word! Should look into my moan – And mock me with you after you were gone" – Dear. I don't take things in to my wooden head very easily – do I understand rightly that Nannie goes away to Italy very soon? If so perhaps I'll look in Tomorrow morning, & <u>if I don't</u> may hap <u>she</u> will come to me about 3 o'clock for half an hour.

I hope you are as well here darling soft dear as you were in the country. Love to the pets from

<u>Nell=</u>

It's not <u>funny</u> that people can put on black clothes! I always thought it – now I <u>know</u>

SMA, SCB6-25

292. To Major Pond, 9 October [no year]

October – 9th <u>Saturday</u>
LYCEUM THEATRE

Dear Major Pond[1]

I am in the country for I've been much troubled & ill lately[.]

Edith – my daughter – is with me – but I want her to hear Mr Beecher on Monday – Please be my friend – <u>as usual</u> – & find me two seats – one for her – & one for my

[p. 2]

Aunt Mrs Rumball & will you send the tickets to Mrs Rumball

33 Longridge Road
Earls Court

With dear dear love to the Beechers

Yours very truly

E<u>llen Te</u>rry =

CLAREMONT
Headed notepaper for Lyceum Theatre.

1. See n. 1 to letter 198, above.

293. To [Charles Reade], [n.d.]

Wednesday evening

A letter I found waiting for me on my return after seeing you this morning relieves me of all heart ("crocodile!") feeling I had in the matter we talked over = (the difficulty I felt with regard to considering Mr Taylor personally, I mean.) Mr Neville has engaged himself deeply to Miss Foote – I can't stay to tell you the whole thing but the very plain words of the "summing up" are ~~Mr Taylor~~ No: Mr Neville

[p. 2]

doesn't want me! –

Now will you give me £30 a week (the sum I've all along made up my mind (my own private mind – the public one was £40 or £50!!!!!!!!) to have! ____ & then let me play "Helen" = I've read it, & think it very fine – but not so fine as "Phillipa" –

Miss Foote gets £15 = she will probably ask for an increase of salary for this new part – that will make it £20 – Do you think I am worth only £5 more than

[p. 3]

Miss Foote?

Write me a line or two like a beautiful man by return of post (Miss E. Terry. 3. Cambridge Gardens. Notting Hill.) if you will please for after hearing from you I shall follow my heart (it went by telegraph to Harpenden this morning, before I saw you & Mrs Seymour) I shall follow it straight & at once –

I didn't think of it before but I will enclose T.T's letter recd to day =

Be quick sweet Mr Reade & *get* *well*

SMA, ET-Z2,229a
Annotated 'This is a charming character a really sweet loveable tender woman as false as Hell. False to her her [illeg.] False to her friends False to herself'; annotated in another unidentifiable hand '(written by C. Reade)'.

294. To Ada Rehan,[1] [n.d.]

Friday –

I feel like a bit of leather, & what is the good of "a bit of leather" sending to you, but I do send over this line to tell you that I love you, or rather *shall* once more when I can love, – or hate, or feel anything at all <about the 24th I guess> – some, I think are born tired – I'm one of 'em. – Weren't you pleased with what The Telegraph said of you? I was –

[p. 2]

& I cut it out & sent it to Teddy at school – who will delight that they should see you as you are – When this confounded <24th> is over, & our plays are "out", & the beastly (!) east wind reared round, then besides pleasanter things, I hope you'll let me come for you, & take you home with me – I'd love that – Please give my love to Mr Daly & Mr Drew & Mr Lewis and to Mrs Gilbert, & to all of them & believe me yr affectionate Bit of Leather

E.T. =

Poor H.I. is almost dead-beat

UPENN, MS.Coll.191, f. 153

1. See n. 2 to letter 202, above.

295. To A. Adam Reilly, [n.d.]

My dear Mr Reilly

Very many thanks for the kind wishes contained in your kind letter.

It's over! The first night is over! It doesn't seem possible to me –

The house was "crammed". Mr Stone, Mr Reade and Papa went together – I saw lots of familiar faces in "front", (Bristoleians included) but not yours – however I hope to see it before long –

With kind remembrances

[p. 2]

In which proper, manner, if not quite, from,

Believe me
Very truly yours
Nellie Terry –

To A. Adam Reilly Esqure

V&A